ADVANCE

THE MASTER IDENTITY THIEF

"Providential, intricate and authoritative...Dartanyon's testimony, which mirrors my story in many ways, culminates with praiseworthy, relevant solutions. I look forward to joining forces with DAW to wage war against identity theft in all of its forms!"

—Frank W. Abagnale, subject of the book and movie, *Catch Me If You Can*

"One must applaud the courage of Mr. Williams to write this book. I imagine there are many who would detest and feel betrayed by his revealing the methods and secrets of identity theft. More so, I applaud the courage it took for Mr. Williams to seek redemption and change his life. This is a brave man telling an intricate and compelling personal and important story."

—Barry Berman, screenwriter, *Benny & Joon*

"In *The Master Identity Thief*, Dartanyon Williams tracks his rise and fall as a shapeshifter and con man, providing an up close and personal view of a world of deception, crime, and ultimately redemption. Like Jacob in the book of Genesis, Williams is a hustler from birth and in this book he takes the reader on his wild ride."

—Guy Lawson, *New York Times* bestselling author, *War Dogs*

"When I first met Dartanyon, he was at Lallie Kemp Medical Center in Amite, Louisiana while he was serving time in solitary confinement at Tangipahoa Parish Prison. Under armed security,

YHWH   יהוה

he was brought in for medical attention. During that first intro-
duction, I discovered then he was not only peculiar, but well-read,
and an advocate for his rights and unique perspectives. What I did
not know was the nature of his charges, but over the years since his
release and our reconnecting, I have gained DAW as a friend and a
continued patient. Looking back, I can easily understand why he
was *The Master Identity Thief* and why he now offers the remedies
to America's crisis of identity and medical identity theft. Today, I
am just happy that we are now on the same side of his redemption!"

—Dr. Charlie H. Bridges, MD, urology specialist,
Our Lady of the Lake Regional Hospital, Baton Rouge

"I've committed my life to preparing for battle and protecting the
lives of my fellow Americans. In all my training, nothing has pre-
pared me to fight against identity theft, until I read *The Master
Identity Thief* by Dartanyon A. Williams. My challenge now is
how to help my fellow marines and my country wage this war
beyond recommending this book. We must turn to its author for
the authoritative solutions he offers here. Mr. Williams is to be
commended for sharing his report of both a personal and prac-
tical reconnaissance mission as a former Master Identity Thief."

—Tanecia Jackson, Gunnery Sergeant,
United States Marine Corps

"Like football, in the game of life you win some and you lose
some. But in America's war against identity theft, how can we
ensure or at least improve our chances for a positive outcome? In
his book, *The Master Identity Thief*, Dartanyon provides the best
possible chance for America to win this war."

—Devin White, 2019 Bucker's Award Recipient,
linebacker, #45, Tampa Bay Buccaneers, NFL

"*The Master Identity Thief* is an *eye-opener*. As a law enforcement officer, I must say it was an awakening for me. The intricacies of the crimes that Mr. Dartanyon A. Williams executed—I did not even know existed at that level. Law enforcement professionals from around the world need to take advantage of the "secrets" that DAW shares to help us not only spot but stop identity theft and vehicular identity theft. We would make our work lives easier if we did."

—Jerry Ford, Sgt., Natchez Police Department;
former president, Burk Watkins Fraternal
Order of Police of Natchez, MS

"Throughout my athletic career, I have been on a field waiting for the play to be called so that I could defend our goal line and tackle any opposition advancing on our team. My friend Dartanyon A. Williams' book, *The Master Identity Thief*, is that playbook and America is on the defensive, trying to scramble and sack perpetrators of this crime. Come on...let's geaux!"

—Davon Godchaux, defensive tackle,
#56, Miami Dolphins, NFL

"In *The Master Identity Thief*, it is clear enough for me that I did not know how vulnerable I was, how to protect myself from all forms of identity theft, and how to safeguard my credit and credibility. As a relative leader and role model in the NFL, I can't afford not to know. What Dartanyon A. Williams gives to the world through this two-book project is priceless. This is one of those exciting, entertaining, and equipping manuscripts that will help you to score a proverbial touchdown in this game we call life."

—Jamal Adams, safety, #33, Pro-Bowler MVP,
New York Jets, NFL

"I have known Dartanyon A. Williams since he was a school-age boy growing up in the church. He came from a wonderful two-parent Christian family who seemed to have it all. However, his life took a hard-left turn, and with a spirit of excellence he served the kingdom of darkness. (But God...!) Dartanyon's memoir is an encouraging true story of what can happen when Jesus arrests your life."

—Duck Scott, pastor, Oneonta Baptist Church, St. Joseph, LA

"Dartanyon A. Williams' life transition is a modern-day example of the metamorphosis that will inevitably occur when the favor and anointing of God is upon your life. Clearly, The Ancient of Days has gifted Dartanyon with both breadth and depth of knowledge. Upon first meeting him, I sensed that there was a special assignment on his life. Now that I understand the deep, dark depths of his past, I rejoice, because our Heavenly Father typically chooses those that others would count out. The best of what DAW has to offer the world is ahead of him and not behind him. If I were you, I would not count DAW out!"

—Reverend Earnest Ford Sr., pastor, Jerusalem Baptist Church, Natchez, MS; vice president, Mississippi Baptist General State Convention

"In 2012, my identity was compromised when a perpetrator filed a fraudulent tax return then claimed and received a substantial tax refund in my name, at my expense. We are nearing 2020 and I am still reeling in the aftermath of that identity theft activity. *The Master Identity Thief* by Dartanyon A. Williams is a masterfully created and crafted one-two punch that squares off to deliver the proverbial TKO blow to the crime of identity theft. For those of us who have been on the non-discriminating end of identity theft victimization, this two-volume work is divinely appointed."

—Dr. Lisa S. Vosper, associate commissioner for Workforce Education and Training, Board of Regents, State of Louisiana

"In his book, *The Master Identity Thief*, Dartanyon A. Williams goes into the dark underbelly of the multifaceted identity theft crimes, comes back, grabs a flashlight, and returns to shine the light on the ugliness that has crippled the lives of so many Americans."

—Dr. R. Jamie Spicer MD, MS, pain management physiatrist, North Texas Synergy Pain and Rehab

"Let me warn you that from the beginning of the story, it is disturbing. I'll admit it made me raise my eyebrow and question what kind of person could do such a thing. After spending personal time with DAW, I can say, unequivocally, a mastermind and genius! In the end you're going to thank him for exposing the disturbing crime that is identity theft and for offering solutions."

—Dr. Jay Perniciaro, B.S., D.C., chiropractic physician, Total Care Injury and Pain Center

THE MASTER IDENTITY THIEF
Testimony and Solutions of an Expert Witness

ISBN   978-1-5445-0701-9 *Hardcover*
         978-1-5445-0699-9 *Paperback*
         978-1-5445-0700-2 *Ebook*
         978-1-5445-0702-6 *Audiobook*

DEDICATION AND PRAYER

This two-volume book is dedicated to my beloved parents, Freddie and Linda Williams, who exist as my first victims of identity theft and are the representatives of every identity that I've ever stolen. For without their love and forgiveness, this work would not have been possible.

In response to their loving kindness, I purpose my repentance to be eternally evident, by a prevalent and pervasive apology respecting the victims of my egregious crimes and regarding the people victimized by the criminal actions of others.

I present this work as a peace offering of my penitence and hope that it would be received in the same spirit with which it has been authored. Even so, my humble prayer is that this book be used as an illuminator to shine greater light on crimes perpetrated by dark minds and not hereby used as a lamp to guide into even greater darkness.

Amen.

—Dartanyon A. Williams

The story that follows is my own, though it is based on what I remember and what I feel comfortable sharing in light of such sensitive and disturbing material. Some facts, names, and details may have been changed. The essence remains.

A VOW...

In honoring the vow I made to Yahweh thirteen years ago regarding the declaration of His sacred name, you will find on the four corners of each page throughout this book a different four-letter depiction of the Tetragrammaton (The ancient four-letter Yisraelitish name of Yahweh, occurring 6,823 times throughout the Hebrew Scriptures and validated via archeological findings throughout the known world). The four letters, like the four Gospels, connote North, South, East, and West, which confers the omnipresence of Yahweh. The Heavens declare His glory, and the earth shows His handywork; and without controversy, Yahweh has not left Himself without witnesses to declare the glory of His power and the greatness of His name. For the nihilist man, I issue not a challenge to meaningless debate, but in the Spirit of love and service I encourage you to emulate the Bereans (Acts 17:11), and search with due diligence to see if these things I profess are so.

Additional imagery, meaning, and significance are found throughout the pages of this book; from the numbering of chapters to the intricate cover designs, the material has been arranged to deliver multiple messages to the reader. To gain a full understanding and appreciation of all the deep thoughts, revelations, and answered prayers regarding the formatting, you may choose to fast forward to the appendix to digest the Sacred Name Declaration and Book Design and Layout sections in the back of the book so that your thoughts, ideas, and imagination may give light and life to the messages and meanings I hope to have conveyed with significance and simplicity alike.

Everything means something. May you find meaning and purpose in these pages as well.

CONTENTS

BOOK 2: AMERICA'S DOMESTIC WAR

To: KRYSTAL,

BELIEF - TRUST - FAITH,
HINDSIGHT...   INSIGHT...   FORESIGHT!

YAHWEH BLESS,
DAN
3/18/21

To BECOME IS TO BE!

BOOK ONE

THE MASTER
IDENTITY THIEF

TESTIMONY AND SOLUTIONS
OF AN EXPERT WITNESS

DARTANYON A. WILLIAMS

FOREWORD

The Master Identity Thief: Testimony and Solutions of an Expert Witness is a real-life story written by a former identity thief who shares his story about how he learned and practiced the crime of identity theft. His account of identity theft practice begins in his adolescence with the theft of his parents' identities. As he gradually learned through trial and error as a novice thief, his criminality matured and crimes escalated, eventually elevating him to a master identity thief with a full-scale criminal enterprise. Dartanyon A. Williams (DAW), informs the reader of the intimate and mind-blowing details of his identity theft operations, including the techniques, tools, and trade secrets that he used to master his strategies and define his motivations, including the insatiable lust to satisfy his self-imposed entitlement to money, power, and control.

Williams provides the reader with a view of the daring adventures and dangers of practicing organized criminal activities in the underworld that included numerous arrests and encounters with the criminal justice system that eventually led to extensive periods of incarceration. In his book, DAW is willing to put it all on the table and share his story as a published confession of his sins (1 John 1:8); condition (fruit) of his repentance (Luke 3:8); and cleansing from the unrighteousness of crime (1 John 1:9), to help educate people about identity theft, to reduce or prevent victimizations from the crime, and to help fight the on-going and ever-increasing battle against identity theft in America.

In the latter section of the book, Dartanyon tells the story about his repentance, redemption, and his conversion from the life of an identity thief, i.e., his three-dimensional redemption: consisting of reeducation, regeneration, and rehabilitation. His story is reminiscent of the Biblical story of the prodigal son (Luke 15:1-24), who disgraced his parents, demanded his inheritance, departed his family, and engaged in riotous living, which landed him in the hog pen, a societal symbol of debauchery and a debilitating lifestyle, before making a conscious decision to repent in 180 degrees of redirection and return home to his Father.

In the process of repentance, his Father saw him from afar and met him with forgiveness to celebrate the reunion and reconciliation with his son who was once lost in sin (dead) but was now received and restored (alive) again in love. DAW's story parallels this same narrative and concludes with his parents putting their Christian faith to practice by forgiving the very son who committed sins against their parentage and his inheritance. Many a lesson can be extrapolated from the similarities between the prodigal son and Dartanyon A. Williams, but for our purposes here it is enough to recognize and appreciate the actual and active principles that bridge Biblical parables to human realities.

Ultimately, despite his troubled past and the thousands of people who were victimized by his "schemes and scams," DAW tells about the amazing grace and redemptive love that he finally accepted from God, and the second chance to turn his life around for the betterment of us all. Indeed, freedom from the shackles of identity theft that kept him in bondage for a transformative season of his life is nothing short of a miraculous conversion that enabled him to pick up the broken pieces and help wage a new war against the very type of crimes that he once committed.

Ironically, when Dartanyon was developing the elaborate scheme of "Vehicular Identity Theft" while under supervised probation after having served a federal prison sentence for conspiracy to commit identity theft, Judith Collins of Michigan State University concluded that "What it's going to take is somebody who's really going to be married to this issue [identity theft] in terms of some knowledge and ability and skills and devotion and strict focus on this one single issue... And I don't know who would do it."[1]

---

1 Sullivan, Bob. "9/11 Report Light on ID Theft Issues." NBCNews.com. NBCUniversal News Group, August 4, 2004. http://www.nbcnews.com/id/5594385/ns/us_news-security/t/report-light-id-theft-issues/.

After reading *The Master Identity Thief* and its companion *America's Domestic War*, I am persuaded that Professor Collins and the awaiting world will observe that Dartanyon A. Williams is perhaps the personification of her admitted uncertain solution to thwart the identity theft epidemic.

It is my professional opinion that everyone should read this book, not just because identity theft has a market and crime category of its own and is the one uncontrollable issue that has devastated more American lives than any other single crime in US history, but also because it does not discriminate. Millions of Americans are victimized by identity theft annually. The FTC Consumer Data Book estimated that between 2017 and 2022, online payment fraud will increase by 13.7 percent annually, and digital bank fraud will reach $8 billion, a prediction that suggests credit card fraud will spike despite the efforts of CVV codes, EMV chip technology, and other preventive security measures.

The reality that the story of *The Master Identity Thief* takes place in a rural setting reveals that many people in small towns and rural communities, who may be unknowingly and unwittingly vulnerable to identity theft, should also read this book.

Moreover, in light of the fact that the global expansion of computers and telecommunication devices have aided the rapid expansion of international identity theft, everyone in and around the world should read this book, for it contains the remedies and recipes to solutions for a host of problems that seem to be on a trajectory that will only widen and worsen over time.

Finally, people in the general public who want to prevent themselves from being victimized by identity theft, or who simply have a desire to read the amazing true story of a master identity thief and his redemption from a life of crime—whether for entertainment, edification, or education—*The Master Identity Thief: Testimony and Solutions of an Expert Witness* is a compelling, captivating, worthwhile read.

—Thomas J. Durant, Jr., Ph.D.,
Emeritus Professor of Sociology/Criminology,
Louisiana State University and A&M College,
Author/Publisher, Durant Publishing Company

ONE

IN THE BEGINNING: HER SCHEME, HIS SCAM

Jacob said to his father, "I am Esau your firstborn."
—Genesis 27:19

s I write these words—first scratched onto notebook paper in cell A-12 of solitary confinement, then finally typed with love and care after more than a decade of healing—with everything in me I believe the Bible was written from the inspiration of the Holy Spirit. However, the story that follows is a living testimony of the dark inspiration that human nature can draw from even the holiest of places. While I wouldn't say that the fullest extent of my crimes were drawn directly from or given twisted justification by the Holy Scriptures, my criminal journey began with baby steps and a youthful naiveté, carried out with trial, error, and a dogged determination to get what I thought was rightfully mine.

To be honest, on sleepy Sunday mornings back in the summer of '95, I was only *inspired* to get back home and on with my day.

My parents held Sunday school as a sacred ritual, with no input from us kids on the matter. They would gather us siblings together to walk the quarter-mile or so to Guildfield Baptist Church in St. Joseph, Louisiana, our rural hometown that anyone local just calls St. Joe, all dressed up in our Sunday best. There, we joined the other kids in the hood to sit under the teachings of Ms. Emma Douglas—a.k.a., Ms. Emma Newman, or simply Ms. Emma, as we kids called her. Ms. Emma was a neighborhood matriarch and the undisputed Candy Lady of our little community. With treasures from her candy bag in hand—Super Big Bol gum or some Rice Krispie treats if we were lucky—I'd choose a wooden chair by the window and drift off in my own thoughts until it was time to leave.

I was fifteen years old on one particular Sunday that comes to mind, old enough to have heard most of the stories before but young enough to have no more than a bit of childhood mischief under my belt. I settled into my perch by the window and let the sun warm my face. I laced my fingers behind my head and traced the scar left when a car collided with my bike nine years prior. My broken hip bone and ten stitches had healed, but the bike that my dad bought me from a neighborhood rummage sale just a couple weeks before the wreck was totaled. I remember it all so clearly—one of those iconic moments in childhood. It's a memory that you can feel.

Stuck in a cool classroom, with the world waiting outside the door. When the sun hits you just right, all you want is to curl up in those rays and drift off to sleep.

I knew better than to doze, though, and Ms. Emma's teaching wasn't all bad. I heard her turning to Genesis chapter 25, caught the names Rebekah and Isaac, Jacob and Esau...I could almost see them outside my window, playacting the story to occupy my imagination.

Ms. Emma was in the middle of a four-part lesson on the patriarchs, the founding fathers of the Jewish nation and the Christian faith. I knew the origins of the promise to barren Sarah and Abraham, the birth of their sons Isaac and Ishmael, and now it seems we were to hear about Isaac's plight with his own children, Jacob and Esau.

Ms. Emma read about the birth of the twins from the book of Genesis, how Jacob had hold of Esau's heel coming out of the womb—a hustler from birth, never quite satisfied, always grasping for something more. As her teaching intermingled with my daydreams, Jacob's imagined face looked increasingly like my own. I chuckled at the visual as she spoke of Jacob's scheming nature, sympathizing with his distaste for working the fields—a family and community chore that I chafed against every summer.

She taught that Esau was a skillful hunter and given to game, while Jacob was an opportunist with the gift of gab. The more I could relate to Jacob, the more of my attention Ms. Emma had, though I would have never admitted it. After all, why *should* Esau gain the birthright of the firstborn—barely born first anyway and without the skills to handle such a responsibility?

Jacob's first scam was to negotiate birth rights away from his brother after a long and frustrated hunting expedition. He knew that Esau's appetite for instant gratification was his weakness, and he negotiated the exchange of a delicious meal for a distant inheritance. Esau agreed to a verbal contract with Jacob that, through their Hebrew customs and culture, was as binding as one written in stone. Later in their lives, their adolescent deal would be put to the test when Isaac put his house in order in preparation for his death. His paternal blessing belonged to Esau, his firstborn son, and would be bestowed under the arrangement of a ceremonial meal to be prepared and presented by Esau's own hands.

My interest began to pique as I wondered how Jacob would con his way out of this one. That's when Ms. Emma named Rebekah, the boys' mother. In her unbridled partiality towards Jacob, Rebekah had contrived a scheme of her own. She decided that Jacob had to steal his brother's identity in order to gain his birthright.

Rebekah outfitted Jacob in some of Esau's attire, adding goat skins on his neck and hands to mimic the hairy skin of her eldest son. Testing out the depth of his scams for perhaps the first time in life, Jacob suppressed his fears and colluded with his mother to defraud Esau of his birthright blessing. Together, they conspired to deceive Isaac through the commission of what the Federal Bureau of Investigations would classify today as Aggravated Identity Theft—the world's very first documented case.

My teenage ears only heard the tenor of Jacob's determination and Rebekah's detailed foresight, not the misdeeds and consequences. The cultural system of birthrights seemed wholly unjust, and I admired Jacob's ability to dance outside of the lines and shape the future that he believed he deserved. The seeds had been planted, though not at all how Ms. Emma or the Scriptures had intended, and my willing soul was ready soil, ripe for planting and harvesting.

History views Rebekah and Jacob through the lens of their redemption. After all, in the Biblical tellings, we have the full picture within a few short chapters. Rebekah is honored alongside her husband, and Jacob's name is changed to Israel after he wrestles with an angel in Genesis 32:28: "Your name will no longer be Jacob, but Israel, because you have struggled with God and with humans and have overcome." Israel then becomes the father of a nation—known from then on as the twelve tribes of Israel.

Yet if we pause for a moment before continuing their story, just as I did on that warm Sunday morning in that solemn wooden church building on the corner of Third and Washington, we have to criminalize their conspiracy as aggravated identity theft, if we are judging righteously. Any honest observer of that moment in a person's life would offer criticism at best, and if we're speaking criminally then one must admit that Rebekah and Jacob's actions warrant the scenario of a criminal arrest, at worst. For the next twelve chapters—as many as the sons of Jacob—I must sit in my own moments of criticism and castigation, as well as in moments of criminal arrests and imprisonment, with the darkest parts of my story forever on pause.

In this telling, I can expose the steps I took as my crimes unfolded, but I can offer no excuse for them. Not one person is responsible for what I've done, aside from me. Not the schools, society, or my family, and certainly not the lovely Ms. Emma Douglas.

Yet, as I'm writing and you're reading, I'm also wholly free from those moments.

Divine Providence allowed for Jacob's identity theft to make him the patriarch of Judeo-Christian heritage. With such a complete redemption realized, I hope you'll receive my story in the same forgiving light. I, too, have wrestled with the Ancient of Days and my own humanity—and I, too, have overcome.

Rather than an editorial on the mechanics of identity theft, what follows is the raw reality of my experience. Any attempt at a definitive work would be outdated before it could be published anyway. The criminal mind will always meet and exceed the challenges of technological advancements, much in the same way counterfeiters continue to match the efforts of the US mint.

Instead, I write to seal my story and unveil its lessons for the sake of America and the endless toll identity theft takes. I write for my children to know what I've been through, what I've learned, and how I came to discover my own identity after years of living through the countless identities that I had stolen. I write to lift the mask from the crime as a former master identity thief, with a proactive lens on this world that our security and legislative systems only seem to react to.

Conventional wisdom often requires a societal jolt—a shock to its system, a calculated act of measured radicalism to rev, revamp, and reform the status quo. As one who possesses an intimate knowledge on the subject of identity theft, I'm stepping outside of the prescriptive bounds of a self-help pamphlet or countertop brochure to bring you into a world that no one talks about and hardly cares enough to venture into. It's a world even I've never fully shared before the completion of this work.

At times, reliving my story was painful, and it often felt presumptuous. I spent time re-engaging the criminal mind in ways I've worked so hard to escape. I should confide that between sentences, paragraphs, and chapters I often took breaks from the writing process to engage the kind of prayer that hurts when it's righteous but also heals when it's real. This work was a painful but necessary labor of truth and love, and I have only obscured facts where necessary to protect the individuals who crossed my criminal path.

To the many victims of identity theft—I offer my apologies in advance for where my critics may accuse me of being boastful and where my skeptics might believe I'm only being braggadocios. To them I assert that I am not in any way proud of the intrusions, injuries, and inconveniences I have caused in the lives of others. But only the truth can establish a righteous record and set us free.

Since our current systems of prevention and warning only scratch the surface of the world of identity theft, I invite you to take a walk in my shoes. Follow my story, and we'll see just how far down the rabbit hole can go. With an entire nation of industries, agencies, and individuals at untold levels of risk, and with a legislative body preoccupied with blue-collar criminal infractions and willfully remiss of the white-collar criminal enterprise, it truly is only the truth that will liberate us from the injuries and infractions of willful and woeful ignorance.

Like Jacob, my interest in identity theft began with my father as my first experimental victim. Experimentation gradually developed into the triangulated livelihood of committing fraud, selling drugs, and gambling it to scale (or to loss), culminating in twenty-two criminal arrests—plus one more that came back to haunt me like a ghost, years later—four state prosecutions, and two federal convictions with subsequent prison sentences. While my criminal works surpassed anything I could have envisioned through that warm window at Guildfield Baptist Church, the depths of loss ran far deeper as well. This work is a retelling weighted with humility, as the call and command of true Biblical repentance.

As those of us who have experienced it can attest to, with any fruit of repentance comes a degree of self-sacrifice. As I type each word on this page, I am acutely aware that many a potential and practicing identity thief will frown upon this work. There is real potential for them to undermine it or retaliate against me for it, and still I press on.

To them, I offer a call toward redemption.

To America, I offer this willing sacrifice, to give back where I once stole.

To the world we all shape with each passing day, as nations of standards and principles built on the promises of civil liberties and social privileges, I offer this attempt to make our communities and our countries safer and let the record reflect that I make these offers as a proud American citizen.

Subsequently, it is not the interception of potential physical threat for which I petition, but rather for spiritual interference and intercession. To the reader, I solicit and covet your prayers in whatever measure you see fit, in support of the greater work that this book commences.

Come what may, cost what it might, let Yahweh's will be done, and may He be pleased with this work and all that it inspires.

> *If Yah be for us, who can be against us?*
> —Romans 8:31

Selah.

TWO

MY BEGINNINGS

Whoever robs his father or his mother,
And says, "It is no transgression,"
The same is companion to a destroyer.
　　　　—King Solomon, Proverbs 28:24 (NKJV)

started cutting grass at the age of ten as an external
household chore and neighborhood side hustle, as well
as in preparation to join the family's Mom and Pop lawn
maintenance business. My grass-cutting companion was
one of those old school, 1980s Snapper riding mowers—
the red ones that will leave you hurting and hemorrhoidal if
you ride them long enough. By twelve, I would cut grass for
Lake Bruin property owners every Wednesday starting in the
spring, then work in the fields every day of the week once
summer came along.

Tensas Parish, Louisiana, which was my family's home for much of my childhood, is driven by agriculture. There was and remains cotton, corn, wheat, and soybean fields covering thousands of acres, all owned by individuals who've kept that property in their families for generations. We were mostly kids working those fields—mostly kids from hardworking families, many of whom have been there just as long as anyone else, but whose grandparents didn't own any fields.

As children, we were hired out to chop the smothering weeds from the root bases of cotton stalks that our parents had picked by hand only two generations prior. The rows stretched on for miles in any one direction with no relief in sight and no reparations in mind, let alone discussed. Stakeholders and outsider justification said those fields made plenty of work and kept it available for communities thirsting for any opportunity they could get. We just called it the "Hoe Field."

I hated every step, every chop, every puff of cotton that came from those awful fields.

During the summer months, the sweltering heat under normal conditions felt in excess of one hundred degrees—though there's nothing normal about chopping cotton as a teenager, fully exposed to the elements, with no shade for miles around. And all for the measly daily wage of twenty-six dollars for seven hours of work.

Yes, the work was technically optional, but with limited resources and access, those so-called opportunities chafed—and as vestiges of an age of outright slavery, they should've.

Through the passage of time and some nominal law changes, the overseers that once cracked whips in those fields transcended into crop dusters spraying carcinogenic chemicals. Agricultural science in Tensas Parish had evolved into generational genocide, with unnamed, uncounted residents of Tensas Parish dying slow deaths from these poisons, living long lives under economic suppression, and echoing a troubled history that we never speak of for fear of disrupting the status quo.[2]

Those fields were nothing more than seasonal occupation for those of us who aspired to work with what we had in order to gain what history had not given. The fields that we worked belonged to community leaders who only held their positions as their own kind of Jacob-and-Esau era birthright, their land passed down through the generations from plantation to present day.

With the agriculturists, farmers, and landowners also holding the seats of councilman and committee member, only these "leaders" retained the right to wave new developments in. And why wouldn't they restrict them? New opportunities might break the cycles of power that benefitted them and their families. As a teenager, I remember when Fruit of the Loom identified our cotton fields for their purposes, yet the whole

---

2   To my knowledge there has not been a single study by the
    Environmental Protection Agency nor Louisiana State University
    Agriculture Center that shows or disproves the harmful effects of cotton
    poisons and other deadly chemicals blanketed over the domicile of
    rural communities, specifically, Tensas Parish. As I write, LSU students
    are working on reducing chemical usage in the region: https://www.
    lsuagcenter.com/profiles/jmorgan/articles/page1569507376903

region voted against the move. No factories, no competition, no industry—and no jobs or real opportunities—are allowed into areas like these. As an alternative to the Tensas Parish region, Fruit of The Loom took their $50 million factory and job opportunities to the neighboring parish of Concordia and set up shop in the city of Vidalia, Louisiana.[3]

If we're talking about schemes and scams, those of the evil men of decades past are still alive and well, merely politicized and packaged under different names. To be perfectly blunt, slavery has only been reformed over the years, not removed, and it often takes on the face of economic control and child labor.[4]

Such were the unfavorable and unattractive limitations that incubated my immature reasoning. The fields I tended in Tensas Parish showed me a societal game that I couldn't win—an unjust birthright delivered to me even while I was grasping at its heels. Even after I was grown and gone, I continually revisited that region of cotton and crime throughout my life. Until my pursuit of a true conversion was complete, it would only yield the rotten fruit of bad choices and even worse outcomes.

---

3 "Fruit of the Loom to Build New Louisiana Plant." UPI. UPI, May 12, 1993. https://www.upi.com/Archives/1993/05/12/Fruit-of-the-Loom-to-build-new-Lousiana-plant/4311737179200/.

4 Fernández, Valeria. "The Young Hands That Feed Us." Pacific Standard, July 9, 2019. https://psmag.com/social-justice/the-young-hands-that-feed-us.

The summer before I turned sixteen would become my last ever with a hoe in hand. I'd decided it. I couldn't take it anymore and didn't feel a need to.

I've always been one to work hard, but never at a menial task and hardly ever at manual labor. The hoe fields were both, and the sun made me feel sluggish and annoyed. I couldn't help but daydream—a constant escape, always available right there in my mind.

Through the heatwaves rising in the distance, I could see the story of Jacob and Esau playing out again, still envisioning myself as the cunning Jacob subverting the system. This time, more current details were coming into view. If Jacob wanted a generational birthright, I wanted the life promised to me on TV commercials and sitcoms and Al Pacino's *Scarface*. They taunted me like a mirage in the distance—Capital One's "purchase power" dancing in front of me, just out of reach. I could see myself living that glorified life of a successful drug dealer, with just a few transactions, arrests, threats on my life, and theft of my accumulated wealth all awaiting my arrival to a life of crime. If Scarface did it, so could I.

I was convinced, though self-deceived, that Jacob and I were exactly alike and that God favored us similarly. We both just had to scheme and scam our way into the next level of blessing.

In that world, I had access. I had means. And I'd been thinking about it more and more as the summer progressed. With one little card, that world could be mine—and I determined it should be. A better, bigger, and brighter life was awaiting me. Like Jacob, I didn't belong underfoot, watching brute force win the prizes. I was smarter than that, and my sense of enti-tlement would be neither abated nor abandoned until I got what was mine. This was the thought pattern that fueled my unbridled lusts and untamed ambitions.

I should be clear here that I wasn't angry with my parents. I was, however, unjustly dissatisfied with the life they'd led us to. I say unjustly, because what did I truly need that I didn't already have as a child? In what way did my parents neglect or deprive me? By all accounts, my mom and dad provided a normal, healthy lifestyle for me and my three siblings.

We were considered a middle-class family in the community with monetary means provided by my dad's employment with the LSU AgCenter Northeast Research Station and extra income supplied by the family's lawn service. My mom stayed home with us kids, and our needs were met in ways that my neighbors and school friends couldn't claim. My siblings grew up without the temptation to sink to the levels that I did. But young Dartanyon was convinced: I was *owed* this life. I was determined to access more than either of my parents was willing or able to give.

During the noon hour on a hot summer day, just before the hoe field shift ended, I set the hoe down and set out to get *it*—by that, I mean whatever I could. I was convinced that stealing my dad's credit card would allow me to change my circumstances, so I resolved to gain that purchase power. To unlock that world, that birthright I craved more than Esau craved soup, and make it my own.

If I can only stay focused, I got this, I thought. I was sure I could manipulate it like my tests and teachers or the street corner games I'd seen played a thousand times. I didn't realize that the lure of lust and vain aspirations were moving targets, or else I didn't care. I was locked into the chase.

Growing up, I was a curious kid who found school boring and bothersome. That's not to say I didn't excel. My eidetic memory allowed me to pay just enough attention and take just enough notes to bring it all back at test time. School was a game. To prove I was the smartest in the class, I beat everyone at test time. I beat everyone eating lunch in the cafeteria. I won my way into the advanced academic Beta Club, then rewarded my intellectual demonstrations by becoming the class clown. The point of school was to get lessons out and not fail—with that achievement in hand, I was sure I had the right to goof off, much to the chagrin of my teachers.

Aside from the Beta Club, there wasn't anything more I could access that might hold my attention in or out of school. If you haven't lived in a rural community, it might be difficult to picture how little we had access to. We didn't have a YMCA or Boys and Girls Club. Besides the underfunded athletic programs, we didn't have before and after school extracurricular activities like the all-white, de facto segregated Tensas Academy did just up the street from Davidson Highschool. A concrete slab and cast-iron basketball goal doubled as our playground and community center. We didn't even have computers in the public library. We went to school from eight to three, then had to figure out the rest of life on our own.

With a population of approximately thirteen hundred people, not even the adults had much to do. As a young child, I remember relatives congregating on paydays to host and play table card games at each other's houses. Eventually, my interest was drawn out to street corner gambling, which ultimately introduced me to marijuana as well. If you weren't smoking marijuana by sixteen, you were peddling it. I had no interest in smoking, but I could see the wheels of society turning and wanted to figure out how to manipulate those wheels myself.

Like most kids in impoverished communities, African American kids in particular, our books were hand-me-downs from metropolis schools—hardcovers with the signatures of two, three, four students already there in front of mine. Like the stuff of movies, our curricular design was the all too real OBY—"Only for Black Youth"—designation, a planned and purposed disparity perpetrated throughout America's public school system.

With only a lifetime of minimum wage and agriculture to look forward to, and a school system that did not seem to care what happened to us beyond our hours at the desk, what did I care whether my education was a success? I didn't have to try to get good grades and get by in school, but it wouldn't matter to me if I did. I didn't want the life that applying myself to my education would bring me.[5] I also didn't want to end up used up by drugs...but that's where I saw a path out. If I was always going to be battling against a flawed system, why not step outside of it and get some wins instead? I could access some cash to make an initial marijuana purchase, then sell that to fund

---

5   In his book *Miseducation of a Negro*, Carter G. Woodson foresaw my
    experience sixty years before my arrival to it.

street corner gambling, which I knew I could win, then reinvest it back into drug dealing.

Without realizing it, I was signing up for the self-funded Black enterprise that economic inequality and social disparity orchestrates for the urban community.

This was not the example modeled to me in my home. Both of my parents were raised in similar educational environments, and they went on to lead lives of industry and integrity. They gave me the best that they could under the circumstances, creating a stable family in spite of being surrounded by poverty and broken homes.

Like any worthy member of America's proletariat, my dad, Freddie Williams, Sr., is the epitome of hard work, the embodiment of good industry, my childhood version of Captain America, and a man after Yahweh's own heart.[6] He is the real life embodiment of what every fatherless child imagines and hopes for. When he wasn't mowing acres of land for the resident specialists who lived on university property, he shucked corn and sharecropped cotton in the employ of LSU AgCenter. Mild-mannered and self-reliant, he always took care of our family, working faithfully for a modest hourly wage as our sole breadwinner. My dad is one of a few good men. I'm proud to embrace and celebrate him and will forever honor him as my father.[7]

My mother, Linda Williams, dropped out of school in the eighth grade when she got pregnant with my sister Samantha, which motivated my dad to take care of her as she

---

6   Acts 13:22
7   Ephesians 6:2

demonstrated motherly love while raising me and my siblings. She was a homemaker and a true nurturer, though she was always more pragmatic and disciplinary than my father, and remains so to this day even as she ages gracefully. But my mother wasn't restricted to domestics. She was no stranger to hard work.

My mother labored seasonally and seriously in Tensas Warehouse ginning cotton on Eli Whitney's modernized machinery. Before the cotton trailers made it to the warehouse, she also worked in the fields "stumping cotton" during the autumn—a manual process to compress the very cotton that I had chopped weeds from during the summer and that my dad had freshly picked in the fall. No matter if she was ginning in the warehouse, stumping cotton in the fields, or baking cakes in our kitchen, she was always the more street savvy of my parents. I tell people that I got my kindness and generosity from my dad, but the hustle and grind in me came from my mom. These days, she'll testify to the same.

The bottom line is that my parents didn't raise me to rely on societal limitations and access to opportunity like a crutch, nor to wield them as excuses. They made the best of what they had and raised us kids to do so as well.

As much as I admire their example in retrospect, none of their credentials were of any immediate concern to me in adolescence. My blinders were up.

It was July of 1995, and I had about ten months before the next hoe field season started. If I started right away, I could make that mirage of an idealized future come into focus without ever stepping back into the fields that were bedded by the same plantation dirt and piteous dust of America's greatest moral debt to humanity—the enslavement of her own children for more than four hundred arduous years. All I needed was a little *purchase power* to jumpstart my escape from economic slavery and agricultural incarceration, not comprehending the literal imprisonment that was likely to follow.

Some kids can't keep their hands out of "grown folks affairs," and I'll let you guess whether I was that kind of kid. Thanks to the constant observation of my parents' comings and goings, something specific had piqued my interest: an envelope from Capital One, laying right there on the kitchen table. No matter how sinful my thoughts became, however, I could not conjure enough audacity to arbitrarily take possession of said envelope. I was born of parents from the *old school*, where lessons of respect were conveniently taught in the quasi-classrooms of corporeal discipline—and the mail was one such lesson. My siblings and I were not ever given access to the mail or any other documents of importance. This was a right reserved for adults, of which our household only had two: Freddie and Linda Williams.

These restrictions only quickened the motion of sin that had begun to work within me.[8] The lust of my eyes required that I "disregard the commandment of my mother and break the law of my father."[9]

---

8   Romans 7:5
9   Proverbs 6:20

Put simply: I had to find out what was inside.

I decided that one of two things needed to happen: either the envelope had to mysteriously disappear, which would create unnecessary suspicion, or I had to wait for my mom to sit at the kitchen table when she paid the monthly household bills. I thought I could feign interest in unrelated matters while keenly observing her management of the coveted envelope.[10] This option would require perfect timing, and there was no guarantee that I would be at home when my mom began to sift through the mail, but the former option carried much graver consequences.

The risk of peering over her shoulder seemed the lesser of the two risks, and I was sure the attempt would be worth the payoff. If I could become an authorized user on my dad's card, I could access the cash that would launch my street-savvy empire. Once I flipped my borrowed wealth in the drug and gambling circuits that I was also sure I would dominate, I could pay the bill before the month's cycle restarted and no one would be the wiser. All I needed was the account number that must be waiting somewhere inside that envelope.

As my aspirations grew, so did my impatience. Without understanding how the economy of a home was generally managed, I began to think that it was unusual and unfair for her to pay the household bills only once a month. My dad was

---

10 This is exactly as juvenile as it sounds, yet if you look for ways to prevent identity theft, one of the first things they will tell you is that people try to look over shoulders to spot useful information. Believe me, this option only scratches the surface. More to come on that as you read here and in *America's Domestic War*.

the only person who retrieved mail from the post office, and that too seemed unfair. Of course, as the child that I was, I didn't yet know that to him the post office box was a lifeless vacuum of monthly bills that sucked away the livelihood he worked so hard to earn. I greedily imagined it was a treasure trove of opportunity.

Every evening, I anxiously expected to catch my mom at the kitchen table tearing through envelopes and furiously writing checks. Meanwhile, those tantalizing Capital One commercials seemed to come at a greater frequency and volume than before. Could it really be coincidental, or were they airing as a sign of my calling to my own personal niche in the credit card industry? *I see you, Capital One! I'm coming for you. It's only a matter of time before your hypnotic purchase power is mine to possess.*

Typically, my mom would attend to the bills as an evening chore. On this particular day, she elected to pay the bills when my dad was on his lunch break. Undoubtedly, this choice was thanks to the kind of quiet noon hour that only a summer afternoon can facilitate, when my siblings and I had made an ephemeral diaspora of the family unit.

When the streetlights came on, I came home full of hope that this would finally be the day my mom would pay the bills. To my dismay, the table basket that should have been piled high with a pre-bill-paying cache of mail, was eerily empty. The household mail had already been processed, and I was nowhere near anyone's shoulder when it happened.

It's hard to say which began to race faster: my heartbeat or the thoughts of disaster that flooded my mind. That card number was my means to financial gain and the pseudo-independence I craved. What now? The rest of the night, I was anxious and irritable, with no appetite and no idea what I was going to do, so I retired to my room to collect myself lest one of my parents confront me about my unwelcoming deportment.

Distraught and overwhelmed with disappointment, I began to think that somehow my parents had found out about my scheme. What if the break in routine was part of their necessary precautions to protect themselves? What if they knew and my whole plan had unraveled before it began?

Eventually I calmed down enough to remember I hadn't shared my aspirations with anyone but the man in the mirror. I might have been a troublemaker, but this was one trouble no one saw coming—and after all, I hadn't done a thing yet. I couldn't afford to abandon my aspirations to mere assumption. This would require an investigation that was best conducted in the dead of night.

I knew my parents slept with their bedroom door closed and were not light sleepers. If I could wait until the household was securely and soundly asleep, I could rummage the kitchen trashcan and table area to gain a clear picture of the day's activities—and potentially access that mythical envelope—without fear of reprisal.

Thanks to the sudden onset of excitement-induced insomnia, I had no trouble staying awake until my entire family had fallen asleep. I tried to play possum and wait until 1:30 a.m., my target hour of safety. Once the sounds of sleep rose from each bedroom, however, I decided that 1:00 a.m. was more conducive to the search and seizure I had planned. At approximately 12:40 a.m., I eased out of the bed so as not to disturb my brothers and padded into the kitchen.

Shaking with jitters as if I'd washed a bag of sugar down with coffee and an energy drink, I sifted through the trash. I was way too nervous and overly cautious to search efficiently, and I found myself hearing every creak and groan in the walls and ducts. Doubling as my own lookout, after the fourth or fifth pause to tiptoe to the living room to make sure my mom wasn't up to go to the bathroom or to catch me in the act, I was finally able to concentrate on my work. My last look was the longest and produced a find that would elevate my thinking, enhance my criminality, and unlock the passage to countless vulnerable identities over the ten years that followed. The envelope that haunted my dreams was there in my hand.

If you stay with me on this journey, you'll see how extensive identity theft truly is, down to the thought processes and circumstances that can turn normal people into identity thieves. But I would like to pause here to posit a constant reminder: I am not in any way proud of what I'm relaying in telling my story. I can feel the sweat, hear the commercials, picture my teachers' faces…This has been a bittersweet walk down memory lane.

For a more direct discussion on the creation and impacts of identity theft, flip to the second volume of this book – that places my crimes in your context.

THREE

EXPERIMENTAL DISCOVERIES: A PATIENT PRACTICE

Patience is a high virtue...but virtue can hurt you.
—Chaucer

held the Capital One statement up like a treasure, then devoured every bit of information it could give me. It told me that my dad had a maximum credit limit of five thousand dollars, with only about three hundred dollars on the balance. It told me there was a cash advance allowance of half of the total credit limit, too—more than enough to get both my illegal exploits off the ground. To gain access, however, I would need more information, and that piece had been detached from the statement in my hand. I assumed that was part of the bill payment process and went back to the table basket for the missing piece of my puzzle.

After only a moment's hesitation, I found and confiscated the envelope designated for Capital One's billing department, then put all the other mail back in place just as my mom had arranged it. My dad would pick that bundle up and drop it all off without any care to read it, coming or going. So I tucked the discarded billing statement and packaged payment in my nightwear, tiptoed back to my room, and hid the two documents under the carpet in my bedroom closet. That night, or what was left of it, I dreamed of the opportunities that daylight would bring.

By the time I woke up, my dad had already left for work. I bypassed my morning personal hygiene routines and went straight to the kitchen to see if the outgoing mail had left the table basket en route to the post office. To my relief, the stack of payments that I held in my hands only a few hours earlier was nowhere in sight.

I'm not sure I had ever completed my daily chores so fast as I did that day.

As soon as I was free, I collected the secured documents from underneath the carpet and went to one of my grandmother's—Ida Mae Harris-Turner, another cornerstone of the community and one of my very favorite people—unoccupied rental properties around the corner. Eagerly, I sat down to study the documents in private.

I didn't stay there for long, for fear of a relative discovering me in the midst of my research. When I got too anxious, I relocated to Mr. Elvasus Fields' cow stall out on Duck Pond, a lone road that travels beside a levee that restricts the Mississippi River from breaching into a massive field where cotton used to be harvested. Duck Pond ironically didn't have a single duck or pond in sight, but it offered the serenity and seclusion I needed to figure this scheme out.

Just as I hoped, the envelope contained a fifty-dollar check made out to Capital One, along with the payment stub identifying the account that it should be applied to. Sweating bullets in the sticky Louisiana heat, I transcribed as much information as I could from both the personal check and the payment stub, writing quickly on the back of the statement that I fished out of the trash. Then I left my reference documents securely hidden in a storage bin where the cow feed was kept and went home to repackage and send off the payment stub and check before a late notice could alert my parents to foul play.

Encouraged by the ample information I was able to glean from just two pieces of paper, it was time for step two: to make use of the 1-800 numbers on those relentless credit card commercials in order to determine my scam's full prerequisites. Long before burner cellphones could provide anonymity, I simply used the cordless phone in the back of the house. Or, since my parents loved to pick up the phone on the other end of the house to eavesdrop on me and my older brother Lamont's communications with our female friends, I would write down the number from the ad and take it over to my friend Sammy Ghoston's house just across the street for uninterrupted, unlimited experimental calls—dialing *67 first, of course, to block the number and all suspicion on Capital One's end.

Each time the operators picked up, I mimicked various things I'd heard on TV, from other adults, or from the customer service representatives themselves. I called in using various pseudonyms while feigning interest in different offers. Hearing their rehearsed telescripts over and over taught me how to use their lingo more naturally. Each conversation was calculated, and each one became easier and easier as I realized that the interaction depended only upon common courtesy and mutual cordiality.

"I would like to access my account, but I don't have my credit card handy."

"Sure, sir, no problem. I just need your name and social security number."

Click.

Alright, so I need to find his social...

Before long, I knew exactly what I needed to provide in order to set myself up as my father's authorized user. In order to cover all of my bases, I would need his complete name with middle initial, social security number, date of birth, home/work phone numbers, complete mailing address, and mother's maiden name—all easy details to satisfy. The personal check made out to Capital One had given me his birthdate, driver's license number, and complete mailing address. I discovered his social security card and number in his wallet that always rested in the headboard of my parent's bed when he wasn't working on the weekends. His home and work phone numbers were automatic knowledge, and to get his mom's maiden name I simply called my beloved grandma Ida (after all, I was her favorite, too) and asked her what her last name was before she got married.

Within two weeks of stealing my dad's credit card account information, my reconnaissance was complete. I was sure my knowledge of the credit card business surpassed that of the average credit card holder. I was probably qualified to be employed by the credit card industry—and I was certainly ready to end my practice runs and call Capital One for real.

From an intellectual standpoint, I was armed and ready to conduct fraudulent transactions in my dad's name. However, there was still the dilemma of the mail and how it was something just grown folks should worry about. Surely my parents would intercept the additional card I was ready to request. For about a week, I pondered my options and gathered more information.

I noticed that my dad occasionally checked the post office box on his lunch break, but his regular routine was to do so at the end of the day. I also learned that the post office in St. Joseph processed mail at nine in the morning, so I needed to gain access to the incoming mail between nine and noon. My mom did have an extra key, but I couldn't simply "borrow" it off of her key ring. I couldn't chance a random discovery sabotaging my plans.

I mulled over the problem constantly—in bed, at play, watching TV, mowing lawns…when the solution finally struck me like an epiphany. If I had my own incoming mail to wait for,

YHWH

and if I harassed my parents about its arrival every day, they'd eventually grow tired of my nagging. Then I wouldn't have to break my dad's habits or take my mom's key. Eventually, they would just let me check the post office box for them.

I contacted a few mail-order companies and organizations to request information, and at the same time started asking my parents about the mail right away. It took patience, but I had time. They would have to start taking me seriously at some point. To my benefit, though I didn't know about consumer-mailing lists at the time—back before privacy laws were reformed to restrict the trade of American consumers' information—my name was sold to a network of companies, and I received even more information and offers than what I requested.

Every day, I would ask about the mail, waiting for the day when one of my parents would announce the arrival of mail in my name. After two weeks of harassing them, it finally happened. Lamont and I were waiting in the truck after a long day of mowing lawns, and my dad emerged from the post office with not one but *two* hands full of mail and a slight smile on his face. I'd received mail at his post office box, and he approved of my trajectory toward adulthood.

Lamont watched with jealousy while my dad handed me the stack of envelopes and asked me to sort out mine from his. At home, I sat down at the kitchen table, in the full view of everyone, and sifted through my mail. I aimed for an air of ambivalence followed by spurious disappointment—where was that *one* item I was so anxiously awaiting? With the evidence of actual incoming mail in my possession, I could no longer be dismissed so easily. My reward was the freedom to check the mail occasionally, and I kept up the eager act until the day came at last: my mom let me use her key.

I covered my tracks as well as I could. Just in case the mail turned up empty, I always went with an older envelope stashed in my clothing. Whenever I returned, I'd have proof in hand that my mom was doing the right thing. Two months later, I had more mail coming into the house than my parents and siblings combined. One morning, she denied my request to use her key, but directed me to use a spare key that she apparently kept in a decorative cup on the entertainment center, as long as I was sure to put the key back every time.

The literal key to my scam had been lying under my nose the whole time. In fact, that same cup filled with various keys still rests peacefully on its perch to this day.

I pulled the key out of the cup, clutched it in a victory fist, and walked out to the post office on cloud nine. *It's on.*

That same day, I called Capital One and breezed through their security questions, sprinkling conversation throughout the call with the ease of a seasoned cardholder. Under the pretense that I was Freddie Williams, Sr., I advised the courteous and kind customer service representative that I needed an additional card with a PIN number for cash advances. The representative processed my request without the slightest suspicion or hesitation and advised that I would receive the additional card in approximately seven to ten business days.

In my adolescent mind, I heard her say it would be seven to ten days *before I would become unrighteously rich.*

For the next week I checked the post office box every day no later than 10:00 a.m. The bronze government-issued key lived on my person or under the carpet in my bedroom closet, with a scripted response ready if my mom ever asked whether I'd put it back in its home on the entertainment center. *Oh, you just reminded me! I'll put it back now.* I started to deliberately leave my junk mail in the box, in spite of my early and often visits to the post office, giving the impression that my interest in the mail was waning, when in reality it had just reached its peak.

Four days after my successful call to customer service, an inconspicuous, unattractive white envelope showed up in the family PO box. Accompanying it was a smaller, flimsy envelope that held a four-digit PIN (Personal Identification Number). The weight of the first envelope betrayed its innocence, and I tore into it to find a gorgeous green piece of plastic that symbolized my fruitful efforts and access to good credit and gateway to purchase power.

For this dream, I couldn't just pinch myself. I had to run the card and see if it worked. A cash advance of forty dollars proved it was real. And until my greed and growing gambling habit would get the best of me, my destiny was mine to command.

The cash advance limit of twenty-five hundred dollars came fast when my original plan to "flip" the money gambling or selling drugs and repay what I had stolen ran into a snag: I still had to figure out how to not lose everything gambling. I started looking for other ways to maximize the remaining credit limit while paying the minimum payment and trying not to get caught. I convinced myself that twenty-five hundred dollars' worth of punishment and restrictions would probably be the same as five thousand dollars' worth, which allowed me to expend the remaining credit limit while any spending at all was still a possibility.

To this point, my experiments only extended to credit card fraud. But as I thought back to that personal check resting inside that very first envelope, I realized there was another potential line to funding just within my grasp. I thought more cash could help me work my way out of the hole I'd been digging shooting street corner craps, a.k.a., dice, but unfortunately for me, I didn't put as much thought into check forgery as I had into the Capital One scheme. I stole a check from the back of my mom's checkbook, wrote it to myself for five hundred dollars, forged her signature, and walked to CrossKeys bank to have it cashed.

The bank promptly called my mother to verify the transaction. Shrewd as she is, my mother told them to cash the check and instruct me to bring the money directly to her. (Didn't I say my mom was street savvy?) She even made sure they gave me all large bills so I wouldn't lose anything on my way home to face her. The bank lady didn't know I was busted, but I knew. She covered for me on that occasion publicly, but upon my arrival home, my mom slapped me across the head, threatened to knock it off my shoulders the next time, and sternly warned me that if I ever stole from her or my dad again she'd call the police and press formal charges.

Little did she know, I had already stolen thousands off their credit card—and I figured it was probably enough for her to shoot me with the policeman's gun herself if given the opportunity.

It would only be a matter of months before I slipped up there, too. Capital One made a surprise courtesy call to my parents, during which they spilled the beans about my spending sprees. Unlike my father, who remains liberal and lenient to this day, Linda Williams is a devout, conservative, religious homemaker and a pragmatic realist with a passion for *keeping it real*. Her hands were on the phone to call the police, just as she had promised, rightly raising hell and expecting consequences. But before she could dial the number completely, my dad hit the receiver to end the call. He assured her on my behalf that I would repay the money I had stolen without bringing the police into the conversation.

I never did. In fact, I only learned that I needed to secure legitimate personal identification and a way out of town.

Our tiny town didn't have driver's ed, which meant waiting 'til your eighteenth birthday to get a driver's license. As soon as that day came, I passed my tests and found my way to the nearby town of Ferriday, Louisiana. Here, I could rent a new post office box in my name, without the watchful eye of St. Joseph's amicable postal employees, who knew my parents personally and would certainly report anything suspicious back to them.

With a new address in a new town, I took the next step in identity theft by opening brand new credit cards in my dad's name. During the application process, I added myself as an authorized user, with a card that had my own name embossed on it. To bypass my last mistake, I gave this different credit card company my number as "Freddie's" home phone, and Lonney Graham's gas station payphone in Ferriday as his work number.

With just a little experimentation needed this time, two separate credit cards were approved for credit limits of five thousand dollars each, with cash advance allowances up to twenty-five hundred dollars.

I was on to something—a lucrative scam that few my age knew about and still fewer were committing. Kids that age have the audacity to sneak out of the house, maybe even steal their parents' car, sneak boys and girls into the house. They don't know how to engage in the complexity of identity theft. I, on the other hand, had new money, a new look, and new means to gain traction in my street hustles. My peers recognized me for drug dealing and counted me as an intellectual—a real life version of *New Jack City's* prototype. I hadn't yet reached Scarface levels, but I thought I was "all that" and more.

In reality, I was little more than a snake that bites its victim and moves on without a second thought for its next prey. I'd stolen my dad's identity, my mom was coming next, and I couldn't wait to steal yours, no matter who you might have been.

The size of my eyes grew with the depths of my pockets, and while I had the money, I still lacked the credit worthiness to acquire the larger possessions I lusted after. Once again, I turned to my parents to help me out, unbeknownst to them.

The waters had already been tested, and my victims had been tried without any debilitating consequences. With the confidence of cash and perfect credit at my convenience, I found my way to Ferriday's Lakeside Ford in search of the right vehicle and, more importantly, the right salesman.

I needed someone who was desperate and underpaid, willing to put his scruples on the backburner and not look too closely in order to close the sale. Before stepping on the lot, I first shopped the dealership's employee directory by phone—using various names each time I called, of course—asking about different vehicles that were of no real interest to me. I did this to get a sense of the dealership's shared mentality and to identify the personality of the salesman who would unwittingly help me carry out my scam. Like my test calls to Capital One, I employed casual but calculated conversation to reveal an unscrupulous, unwitting partner in crime.

Having already feigned familiarity and endeared myself by phone, I went to my targeted salesman with a Lincoln Mark VIII in mind. Thanks to the fifteen thousand I'd spent of my dad's credit and a growing income from my drug dealing efforts, I looked like a man of money and means. The salesman was ready for me and the commissions check I represented. He was so ready to sell a car that I felt more confident and excited than anxious.

During the test drive, I advised the salesman that my dad would be helping me purchase the car once I made a final selection. I decided the car would suffice, so I told the salesman that I would have my dad give him a call so that they could work out the details. I explained that my dad worked offshore for extended periods of time, and that I did not want his unavailability to delay or impede the purchase process. The salesman assured me that he could facilitate the transaction in some way, offering to drive the paperwork personally in order to get Freddie's required signature.

To demonstrate the sincerity of my good intentions, I took the initiative to present the thousand-dollar deposit that would secure my return to the dealership and complete the purchase. Just ten bills with Ben Franklin's face on them had won me a pearl white Lincoln Mark VIII—that and a few phone calls, posing as my dad as always.

Playing the dual roles of benevolent father and mischievous son, a couple of days after I parted ways with the salesman, I called the dealership back. My first fraudulent calls at fifteen were on landlines, but it was now three years later, and I had access to pre-paid cell phones. I purchased two of them to provide my "dad's" home and work numbers for the application process that would satisfy the financing bank more than the personnel from the dealership.

When speaking with the salesman under the guise of my dad, we discussed numbers and negotiated a deal. Once we'd settled on an arrangement, I advised the salesman to call my "son" to inform him of the final arrangements. Later that same day, I celebrated with the car salesman like he'd just won the Super Bowl as he announced that my dad's application for the loan had been approved by Ford Motor Credit with the fees for tax, titling, and licensing included.

The salesman, who was also a Black man, generously introduced me to the notion of "white man's credit" and explained how beacon scores factor into the approval of various loans, how my dad's credit score of 783 exempted him from providing proof of income, and how these numbers serve as a type of grading scale for preferred interest rates. This information was genuinely helpful—despite his complete ignorance to the scams I'd run through him that day. I absorbed the valuable information, though not fully understanding that even in the credit market race plays a factor. The long-held perversion of credit scores, loan selection, and partiality in lending practices based on skin colors created the necessity for Equal Credit Opportunity laws in 1974, though implicit habits had lived on for many lenders. Giving absolutely no regard to my own civil rights, beacon scores would go on to factor into my success as a master identity thief, all thanks to this friendly salesperson helping a budding young gentleman out with his illegal vehicle purchase.

With the deal on the books, I avoided all attempts at securing paperwork through the mail, since I'd already established that my dad worked offshore for as long as ninety days at a time, and always unpredictably—and the salesman had a vested interest in moving this deal along before we lost our thirty-day approval. I assured him that I would take care of it all myself and would return the signatures and required photocopies to the dealership. Knowing that my parents don't receive mail at their physical address, I happily provided their street address to both the salesman and bank, with full intent of calling Ford Motor Credit within days to provide my own Ferriday box as the primary billing address.

Paperwork in hand and a vehicular vision almost realized, off I went to commit a little forgery, photocopy my dad's driver's license, and purchase a full coverage insurance policy over the phone using my dad's personal information. The salesman didn't bother asking me how I got my dad's signature even though he was fictionally working offshore at the time, and

I surely didn't volunteer any information. I suppose that the copy of the driver's license and proof of insurance gave the impression of a legitimate transaction that didn't necessitate questions. In any case, he handed over two keys and one fully detailed Lincoln Mark VIII that no longer belonged to Lakeside Ford—and didn't technically belong to me either, though I had every intention of making payments now that the credit heist was complete.

Despite my new car and new lifestyle of ease, access, and excess, my ride in the fast lane quickly began to feel more like a rollercoaster. Though the overlapping hustles of identity theft, credit card fraud, and selling drugs each supplemented the other, they all worked together to carry my floundering gambling addiction. Once the losses reached my cashflow and my payments became delinquent, my dad found out that the "friend's" car I had been driving was actually a car that *he* had unknowingly purchased. Ford Motor Credit couldn't reach Freddie Williams, Sr. on the two numbers I provided, so they dug until they found his actual home phone and disclosed to him the delinquency of his auto loan account.

Like my mom's cover with the banker back in St. Joseph, my dad never told Ford Motor Credit that he didn't purchase a Lincoln Mark VIII. The thought of ever reporting me to the police hurt him more than my misdeeds had. Still, my parents were devastated and outraged. I swore I could see smoke emanating from my mom's person. Their son had once again allowed the lust for vain glory to outweigh the love for his parents.

While my dad was offering forgiveness and my mother was politicking for righteous retribution, I was not deterred. Even though I could see the way I'd hurt my parents and didn't deserve their grace under my continual pressure, I was still busy trying to figure out how to use my mom's personal information to steal her identity. Once her resources had been exhausted, I would go on to use both sets of grandparents for their identities and access. After that, no one would be off limits.

My parents took responsibility for the debt I left them with. Over time, their unrestricted love cost them their high credit ratings and eventually their son to extended incarceration. However, that same love would also bring me back from the depths of degradation. Until this writing, I've held the details of these intimate familial thefts as a deep, personal secret—partly out of embarrassment and entirely out of love. Today, the only debt between us is one of eternal gratitude and, finally, an unencumbered *phileo* and *agape* love—the familial and unconditional love held up by the Scriptures and demonstrated by my parents even in my darkest days.

But we had a long road to walk to get here.

What started as a plan to jumpstart my enterprises had turned into something much more insidious. As the old adage goes, when you dance with the devil in the moonlight, he will take you further than you ever intended to go and will keep you longer than you ever intended to stay — and I now know he will cost you more than you ever intended to pay.

The appeal of identity theft comes with a limitless supply of financing sources. No one is off limits, though certain factors can make one person more appealing or useful to the criminal mind than another. For more on what makes victims of identity theft most vulnerable, see chapter 3 of *America's Domestic War.*

FOUR

DESPERATE ESCALATION

*Earth provides enough to satisfy every man's
needs, but not every man's greed.*
—Mahatma Gandhi

Just about every year of high school, I seemed to maximize the suspension allowance before expulsion. My offenses were all premeditated and timed around important exams in order to reduce the risk of failing a grade for the year. In my last two years of school, whenever I was suspended, I treated it like a break and easily occupied myself with the usual scams—gambling, peddling drugs, and visiting the ATM for cash advances using my dad's credit card. In twelfth grade, however, I was determined to take school more seriously in the last days of my student status. While most of my class-mates confused themselves with wishful thinking about their impending careers, I considered how I might use school to my own advantage.

Trades were out of the question. I didn't want to learn to weld, I didn't want to work on a car, I didn't want to be stuck in agriculture or anything blue collar—not to say anything is wrong with those honorable fortes. But of the options available to me, an executive assistant program seemed to have the most white-collar prestige that I could muster, so I completed a forty-five-hour college prep program at Shelby M. Jackson Institute, a technical college in Ferriday.

Between this and my on-and-off membership in the Beta Club, it was clear that I was college capable. On the other hand, my attention to detail and strategic planning in the theft of my parents' identities indicated a disciplined and potential military mindset. I narrowed my options down to the US military—potentially as a fighter pilot, I determined—or Southern University and A&M College in Baton Rouge, or SU for short.

At the end of the day, these were only perfunctory considerations. While feigning interest in response to peer and adult pressure, I deliberately failed the ASVAB to rule out the military. This left college as my single choice to "do something" with my life, as my old school parents inculcated.

When it came time to bomb the ACT to disqualify that path as well, I failed at failing. There were no excuses this time. Though my attendance at SU could be justifiably delayed for a year, enroll I did. In that gap year, I decided to move in with my sister, Samantha, in Houston, Texas. My parents saw this as the land of opportunity—a chance to get me away from my connections and reputation in St. Joseph and Ferriday. Perhaps I could make a career and stable life for myself out there.

For me, Houston was just a bigger platform with bigger dreams.

In my sister's apartment complex, I practiced fraud to perfection thanks to some strategic dumpster diving. What was trash to others became my treasure: an endless bankroll. I would use the personal information found on the residents' mail I stole to call the apartment leasing office, posing as an employer who needed to gain more information.

Houston gave me more than just personal data, too. While my original scheme was three-pronged, drug dealing was my early field of choice, and the big city brought big potential. In my mind, I didn't make people use and abuse what I sold them, and I should not be held accountable for their recreational choices. Without giving any consideration to the chemical dependencies and psychology behind drug use, I was convinced that the only difference between me and a pharmacist was societal power. After all, pharmaceutical companies fed addiction on a much larger scale than I did, and always for the same reason that I did: that almighty dollar. Today, the opioid epidemic continues to overdose America through pharmacists, physicians, often under regulated nurse practitioners, by unscrupulous manufacturers.[11]

---

11 While my justifications were imagined, the information feeding them was not. Most recently, see the historic decisions being made to hold the supply chain accountable: ABC News, "Feds charge Rochester Drug Corporation and CEO in first criminal case over opioids, " April 23, 2019; "Johnson & Johnson ordered to pay $572 million for its role...

We were both satisfying a need, both held accountable to higher authorities—me to the local police, them to the Food and Drug Administration, and both of us to the Drug Enforcement Administration. In my mind, there was little to no difference.

This was the twisted justification that my eighteen-year-old mind fed me, and identity theft and credit card fraud became my source of funding for the enterprise.

Life in Houston was short lived, however. As soon as my sister got wind of what I was doing, she gave me the ultimatum to quit or move back to St. Joseph. I elected to move back home that same year, in the fall of 1998, though I did not leave behind the credit card experience I gained while in Houston. What I hadn't gained in information, I earned through contacts—the drug connections I made there would last for years.

I planned to go to college but had no aspirations to retire from credit card fraud or abate my drug dealership. It actually wasn't about college at all. Embracing Louisiana meant getting closer to the one girl who managed to capture and hold my attention from adolescence to adulthood.

I first met Nellie Ann Webster at a junior high basketball tournament in her hometown of Ferriday, and for the next few years we broke up and made up, drifted in and out of other

------

…in Oklahoma's opioid crisis," August 26, 2019; and USA Today, "Drug distributors, opioid maker reach deal with Ohio counties in historic lawsuit," October 21, 2019.

relationships, and always came back to each other. She was *Love and Basketball's* Sanaa Lathan if I were Omar Epps, only my St. Joe-based reputation as a rising drug dealer kept me off the court and riding the bench. If I knew she was out of my league, I kept it to myself until she voiced her commitment to me as her first love—over basketball as well, if you can imagine. I had secured her heart as a trophy that I could never earn playing any kind of game.

Since Nellie lived in Ferriday, and I had that PO box on file, that became my home base. She knew next to nothing about my exploits on the streets, and I worked to keep our life together entirely separate from the rest of my world. For years, I was able to play the role of above-board entrepreneur and doting boyfriend cheering from the stands, as well as the underground criminal that Nellie would eventually find out about. While she was focused on completing her senior year in high school, I was busy making "living" arrangements in three different locations so as not to wear out my welcome with any one host.

In addition to my parents' home in St. Joseph, I chose my older brother Lamont's house in the city of Monroe and my late cousin Jeffrey's (a.k.a., Pee-Wee) home in Ferriday as alternating places to live. Both my brother and cousin welcomed me with open arms, without the broken trust that I'd so egregiously left my parents with.

Lamont and Pee-Wee did set rates of contribution toward their household expenses, and for every dollar that my dad would reject, my mom would require and receive two. She counted my monetary contributions as a type of restitution for the debt I had created for them and wasted no energy on symbolic refusals. The three living arrangements incurred a triple cost of living that required income or enterprise, which I satisfied to varying legal and illegal degrees based on location.

The town of St. Joseph, with its approximate thirteen hundred residents, is one of three towns that comprise the rustic community of Tensas Parish—Newellton and Waterproof being the other two towns. Its idyllic landscape does nothing to convince visitors and passersby that it is anything but a country town. As my childhood home, St. Joseph was most familiar to me and became the headquarters for my drug dealings throughout Northeast and Southeast Louisiana.

The city of Monroe, where Lamont lived, is not a bad city to live in, though like any thriving and growing community, it has its share of social challenges. Monroe is where I engaged legal commerce as the silent partner behind four businesses—the Anutha Level franchises. Eventually, these became failed fronts for criminal income, which would prove to be a poor move for business and criminality alike. I'll forever remember Monroe as my mournful metropolis.

Ferriday is a rather quiet community where everyone knows everybody. Nellie was my only reason to settle there. While I had tirelessly recruited Nellie to be my own MVP, she was a highly sought-after and talented star point guard for the Ferriday Trojans girls basketball team. Her athletic and social prominence didn't intimidate me or dictate the direction of our developing relationship, but it did determine some of her priorities and moves, which would affect mine as well.

My residence in Ferriday lasted only for the duration of her senior year, which came just at the end of my gap year.

Starting from as early as tenth grade, Nellie repeatedly received full scholarship offers from various universities and community colleges. At the close of her senior year, she decided to commit to Copiah-Lincoln Community College just south of Brookhaven, Mississippi. With Nellie going off to college, I had no worthwhile reason left to frequent the city of Ferriday, but the contacts and associations that I made held my interest nonetheless—particularly in the inner city's illegal drug trade.

As I settled into my triple residence, I also grew more proficient in my crimes. Stealing my mom's identity hadn't been as challenging or complicated as I initially thought it would be. All I needed was a woman of like age and physical appearance to be ready to assist me, in the event that we had to conduct a transaction in person.

Incidentally, I had a hesitant but willing candidate in the employ of my local drug operations in the heart of the hood in St. Joe. Her name was Melany, and she has since passed on, into the life where the land flows with milk and honey. She was a bit uneasy about my proposal at first, but her fear was forgotten in exchange for promises of a platonic Bonnie and Clyde future full of fortune.

I had positioned my mom's stolen identity for the "purchase" of two brand new Banshee racing four-wheelers. My merchant of choice was The House of Cycles in Natchez, MS, and my reconnaissance for this mission followed the same strategy that had succeeded at Lakeside Ford. They did indeed have the Banshee four-wheeler in stock, I confirmed. In fact, they had several of the latest models. The salespeople with whom I spoke over the telephone were professional, but also quite eager and excited about my calculated inquiries, which indicated they needed the sales.

I talked to one salesman about all the bells and whistles that came with the Banshee, which later informed my dialogue and negotiations when the time came to make my cameo appearance at the cycle shop. Meanwhile, I coached my partner-in-crime to use the same prepaid cell phones that I used during the fraudulent purchase of the Lincoln Mark VIII. Upon arrival to the cycle shop, I asked for my preferred salesman by name, engaged in small talk, and decided upon the Banshee that would best accommodate my wishes.

From previous telephone conversations, I knew that the four-wheeler could be financed through Yamaha Credit, so I inquired about the credit application process and was advised that credit approvals or denials usually come back within two to three hours after an application for credit has been submitted. The finance manager was a young Caucasian female with a welcoming, if not credulous, personality.

I advised her that my mom was willing to help me purchase the four-wheeler, but that she was sedentary and had physical disabilities that discouraged unnecessary traveling. Just as before, I took the initiative to suggest simply calling her to complete the phone application. I went on to suggest that I'd be willing to traffic the paperwork to her for signing purposes. To reinforce the finance manager's confidence in the integrity of this transaction, I also volunteered to leave a five-hundred-dollar deposit on the four-wheeler as a show of good faith and intent to purchase.

The finance manager didn't object to anything I had suggested. When I perceived that she was totally convinced that I was speaking to my mom on the phone, I passed the phone to her so that she could complete the phone application. The process went as planned and without any air of suspicion. For good measure, I advised my partner to list her employment as self-employed, intended to corroborate the lie regarding her supposed disability.

About an hour after I left the shop, the finance manager called to inform me that Yamaha Credit had approved my mom for a credit line of twelve thousand dollars, although the four-wheeler retailed for approximately fifty-five hundred, and of course I didn't purchase anything at its full retail listed price—then or now. The credit line was plenty to cover the two four-wheelers that I wanted, though I didn't purchase both right away, in order to avoid arousing any sabotaging suspicion. I returned to the dealer to collect the paperwork that required my mom's signature, left the five-hundred-dollar deposit, and shook hands with both the salesman and finance manager.

The following morning, I returned with my mom's forged signature, along with a computer-generated copy of her driver's license and a borrowed truck and trailer to haul away my newly purchased four-wheeler. Back in St. Joseph, I immediately had Melany call Yamaha Credit and provide them with the mailing address where I wished to receive the monthly billing statement, as well as to add me to the account as an authorized user.

I now had the authority to make major purchases without having to traffic paperwork back and forth for a signature. I could sign them myself.

Two months later, with my own Yamaha credit card in hand, I returned to The House of Cycles to buy a second four-wheeler and two thousand dollars' worth of accessories. The first Banshee was now considered used, and I traded it off for its equal value in drugs so that I could revamp my drug operations. The second one was my personal toy.

Nothing and no one could deter me from this season of poisoned prosperity.

With that injection of income, I sold enough crack cocaine and made enough money with repeated investments that I could've purchased twenty Banshees and ten Lincoln Mark VIIIs. As a city-savvy country boy, I was living the dream. I was doing what others were either too scared to do or simply did not know how to execute. I embodied the street philosophy that "the game is to be sold, not to be told"—this was my hustle, and no one else needed to know the details.

August of 1998 came faster than I wanted it to. Nellie moved into the college community of Copiah Lincoln, where she would reside on the lease of a basketball scholarship for the next two years. In the meantime, my enrollment date had arrived and I tried my hand at attending Southern University in Baton Rouge.

Being raised in an agricultural part of the state, I figured a major in Agricultural Science would be befitting of my supposed calling to college. On many occasions when travel-ing throughout Tensas Parish, I envisioned the "White Gold" of the cotton blooms as the green money that buds from coca and marijuana plants. A degree in Agriculture Science would teach me how to germinate, cultivate, and transform slave fields into US Mints by the acreage. But constant reminders of the hoe field quickly snapped me back into reality. I do not remember all the particulars of my enrollment at SU, except that my actual attendance lasted no more than a day or two after the financial aid office cut me a check for my pocket-por-tion of the federal financial aid I had received.

I didn't bother with the hassle of moving on and off of cam-pus to fake my student status for an entire semester. Instead, without any pretense, I lived the nomadic life of traversing between St. Joseph, Monroe, Ferriday, and now the town of Copiah Lincoln, approximately two hours and forty-five min-utes from St. Joseph.

Whenever Nellie didn't come to Ferriday for the weekend or have a basketball weekend road trip, I traveled to her. When I wasn't in Copiah Lincoln with Nellie, I was traveling from Houston to St. Joseph supervising the distribution of my drug operations or in Monroe committing various kinds of fraud.

In Tensas Parish, my growing prominence as a flashy but shrewd drug dealer had begun to settle over the roof of my parents' home. While I never stashed large quantities of drugs on my parents' property, I did hide large sums of money throughout the house. Occasionally my mom or dad would find a stash of cash and confront me about where it came from. I'd reluctantly admit that it was the winnings of high stakes gambling, but neither of my parents were convinced. The shadow of my reputation weighed heavily on my dad's conscience. They decided that their home would not be a haven for a drug dealer, and it was time for me to "get the hell out" of their house for good.

My dad's rental property, on the other hand, was not off limits. It became known as the Gingerbread House because of its distinctive structural design and color, which meant I was now known and identifiable in my own home. My paranoia grew, not only because my social infamy no doubt attracted the attention of the cops, but because private fortune surely aroused the curiosity of robbers hoping to get lucky. I equipped my new residence with a motion sensor alarm system and a 360-degree-view video surveillance system. I also had a total of six unauthorized, unknown-to-the-public street surveillance cameras situated on three different light poles between Third and Fourth street to see cops and aspiring jack-boys from a distance.

To animate my security systems, I also purchased an all-white American Stanford pitbull that I planned to have trained as a sort of guard dog as well as a family pet. My dog's name was Juvy, and contrary to plans, he became the people's pet. He was highly trained and unusually intelligent, but rather than being fearsome, he became my own Spuds MacKenzie.

I spared no expense to provide for Juvy's comfort and convenience. Both my mom and Nellie's parents, the beloved Harold and Sharon Webster, took turns babysitting him whenever I was out of town. Juvy, aka, Ju'Ju, was terribly spoiled, always treated as a puppy even when he became an eighty-pound, fully grown dog. Nellie loved him just as much—their only disagreements happened when Juvy would lay out on the living room couch or stretch out across the bed instead of sleeping on the floor.[12]

Juvy was my closest companion in the absence of Nellie.[13]

When I wasn't with Nellie or counting my money while Juvy watched and waited for some of it to be spent on him, gambling was my only form of entertainment. Fraud and drug deals were my entrepreneurial activities, and high stakes street dice or big money table card games became my recreational pursuits.

During the latter half of Nellie's two years at Copiah-Lincoln Community College, I set my sights on even higher stakes: gambling in the riverboat casinos. Because I couldn't legally enter a casino until I was twenty-one, I would need a driver's license that would provide entry while still validating my nineteen-year-old appearance.

After stealing an older peer's actual driver's license and damaging it, I simply walked into the Department of Motor

12 Although I was far from righteous at this moment in my life, I shared a commonality with the righteous man who "...regards the life of his beast." (Proverbs 12:10)

13 I would be remiss to skip mention of my best friend, Adrien Marcel Brown. We had been partners in crime for years, but Marcel was in prison at the time, serving a ten-year sentence for getting caught with a large quantity of my cocaine at a Greyhound bus station in Houston. He took ownership of both the drugs and the charge in my stead. I love him for that, and I probably bonded more with Juvy in light of his absence. He was and forever will be that "friend that sticks closer than a brother." (Proverbs 18:24)

Vehicles office in St. Joseph, presented the unusable license, and requested a duplicate with a photo retake. The older white woman behind the counter couldn't tell the difference between us, though we look nothing alike, so it was just that easy. Off I went with a state-issued driver's license that proved my claim to be of legal age to access the casinos.

Casino gaming offered way more security, excitement, peculiar personalities, and winning opportunity than gambling on the streets ever could. Whenever I wasn't stealing in Monroe, negotiating in Houston, dealing in Tensas Parish, or visiting in Copiah Lincoln, I was playing Pitch Blackjack, roulette, or five-card Baccarat at one of three riverboats situated on the banks of the Mississippi River in Natchez and Vicksburg. My wagers of sin[14] flowed freely at no less than one thousand dollars on a budgeted day, and not more than three thousand dollars on far too many desperate days of chasing losses.

I also learned that casinos are the devil's den.

They might be legal entities, but they are also the moral equivalent of social parasites, tantamount to me using the profits from selling crack to play a twisted form of Robin Hood—literally robbing the hood to "give back" to the hood. From school to street corners to financial institutions, I had always been the smartest person in any given room. Even when that wasn't true—and I'm sure it wasn't in many cases—I was able to play and win every game set in front of me. That confidence carried me into casinos and promptly sat me right back down. They taught me my lesson.

14 Romans 6:9

For a season, gambling was the disease of my demise and gradually forced me into an unwritten chapter of bankruptcy. The constitution of the concrete jungle in which criminals live and play interprets bankruptcy as simply "doing bad"—and I had begun to do *so* bad that all three of my vehicles were eventually repossessed at the home address I had given to conceal the stolen credit for their purchase. I was left with only one of the two four wheelers I had purchased using my mom's identity.

Nellie had no idea of the depths of loss I'd fallen into until we walked outside to find that my customized 2001 Cadillac Escalade, that was purchased from Houston using the stolen identity of my beloved and late maternal grandmother, Betty Roach-Bradley, had been repossessed within minutes after she had used it to go to the corner store. I had no believable explanation other than falling behind on the monthly payments I had once made, thanks to a big gambling loss I was trying to recover from.

More in line with the truth was that there were so many gambling losses over the past few months that I could not fully recover from any of them. Two months before the repossession of the Cadillac, I had sold the Lincoln Mark VIII to my younger brother, Freddie Mac Williams, Jr., for nickels on the dollar, which left Nellie and I with two vehicles between us—her car and a motorcycle I had purchased using my other grandmother Ida's stolen identity, may both my grandmothers rest in peace.

I believed that I could discipline my addiction, not realizing any vice—gambling, food, drugs, pornography, and more—comes at the impulse of an imbalance that's manipulated by the forces of darkness. With the darkness unconquered, it will eventually and continually manifest itself in some fashion, for the only way to conquer and control darkness is with light.[15]

In August 2001, I lost thirty-five thousand dollars playing blackjack in the Red Room at Casino Rouge in Baton Rouge, then another twenty-five thousand dollars playing blackjack at the Paragon Casino in Marksville—on the same night. Those would be my last losses, though they weren't why I quit gambling. Honestly, those weren't even my worst losses. I was tired.

I was tired of all that losing—of *being* a loser. I was tired of chasing my losses and never catching my winnings. I was tired of hiding my addiction from Nellie and having to lie about my whereabouts. I was tired of living on the edge from hustle to hustle. And with my twenty-first birthday around the corner, the allure of criminal evasion was about to end for the casinos as well. It's clear now that my addiction wasn't to the games on the table but to the game I was playing within society, against myself.

Criminality would not permit permanent retirement, however. With gambling no longer a controlling distraction in my life, I was poised to escalate my endeavors to the next level. Just around the corner from my twenty-first birthday, I would make more money committing identity theft in one year than I had made in the previous five years of selling drugs, committing petty credit card fraud, and gambling combined.

---

15 Genesis 1:2–5

My original sin[16] began with the theft of my parents' identities and would continue to escalate and expand over the years—but the record of my first arrest finds its origins on the property of Carroll High School, back in mournful Monroe.

As my story unfolds, you'll see just how far I would go to expand my identity theft exploits. My criminal enterprise would continue unabated over the course of twenty-two arrests, with no external consequence able to slake my greed for money, power, and control.

But the leader of the crime isn't the only player involved in these games. From the car salesman willing to look the other way to the person at the top pulling the strings, there are many ways and reasons individuals might step into identity theft. For more on the criminal mindset, see chapter 4 of *America's Domestic War.*

---

16 Romans 5:12

FIVE

MISDIRECTED LESSONS

People who treat other people as less than human
must not be surprised when the bread they have cast
on the waters comes floating back to them, poisoned.
                                        —James Baldwin

B y the time Nellie graduated from Copiah-Lincoln Commu-
nity College in the spring of 2000, I had built up a double,
even triple, lifestyle and two separate, concurrent proba-
tionary periods. But my collisions with the judicial system
had begun two years prior when I decided that a brand new,
Windows 98, desktop computer was necessary for a full and
proper expansion of my enterprise. What exactly a computer
could do for me, I honestly had no idea. Still, it seemed like a
reasonable next step on my ladder of greed and gain.

Computers were rare commodities at the time, and it would have been too suspicious for me to ask for one directly. The best way to keep my acquisition under wraps, I decided, was to steal one.

I also decided that a school would provide the easiest access to said computer, especially a school in the hood, because to my thinking, a more rural, underfunded school might not be as secure. Even if it had some kind of burglary protection, I couldn't fathom anyone showing up in a timely manner in response. Being only a year removed from high school, I saw how little attention our schools in the urban community received, and I took that to mean the authorities simply didn't care. My naivete would soon get the better of me, and not for the last time, as I tested my perception of the world against the details of reality.

Carroll High School was my target for this electronic acquisition, and I selected a male accomplice to join me. Acting as a would-be tourist in the town of Monroe, I explored the city by day and went on reconnaissance missions by night, plotting my attack and planning my escape routes.

On the appointed night, in late February 1998, we snuck up to the rear entrance of the school. With my accomplice on the lookout, I used a couple of simple glass cutting tools to gain access to the school's computer laboratory, feeling smug about our stealth and perceived sophistication. However, neither of us was quite sophisticated enough to account for a silent security alarm, which had indeed been triggered. While I was acquiring the goods and heading for the exit feeling nearly home free, the Monroe City Police Department knew that a burglary was in process and was well on their way to meet us.

In retrospect, it makes perfect sense for the cops to approach the scene just as silently as that alarm. At the time, I thought we were in the clear as I handed part of the computer out to my accomplice and climbed through the window to exit the building. Halfway through the glass, I heard the click of the radio on one of the approaching officers.

So much for sophistication.

In a hard whisper, I told my accomplice to *run*. By the time my feet hit the ground, the chase was on. The cops had every advantage in their pursuit, except for that of youth and agility. About a hundred yards in, we thought we'd lost them. My accomplice got away, while I slipped into the bushes to wait for a clear route home.

I didn't know that a canine—a Belgian Malinois the cop called Thor—had been hot on my trail. I didn't know he would sniff out my hiding spot.

I certainly couldn't have known the cop would point the dog right at me, look into my eyes, and let go of the leash. There in the bushes, with nowhere to escape, Thor tore a gash in my left leg that sent me to the hospital on the way to the parish jail.

Twenty-six stitches later, I'd developed a foundational disdain for law enforcement and was quickly acquiring a fresh distaste for incarceration.

I've never been one to sit still and wait, and in jail I had no way to hurry things along. The concrete walls and ceiling were closing in on me, and I tried to get comfortable on the iron seating designed for anything but comfort. My best choice was to hit the payphone every time the room seemed to shrink—*what the hell was taking my parents and the attorney so long to get me out of there?*

My sudden case of claustrophobia aside, I had other people to contend with, too. I could hear conversations and had been watching the way people were interacting with each other. When another inmate asked what I was in jail for, I told him I'd been a suspect in a drive-by shooting. I held my breath, hoping the lie was grave enough to hide the truth that it was my first time in jail and that I was scared to death of staying. It worked.

That momentary win gave me the bravado I needed to flip the script on that interaction. Instead of waiting for more questions, I started asking them. I got the upper hand. Within hours of my first arrest, I was learning on the fly just how important composure is for prison survival, and the game occupied my mind until my bond came through and I could breathe fresh air again. I limped out with my parents and my paperwork, relieved to be rid of all that had gone wrong on that terrible night.

```
Lesson 1: Just like the US Army, in jail you can
"be all you can be" — truthfully or not — as long
as you act like you believe it.
```

My mission to steal a computer had failed criminally, but now I had a new vision. I also had a floating court date, though it offered very little distraction from my work at hand. In my reconnaissance of Monroe, I discovered untold treasures that lay behind storage room doors in the better-franchised hotels. Every time the front desk would swipe a card back and forth in their manual scanner, the scraping sound was that of a carbon copier. Behind closed doors, there were boxes and boxes of receipts for each of the hotel's transactions, with a copy of the card attached. For check-in receipts, I could usually find a copy of the patron's driver's license attached as well—all standard ways to "secure" the check-in process.

Once I gained access to these backdoor storage rooms, I found I could easily walk out with boxes at a time—thousands of copies of data covering every major credit card, corporate cards, commercial, and personal cards, alongside the driver's license or acceptable form of identification. With a stash of burner phones and some practice in the over-the-phone and in-person device fraud that had earned me my vehicles and credit cards, I had a good run of shopping ahead of me.

Six months later, in August of 1998, Monroe's Pecan Land Mall loss prevention personnel caught onto one of many shopping expeditions. I was caught completely by surprise when they apprehended me for felony theft of goods—my second felony arrest that year. This time, I made sure to reserve some of my growing cash flow for bail. The walls weren't so tight around me as they had been after my run-in with Thor. Knowing that I had what I needed to be out the next day, I was feeling like a self-made man. The next morning, my only thought was of ways to recoup my losses.

Lesson 2: If you keep cash on hand for bail, jail
is only a temporary detour.[17]

---

17 As I would later learn, this isn't the case for federal jurisdiction.

Big screen TVs always turned a quick profit—I brokered them as pre-sold items, ready to turn around for fifty to sixty percent of their retail value, depending on the customer, with a zero-dollar investment. Unfortunately, this was the era of the *big* screen, true to its name, that required at least three men to move. The credit card numbers weren't my problem. It was getting them out of the store that took some finesse.

Before then, I had utilized the paid by phone/customer pickup option at least a dozen times. That was my plan in October of that same year, tried and true. I did my due diligence the evening prior to make sure they were in stock. I called in to initiate the order. As always, I confirmed the successful transaction by asking for the approval code generated by the credit card terminal. This told me whether the sale was approved, declined, or compromised—in other words, whether or not to show my face.

My plan went off the rails when the associate and/or management offered me free delivery. Without an address for delivery, I was caught completely off guard and said "No, thanks!" rather than accepting their generous offer like any legitimate patron would. Then I took some time to compose myself, no doubt raising even more red flags for the associate and for management.

Three days later, I arrived at the appliance store on Hwy 165 in Monroe, driving a rented U-Haul truck. I never even saw the TVs. Instead of loading up my wares, cops dressed in plain clothes loaded *me* up and took me back to Ouachita Correctional Center, charged with a third felony: theft valued at more than five hundred dollars.

Lesson 3: Never decline free delivery, and never
delay pick up once an order is paid for.

———————————

Three felony arrests and less than a year into my escalating escapades, a regular bail bondsman and some preferred criminal defense attorneys had become usuals on my growing payroll, making an honest living off my dishonest deeds. The bondsman had working relationships with the judges and jailer, so if I called him first, I knew he could get my bail set and the whole process expedited.

The system felt like mine to work...until that floating court date came around in November. Jail was becoming familiar, but the courtroom was uncharted territory.

At the time, I had one of the best criminal defense attorneys in Monroe, Mr. Lavalle B. Solomon, Esq., who promised to be by my side. Even this relief, which was held at a great and worthwhile expense, was not enough to bring my appetite back or to occupy my anxious mind. After all, it was me who would be on trial, not him.

Stepping into the courtroom intensified my concerns. To this day, I believe courts were intended to intimidate at the level of someone's imagination of what the Heavenly courts must be like. The judge towers over the room playing God to a convincing degree. The prosecutor takes on the role of the Accuser of the Brethren, and the defense attorney stands by as your Savior and Advocate.

Of course, "the devil" and his people in this scenario are typically in the right.

The intended impact hit me with its full force as I shuffled in with butterflies in my stomach like I was about to stand up and speak before a million strangers, and not just the few who wanted to see my case closed, for better or worse. Even though my attorney had given me a speech about preliminary hearings, arraignments, and that I was to just say "not guilty" then we'd be done—I hadn't experienced it before. I had no experiential idea of what the process entailed. A decade prior, I might have felt this same way walking into the dentist for my first filling. No matter how much you tell me about local anesthetic, it all sounds gruesome to a kid who's never been there before.

My mind ran wild with possibility. For all I knew, I'd be tried, judged, and crucified in one leveling blow.

I looked around at the room full of people and expected to go last like I always had in school, with *Williams* appearing so far down the alphabetical list. When they called my name first, I was shocked to learn that the alphabet had no bearing. The more prominent the attorney, the more prioritized the case.

Mr. Solomon was the guardian angel on my shoulder, whispering answers in my ear as the judge ran through his procedural questions. Five minutes later, just as he had prepared me to expect, we were done with questioning and turning to leave the room—when a sheriff's deputy grabbed my arm and directed me to the empty jury box.

Apparently, a warrant had been issued for my arrest when I'd failed to appear in traffic court for a speeding ticket I got previously in Woodworth, Louisiana, and again when I'd been found to have issued floating checks in and around Monroe.

Having insufficient funds isn't criminal, but deliberately writing checks on a closed account, evidently, is.

Rather than leaving with my attorney that day, my worst fears came to life as I was escorted back to familiar territory, the Ouachita Correctional Center. On my way in, one of the jailers recognized me from my previous visits and shook his head.

"Son," he told me, "you ain't gonna stop comin' in here 'til you hit the lottery."

And he was, more or less, right.

Lesson 4: Expect the unexpected.

Lesson 5: As long as you can afford it, you can buy the right relationships to finance and finagle your way out of certain situations.

———

Teenagers and young adults don't have much to do in St. Joseph—or in any parts of Tensas Parish, for that matter. Fishing and hunting are pastimes of choice for both kids and adults, especially when high school athletics are seasonally unavailable. I was never interested in any of these forms of traditional entertainment, so I spent most of my time making and spending money, riding and racing those fancy ATVs I acquired, and participating in the community gambling circles via table card games and street corner dice games.

Because I brought more money to the neighborhood gambling experience than my competitors collectively owned, the boys in the hood and anyone hosting a card game looked forward to my visits back to St. Joseph. For me, I enjoyed the camaraderie more than the profits. Food, fun, laughter, and good-natured disagreements spread across my visits like a buffet of entertainment.

However, at the time gambling in any form happened to be illegal in Tensas Parish, save for the scratch tickets and Louisiana lottery that was introduced under the political misrepresentation of educational system funding. And, as I would learn the hard way about six months after my Ouachita woes were resolved, shooting dice in public was the most exposed form of this indiscretion.

In the parking lot of Bates Store in May of '99, dice in my hand and my back to the street, we were ambushed from three different directions by patrol cars from the St. Joseph Police Department.

Never mind the secretive, increasingly skilled, white-collar exploits that funded my part in these games. We were in the hood and on the block, a hot spot for drug dealing and one that was under constant observation. I was arrested and charged with "gambling in public."

As expected, I posted bail just as soon as I was processed and went back to the block to tell the fellas that our games would continue *inside* Bate's Store on the pool table. The owner could take a house cut and we could cut our exposure risks. After all, I was becoming a magnet for police—at least when I played the part and committed the crimes they expected of me.

Lesson 6: Never shoot dice with your back to the road.

Identity theft and fraud thrived in Monroe. Gambling grew and failed in St. Joseph. And Houston became the hub for drug supplies that I began to traffic throughout north and south Louisiana. The season often dictated my activity thanks to supply and demand. In the summer months, the supply of marijuana is low and demand is high, thereby driving up its premium. At other times, cocaine was on the docket and provided the bigger return.

On countless occasions and every time previous to June of 1999, I let a mule—a driver, more or less, if you haven't seen the Clint Eastwood flick yet—transport my orders from Texas to Louisiana. But when the supply was low and the demand was high, the stakes demanded that I man the money and monitor the purchase myself.

Trafficking drugs is like shooting dice: As a drug dealer, you have to get lucky every day to sustain, survive, and thrive. As a cop, you only have to get lucky once to capture, confiscate, and conquer. It's only a matter of time before you crap out, and six arrests told me my luck was no good.

Just a month after being picked up for that ill-planned game of dice, I rode along with the mule and had made it all the way up east-bound I-10. We passed all the tricks and traps set for us along that drug interdiction corridor, and I was in the driver's seat and ready to be home. It was two in the morning, my guy was next to me knocked out cold thanks to a hit off of the marijuana we were transporting, and I just wanted to get in bed. Stupidly, I went ten miles over the speed limit on the last stretch of Highway 84, and my speeding alerted the police before I could make it out of Rapides Parish and into the familiar territory of Catahoula Parish.

I knew it was over. My vehicle was filled with pounds of marijuana. Not just any marijuana, either. The good stuff that's so potent and mind boggling that it has the unique ability to refresh memory, the smoking-but-not-inhaling, Cheech and Chong, *reefa*—back before vacuum sealing. And we'd violated rule number one: Mary Jane had been kissed in the car.

I think that cop could smell her addictive aroma before he even opened his door.

Rapides Parish Sheriff's Office took my hydroponic weed and locked me up, in unfamiliar territory with no local contacts or connections. This time, I felt more comfortable navigating the unfamiliar. I called my bail bondsman out of Monroe, who in turn contacted his counterpart in Alexandria, Louisiana. I was out of jail—on new drug charges, of course—later that afternoon. Back to St. Joseph I went.

Lesson 7: Never ride in the car with your product, never smoke it in the car, and never, *ever* let your guard down.

Back home, I felt like I'd made it. To my peers, I embodied their hip hop dreams. Being a hometown celebrity has its perks and its drawbacks, though. While I was admired in the hood for my material acquisitions, I was despised by local law enforcement. The feeling was more or less mutual.

Tensas Parish Sheriff's Office wanted me for drug dealings throughout the parish but could never catch me in the act—they hadn't been so lucky as Rapides. The cops knew I was responsible for 99 percent of the drugs in and throughout Tensas Parish. They just didn't know how any of it moved.

St. Joseph police didn't even try to hide their surveillance of my movement, which typically happened on foot or on one of my fastest ATVs. Less than a week after my aromatic commute, Rapides Parish notified Tensas Parish of a large seizure that had been headed their way. I was a hot topic, and they were determined to make an example out of me.

On the morning of July 6, 1999, I hopped aboard my modified Banshee four-wheeler to make a run to Lake Bruin. That's where I cut grass every Wednesday as a kid, and an unoccupied lake house had become a storage site for my product, since the marijuana that Rapides had gotten from me was not my only source of inventory. That day, I was planning to fill and move a backpack full of cocaine at a street value of one hundred fifty thousand dollars, already arranged for transference to constituents in Concordia, Franklin, and Madison Parishes.

I rode the levee all the way to Lake Bruin without a hitch, made it to the lake house without impediment, then accessed my stash and set my sights back towards the city limits. Unbeknownst to me, just before leaving the city limits of St. Joseph I was spotted by an unmarked police vehicle. As long as I had been on the levee on my ATV, I was legal and not worth the pursuit. But the moment I touched the street pavement, my off-road vehicle became a probable cause for stop, search, and seizure. On my way to the lake house, I didn't see the deputies boxing me in, ready to pounce.

On my route home, I didn't think much of the patrol cars coming from both the left and right. That changed when each of the cars increased in speed as soon as I was directly in their sight. It was me against them, and their lights and sirens were like a gun at the races. I could either take a felony drug charge valued at a mandatory minimum of two decades in prison, or a misdemeanor flight from an officer charge valued at a couple hours to process in and out of jail on bond.

I took my chances.

They had their cars and trucks readily equipped with canine cops, but I was on a modified Banshee—a racing ATV. The patrol units were clearly no match for speed. And because I knew they knew who I was, I had a growing sense of confidence that they were no match for *me*. With the fear of capture fading by the moment, I zig-zagged my way around my town, concentrating the patrol cars before spinning out and speeding away.

Thanks to Thor and his keeper back in Monroe, I knew I couldn't outrun their radios, so before the game could end, I had to dump the dope. What could be the last place the department would look, and that they'd never risk exposing even if they did find it? I didn't have to think long. Back in the city limits and with about a mile of mazes between me and the chase, I cut over to the neighborhood where I knew Sheriff Ricky Jones lived. Tucking the Banshee in behind a neighbor's home adjacent to the sheriff's house, I ran across their fenceless backyards and tossed my backpack into the crawl space beneath his house.

Back on my Banshee, incriminating evidence safely tucked away, I cruised the three blocks up the street to the station to turn myself in.

On my way, I made use of the other lesson that Thor and Monroe had taught me. That Rodney King taught me, and that we're still learning with blood and tears, with Freddie Gray, and with Michael Brown, and a list that keeps growing as I draft this book: the threat of police brutality was real and present and had to be accounted for.[18] I called my parents and a couple of homeboys and asked them to meet me there, with cameras in hand. I had them take pictures of me just before I walked into the police station. Like an insurance policy verifying the original state of their covered goods, I wanted to make sure I came out of that station looking just like I had when I walked in.

My Banshee was impounded. Their interrogations and corresponding investigations regarding the contents and whereabouts of my backpack were unsuccessful. I posted bail just as soon as it was set that afternoon.[19]

Lesson 8: You drew first blood, but I'll get the last laugh.

---

18 Three such tragedies occurred in my own backyard with the deaths of Alton Sterling, Josef Richardson, and most recently Christopher Whitfield, whose crime was hunger. Most egregious of them all, regardless of home state, is Atatiana Jackson, shot in the comfort of her home while spending quality time with her nephew. https://amp.cnn.com/cnn/2019/10/14/us/fort-worth-police-shooting-atatiana-jefferson/index.html.
19 Today, Sheriff Jones and I are good friends, and we share a good laugh every time we revisit this story.

At the end of summer, all the kids were back in school, including Nellie. My double life was becoming a challenge, running from the cops one night and making it to a basketball game the next. I had confined myself to that small region for too long, and I became a coveted prize for local law enforcement. Ready to get out of St. Joseph and head back to Monroe, my vehicle attracted the attention of a patrol car before I could even get out of city limits.

We crossed paths in opposite directions, then five minutes later he came speeding into my rearview mirror while I cruised at a comfortable 52–55 mph along Highway 65 south bound, just at or below the limits. For the next five minutes, we rode in tandem. Despite the intimidation of police presence over my shoulder, I remained calm, waiting for his siren and lights to signal the inevitable traffic stop. I hadn't given cause for one at that moment, but he knew me and my car and the havoc I'd wreaked the month before. On we drove as he ran my plates and called me in, then the lights came on.

This time, I had no reason to give chase. When he stepped up to my window, the officer told me I had been stopped for doing 71 in a 55 zone. He told his lie as easily as I might've if I had anything more than pocket money and traveling clothes on my person.

Blatantly but respectfully, I told the officer that he wasn't representing his badge in a truthful manner. He was lying and needed to reinvent a different reason for pulling me over. Instead, he doubled down.

After verifying my registration and insurance, he revoked

my driver's license and announced that he was placing me under arrest for "driving under a suspended license" and speeding.

Lesson 9: We're both out to get what's ours, at any cost.

In all of my interrogative encounters with law enforcement officers, I've never been able to fully nor partially appreciate how they can strategically and deliberately tell an abundance of lies in an apparent search of the truth, but can charge a suspect for rendering a false statement. This is an alleged interrogation tactic of the lesser evil, but is nothing more than a double standard that I'll never be able to accept by ignoring it. If you want the truth, initiate the truth you've sworn to represent, present, and preserve.

Granted, I might have avoided that suspended license if I actually paid any of my various traffic fines and fees. But I couldn't be bothered. They were going to keep arresting me, and I was going to keep bonding out. It was our dance, and as long as it kept them away from my real bankroll—the fraud that they hadn't scratched the surface on—I was willing to keep on dancing.

Yet again, I was under arrest. This time, for no reason other than revenge. Nine times must have been the charm, though, because I didn't even flinch. The sooner he took me to jail, the sooner I could bail out.

I was free in less than two hours, got a ride to my car that was still parked on the side of the road, and resumed my trip back to Monroe.

From my first encounter with law enforcement, I could tell what our relationship would be like. They had no regard for me as a person, and I returned the favor by disregarding their office. I was in the wrong, of course, but so were they. This ongoing adversarial dynamic shaped my view of the world and shifted everything toward survival, coping, and playing my part in the game. I can't tell my story without including the narrative of *bluetality*—brutality from the men and women in blue—profiling, and targeting young Black kids disproportionately to their peers and their collective crimes.

As soon as I learned I could hide in plain sight if I avoided the "crimes of a color" that our hood was monitored for, I decided to play the part of a white-collar criminal instead, and embraced my role as the master identity thief.

They didn't even see me coming.

SIX

IMAGINED INVINCIBILITY

*A proud man is always looking down on things and
people; and, of course, as long as you are looking
down, you cannot see something that is above you.*
— C.S. Lewis, *Mere Christianity*

Nellie held the attention of University basketball scouts through her two years at Copiah-Lincoln Community College, and in 2000, she had scholarship offers to choose from. Southeastern Louisiana University (SLU), located in Hammond, recruited Nellie hard, and she accepted their full scholarship offer for her remaining two years of eligibility. Rather than sending her off to Hammond without me, we moved there together—two country kids navigating the mazes of growth and maturity, arm in arm.

As a point guard, she was the center of attention both on the court and off, with the program's advertisements revolving around her. Nellie was a star at SLU and my one ray of sunshine left as I slowly buried myself beneath my ambition. I couldn't imagine losing her, but as she rose to stardom, I also couldn't imagine deserving her.

Nellie should have had so much more than I could give her, so what I lacked in character, conduct, and commitment, I recouped in capital. I spared no expense on the townhouse we chose off-campus or the décor that married her touch to my taste. No less than the best would do. On one occasion when her mom, Sharon, accompanied us to shop for decorations, in response to her question regarding the budget I simply replied, "The sky is the limit!" And I meant what I said.

She and the Lady Lions lost out of the 2002 March Madness tournament in the third round, and at the same time, she aged out of the NCAA. Now she had a choice between keeping the scholarship that covered the rest of her bachelor's degree or attending tryouts for the WNBA. Although she traveled to Detroit to honor her exclusive opportunity to play professional sports, her heart wasn't in it. The sociology degree path in front of her held more promise than the seventy-five thousand dollars she was estimated to make in the league, and that was the end of her basketball career.

While Nellie was in Detroit at the tryouts, I was shopping for a way to honor her successes in basketball and academia. I identified a fully loaded Nissan Altima that matched her character and a new model Cadillac CTS that aligned with my own aspirations. She opted for the Altima, which I gladly convinced her parents to willingly lend their credit for—but I used my car shopping efforts as reconnaissance for a future purchase. Within the year, I'd used the identity of a stranger with a 752 beacon score and the efforts of a well-compensated Field Operative to obtain my next two Cadillacs (one black EXT luxury truck and one pearl white Deville sedan), then months later a brand new '03 Nissan 350Z as the burnt-orange, fully loaded cherry on top. If she had a clue then what I was into, she didn't let on, nor did I care to entertain her conveyance of hearsay, so long as I could avoid validating the rumors or arousing her silent suspicions.

Exchanging St. Joseph for Hammond would prove to be the most lucrative move of my criminal career. I left my silent partner businesses active in Monroe, which served as a front to launder some of my income and to justify the three-hour drives back to connect with the Info Operatives I recruited and trained to supply me with stolen identities and credit card numbers. I also moved a relative, my cousin Dee, into the house in St. Joseph, which was just south of Monroe on the route down to Hammond. That way, I could keep it as an alternate residence when I returned to the area to monitor my ongoing drug operations.

Not only were we thriving financially, but in April, 2002, we learned that Nellie was carrying our first child—which also happened to be my third. The recent births of my oldest daughter, Emoni, and my only son at the time, Darquise, had put a strain on my relationship with Nellie, as one might expect. They were stair-stepped and young still—children that I loved and provided for but did not see as often as I should, born as evidence of my indiscrete choice not to care for Nellie as I should.

This pregnancy, on the other hand, was one we could both enjoy. In between my bi-weekly visits back to Monroe and St. Joseph, ostensibly to check in on my business investments, I joined her for her doctor visits and sent her on weekly hot rock massage appointments and milk baths at the local spa. I relished in spoiling my newest baby by first spoiling her mother.

By the age of twenty-three, just before our baby was born, Nellie had almost graduated and I had well surpassed a seven-figure income in ill-gotten gain. The experiments I dabbled in from my teen years would soon expand into a full-scale operation, with forty operatives and seasonal, organizational objectives. The skills I developed gave me near unlimited access to shopping sprees both for a financial turnaround and for personal enjoyment. And the lessons I learned from my previous run-ins with law enforcement allowed me to continue to rack up cash alongside arrests without fear or a second thought, even while on supervised probation.

Those three years, between the ages of twenty and twenty-three, by modern day standards, would prove to be the richest days of my criminal career—though they set the stage for devastating consequences for our small but growing family.

When we first moved to Hammond, I stretched my wings using the unwitting help of both my grandmothers. With their identities, I purchased a Cadillac Escalade and a Suzuki GSX1300 motorcycle for no other reason than pure greed. These vehicles doubled as alternates to each other as I traveled back and forth between exploits. The random home visits and routine drug screens that came with my probationary period were annoying but simple enough to dodge. My home in St. Joseph became a staged residence as well as the center of my drug operations throughout Tensas Parish and surrounding areas. At my real home in Hammond, I orchestrated identity theft operations that covered Louisiana, Mississippi, Texas, Alabama, and all the way up to Missouri, not including my counterparts who flew in almost weekly for identity theft consultancies.

It took a couple of months to become acquainted with the business community in Hammond before I could launch this enterprise, which was time that I interspersed between basketball practice for Nellie or feeding the casino addiction that plagued me until my twenty-first birthday.

My first victim of fraud in Hammond was a young white female owner of a cell phone store. I used a stolen identity to purchase five Nextel cell phones, then provided a duplicated photocopy of the driver's license when I went to pick up the phones. She was clearly enamored with the size of the transaction, indicating how rare it was for her privately owned franchise store to run higher volumes when the larger, corporate-owned stores attracted most of the business. Like the car salesman I regularly sought out, her excitement for the sale overshadowed my dubious explanations. She had no qualms about my self-produced photocopy of the driver's license and was rather satisfied with the fictional account of why I delivered the identifying document instead of the actual purchaser, who I claimed to be my dad.

Experience taught me that such lax, almost eager cooperation was an unspoken invitation to collaborate. On subsequent visits, I prodded her conscience by offering to sell her brand new, high-end electronics at a discount of up to fifty percent off the retail prices. When she countered with questions about specific products and brands, I knew that I had gained her as a customer and eventual Info Operative. Over the duration of my stay in Hammond, she and I would produce hundreds of thousands of dollars of pure profit, filtered through her hands and passed into mine.

My networking efforts continued up the street and around the corner from the cell phone store, where I met an interesting young white male owner of a jewelry store that sold high-quality diamonds and made custom jewelry. We'll call him DG, because I always considered him to be the Diamond Guy. The dental jewelry I had indulged in captivated his attention, though not overtly as an identifying marker of a criminal in the way that various law enforcement agencies were zeroing in on them. DG told me that he had simply never seen diamonds set so perfectly in a person's teeth. Later, he would admit that he had profiled my appearance and categorized me as either a drug dealer or a rapper—typical stereotypes for the appearance of young Black success, grouped in with athletes—but we both let his presumption lay for a few encounters. When he finally felt comfortable enough to ask whether I had access to cocaine, the door was open and we could proceed.

DG was a well-organized business owner but undisciplined in his spending. One day, as he vented about his impending financial woes, I proposed that he falsify the sale of a few pieces of high-end jewelry by running some of the credit card numbers I had through his credit card machine. A day or so later, he called and asked that I meet him with four credit card numbers, which I obtained from my Info Operative in Monroe. His paranoia kept him from conducting the initial exchanges of information at his store. Instead, he wanted to meet me at different locations. Over a period of four days, he took the stolen information that I'd given him and ran falsified purchases through his credit card machine at more than ten thousand dollars each.

Three days later, all four transactions were cleared for withdrawal, and we met at a gas station to divide my 40 percent from his 60 percent he always took to cover the fees and taxes that were a part of each fraudulent sale. He opted to watch for chargebacks rather than continue right away, since the identity owner could still catch and dispute the charges with the credit card company within thirty days, leaving DG to suffer the losses.

From DG, I learned all there was to know about credit card security from a merchant's perspective, as well as how to select diamonds based on their color, clarity, cut, and total weight. These one-on-one lessons after business hours prepared me to eventually purchase high-end diamonds from his local competitors and resell the same to him at reduced wholesale prices.

In my conclusive evaluation of high-quality stones, I can appreciate that in the estimation of eternity, diamonds are earthly material only valuable within the limitations of time. So really, all I learned is that diamonds are only worth what people are willing to pay for out of ignorance or pride.

Despite constant cash flow from drug proceeds and fraudulent credit card transactions, my cost of living was at an all-time high. I learned to acquire wealth through trial and error, but retaining it was more error than not. The more money I made, the more I spent on meaningless possessions. This was the same timeframe in which I learned the dangers of casinos, as well as while undisciplined generosity took its own toll on my finances. There wasn't a soul, from family members to fair-weather friends to frenemies, who couldn't count on me. Long before the "income tax refund anticipation loans" and without the exorbitant interest rates on payday loans, most of the people in my life found that I could provide interest-free loans—turned costly donations—and directly or indirectly finance their needs and wants right from the linings of my pockets.

It wasn't until I stopped gambling that I realized I'd been flirting with a definite end and financial ruin. While I initially saw gambling, drugs, and fraud as a self-financing pyramid of wealth, I now placed drug dealing as the foundation and eliminated gambling from the scenario altogether. This full revelation came in the fall of 2001 when the devastating attacks of September 11 rippled across the country. Even the motions of sin seemed to be at a standstill as hardened criminals like me unearthed enough conscience to pray for the comfort of families, the efforts of emergency personnel, and the swift capture of those who were responsible. While we do observe an annual National Day of Prayer, this occasion couldn't wait for the first Thursday in May. America sustained a wound that required our collective humanity to heal.

The donation cans on store counters and fundraising T-shirts all called to mind the first responders covered in ash and the family members of the victims covered in rubble. I contributed whenever the opportunity arose, but my melancholy over 9/11 was, unfortunately, not wholly selfless. The drug drought following the tragedy caused heightened security at America's every border and port of entry. Desperate drug dealers had to make new connections, and everyone was in search of new supply.

At one such networking attempt down in Hattiesburg, MS, I was looking for a connection with someone named Super Dave when I ran into a guy we'll call Scotland. He was a legendary St. Joseph homeboy who had been on the run from the authorities for years. The rumors of his fortune and fame had partially shaped my motivation as a young drug dealer back in St. Joseph. If Scotland could go from country boy to living large in the city streets, then I was sure I could rise to meet him there. That day had finally come, and it was clear that Scotland heard rumor of my prosperity and various exploits in crime.

The more he and I talked, the more our conversation drifted toward my white-collar crimes. I casually but thoroughly relayed the aspects of identity theft and credit card fraud that I had pursued, while he pretended to be impressed. Then to my astonishment, he revealed five different driver's licenses, each originating from different states, that he alternated as a fugitive of the FBI. I thought back to my visit to the DMV when I counted on the old woman's inability to decipher my features, while Scotland surprised me yet again: these were fake IDs produced by a guy in Houston. Not just any guy, but *his* guy—and he was willing to make the introduction.

Scotland dialed his connection right then, and after a five-minute conversation I had plans to drive to Houston the very next day. Super Dave wasn't even on my radar anymore—this was the missing link I didn't know I needed. Scotland chuckled at my excitement until I slipped an unsolicited five thousand dollars into our parting handshake. He had given me "Free Game" as an OG—Original Gangster—thanks to our shared opinions and humble beginnings, and I didn't mind manifesting my monetary appreciation. I was completely serious, and Scotland assured me that I wouldn't be disappointed.

———

I took a friend named Tyrese with me to Houston, alongside a few stolen identities and credit card numbers so that the master Printer could reproduce them as a demonstration. In the parking lot of the Galleria Mall in Houston, my new contact introduced himself as CC Man—likely alluding to carbon copies or credit cards, though I never substantiated my assumptions. We got right to work.

Tyrese and I trailed CC Man to his apartment, which included a room that rivaled a small printing shop. His studio was equipped with high tech printers, scanners, embossing machines, digital cameras, laptop computers, desktop computers, and everything else that one would need to commit some serious fraud. We wasted no time with idle talk. I presented victims' personal information for the demo, and he pulled out a book that held a detailed description of each of the driver's license designs for all fifty states, US passports, and US Military ID cards, each with their encrypted security features. Ironically, the volume wasn't anything special—just a book right off the shelf at Books-A-Million intended to help merchants guard against fraud.

After I tasked him with the states and cards I required, he handed me two 10x13 business card portfolios to peruse while he worked. In them, I saw hundreds of counterfeited cards representing American Express, Discover, Mastercard, and Visa credit cards. He spoke casually as he clicked and sorted and executed his trade. The particular collections I was holding had been recently compiled. He said that he had completed the jobs over a three day period for two Russian and Nigerian clients, suggesting that as a Black man from an urban area I had shown up late to the game, barely in time to cash in on the riches that organized crime had shifted toward. According to CC Man, those clients regularly spent no less than fifty grand on his services each month. I'm not sure whether my face betrayed my surprise, but that volume made my two sample cards seem like a waste of his time. I had no idea how fast my own spending would scale as his services changed the shape and scope of my work.

With his assignment in hand and ready to go, CC Man took a passport photo of Tyrese and made note of his height, eye color, and approximate body weight, all of which he transcribed into the description of the separate Texas and Louisiana driver's licenses I had ordered. Then he shook our hands and told us he would call us the following day when they were ready for pick up, or that he could put them in the mail under next-day services. I had waited too long to meet a connection like CC Man to risk being labeled a wannabe, so I assured him we would stay in Houston as long as necessary.

The next day, CC Man presented us with the replicated credentials and recited some very attractive prices for his counterfeiting abilities. Depending on the type of identification and the details supplied with it, his documents ranged from one hundred fifty to one thousand dollars—all very reasonable for the returns we could get from the right data. If the stolen information was good, it should easily pay for itself. We devised a plan to fax over all the information for the stolen identities and credit card numbers, and to mail both the money and the merchandise in order to cut down on travel risks. Before parting ways, he took a passport photo of me to keep on file so he could adapt it to the identities I would assume in the future.

The scheme was simple yet elegant: acquire identifying numbers and data—SSN, driver's license, name, and address—then recreate the documentation using the image and descriptor of the operative. It was our key to unlock doors that had previously been opened only by elaborate stories, quick thinking, and too many potential slip-ups that constantly risked arrest.

On our way home, Tyrese and I tested our new plastic at a Home Depot using his newly counterfeited Louisiana driver's license. In less than sixty seconds after the sales associate submitted the fraudulent application for instant credit, the account was approved for eight thousand dollars, good at any Home Depot in the country. Tyrese spent approximately

YHWH

thirty-five hundred on two gas generators and two five-hun-dred-dollar gift cards. We loaded the generators and headed for Lake Charles, LA, where we stopped to do some miscella-neous shopping with the Texas driver's license and its supple-mental counterfeit credit card. The transactions were a breeze, my first Field Operative was in action, and my plans were in motion before we even made it home.

Back in Hammond, I immediately started moving the chess pieces around, establishing reliable mailboxes and informing DG of the good news. He was ecstatic to hear of the new and improved security that came with a reliable photo identifica-tion to keep on file. That way, if anyone ever came to inspect his records after an attempted chargeback, he would have recorded, photocopied data safely on file. For my part, the ability to send Operatives like Tyrese into a store with validat-ing documentation meant I could teach more people to exe-cute fraud without limiting the pool to those who could talk their way into and out of situations the way that I could.

Over a period of two weeks, my Field Operatives and I applied for and exhausted instant credit accounts from Jackson, MS, to New Orleans. Before the stolen identities went bad—meaning, before we exhausted their potential and risk started to climb—we acquired three of the five 1ct dia-monds DG ordered, netting a payday of ten grand upon deliv-ery. It was a successful test run, but not enough to sustain an organization. For the month of December 2001, I outfitted myself with stolen identities for five Texas driver's licenses that had my face on them, as well as two counterfeit credit cards for each license, and got to work.

With Nellie absorbed with scholastic and athletic commitments that December, I wasn't as preoccupied with alibis for my goings and comings throughout the day. As long as I wasn't required to stay overnight at a given location, I would always be home by nine. She stayed busy at games, studying, or traversing the campus, while I was busy establishing a private clientele who would keep big-ticket orders for electronics, jewelry, clothing, weapons, and vehicles coming.

My customers came from all walks of life—after all, no matter who you are, where you come from, or how much money you have, everybody likes a good discount. By the time Christmas arrived, my three-grand investment turned into a profit of a little more than fifty thousand, not including any after-Christmas shopping I did for myself. Orders kept coming in after that, as did the growth of my private clientele. The more orders I filled, the bigger the succeeding orders became. The bigger the order, the bigger the profit.

Now I was ready to expand my operations to meet the growing demand.

I first turned to the roster of older former street affiliates who had sold drugs under my direction, then expanded until I felt comfortable with my team. At peak, I recruited twenty Info Operatives and twenty Field Operatives, categorized evenly between men and women, myself not included, with the ideal Operative usually around forty to fifty years old. I then split the Operatives evenly into four teams, each team appropriately aged and racially diverse. They came from all walks of life and manner of profession, actively working in local law enforcement, banks, hotels, hospitals, car dealerships, tax preparation companies, restaurants, cell phone stores, rental car dealerships, and of all places, there was one Info Operative who came from a casino's credit and finance department.

At twenty-two years old, I had become the Superintending Financier of my own forty-person identity theft organization.

I paid each Field Operative a weekly salary of two thousand dollars a week, for which they were required to fill an order list of specific items ranging from electronics to jewelry to clothing to guns. Each order list had a total retail value of approximately twenty-five thousand dollars, which I converted into at least thirteen thousand by reselling the merchandise through my exclusive network of private customers.

Each stolen identity that came with a credit score of 721 points or better could easily bring in thirty thousand dollars after we submitted three to five applications for instant credit through different merchants—this was without the supplemental profit from counterfeit credit cards that increased purchase power while doubling as second forms of identification for the instant credit application process. Each Operative earned a bonus, unhinged shopping spree for themselves once my orders were filled and quotas were met.

My Field Operatives also possessed vehicles of their choice, made possible using stolen identities of course, and I paid the monthly notes and insurance premiums for the vehicles to ensure none of them went bad. Their living and wardrobe expenses were absorbed by counterfeit credit cards, and I gave each of them a monthly stipend of a thousand dollars for housing. They had access to as much rest, recess, and relaxation as their expediency would allow.

My Info Operatives weren't forgotten—they also had a weekly salary of one thousand dollars, in exchange for a minimum of twenty-five stolen identities and/or one hundred credit card numbers on a weekly basis.

To cover our ongoing baseline costs, I set an organizational goal of a minimum of fifteen thousand dollars profit each day, from Monday to Friday, and no less than twenty thousand on Saturdays when store managers were most likely to be off for the weekend. My Sundays were dedicated not to religious observances, but to religiously writing out identity profiles and filling out custom-made credit card order forms that I would fax over to CC Man for counterfeiting for the following week.

I always stayed ahead of my operation by keeping an extra five counterfeited driver's licenses and ten credit cards for each of my active Field Operatives, and two counterfeited credit cards for each stolen identity, just in case CC Man ever shut down or was compromised. I kept an extra ten of each for myself in the event they became necessary to use since none of my Field Operatives were as effective as I was. If all of them were to forsake me at once, I could stand on my own, just at a slower pace.

I believed that taking care of my people meant they would, in turn, take care of me, but as much as this felt like a thriving business organization, it was still a criminal syndicate. And some of my people got too comfortable, too cocky, and too carried away by easy money and the lust and allure of *more*.

By February 2002, however, my teams were fully deployed and operating with great proficiency. My merchant targets were mapped out, broken down by regions and districts within a four-state operation that covered Louisiana, Mississippi, Alabama, and Texas, occasionally expanding to Missouri.

I remember one day, just after we had hit the Zale's and Gordon's jewelry stores all over the state—bringing in hundreds of thousands of dollars—I went to the mall in Hammond with absolutely no criminal intent. As I came down the escalator, I spotted a meeting of sorts, with chairs positioned in a rented space situated for what appeared to be a regional meeting of store managers. As the escalator moved me slowly closer to the group, I started to recognize faces from some of those same jewelry stores, and I could tell some of them recognized me, too. Their little organization-wide meeting had to be about me and my own organization.

I smiled, waved, and walked right out of the mall. Our reach was growing, and we were leaving a mark.

My operation continued to scale despite my random and repeated run-ins with the law, but it had not yet peaked—not as it was about to, just after getting arrested in June of 2002 for attempting to purchase a Panasonic high definition LCD TV from a Best Buy store in Metairie, LA. The TV was meant to furnish a high-rise apartment I had just signed a lease on, which would be monitored by my cousin Dee and used as a temporary safe house in Baton Rouge. That incident landed me in Jefferson Parish Jail, where I met a car salesman turned

Info Operative who was being processed in and out of jail for a few bad checks.

I found this fella through casual conversation as we all waited to be processed. His name was Chris, and he was venting about being arrested for a worthless check he had issued months before. Chris was what we would call a Pretty Boy. His preppy attire made him stand out like a sore thumb, and I immediately began fishing for his occupation. Better than retail, he worked as a new and used car salesman in New Orleans, which partially explained his clothing choices. In fact, Chris started trying to pre-sell me a vehicle while we both sat there in jail, assuring me that he could get me approved for any kind of vehicle I wanted, regardless of how unworthy my personal credit was. Clearly, he was willing to bend or outright break the rules to get a deal done. And he had unlimited, direct access to consumer credit reports. Chris was made for my operation, and I believed I could earn his business in exchange for immediate, bonded freedom from temporal incarceration and a few dollars for his pocket.

I waited until he called his girlfriend back for the hundredth time to see how things were progressing with his bond, and when I overheard him firing off profanities under his breath, I capitalized on my chance. I approached him with a hushed proposal to post his bail if he would return the favor by pulling a few credit reports of people whose names, social security numbers, dates of birth, and mailing addresses I would supply. In his desperation, Chris felt that pulling a few credit reports was the least he could do for me if I were to put up money for his bail.

It cost a little more than two thousand dollars to bond Chris and myself out of jail, which I had held on my person from the time of arrest until the opportune moment.

Chris kept his word, and the very next day I called to have him pull twenty credit reports to test the waters. He came through on every request. Within a year's time, I would use his offer of gratitude to pull thousands of credit reports. I paid him impressively for the credit reports he delivered with beacon scores above 721.

Before I connected with Chris after that fortuitous arrest, I had to intuit the identities that might carry good credit based on several factors. Now, having privileged access to credit reports a phone call away allowed me a window into their finances that even they did not have, at least not on a regular basis. The credit report also put us in a unique position to correctly answer the requisite set of computer-generated security questions that would populate sometimes as part of the instant credit approval process. This powerful access promised a profit of at least twenty-five thousand dollars off of every stolen identity, even on a bad day. The future was bright and filled with fraud, and I took pride in what I had built.

To protect my crimes, reputation, and eventual organization was to protect myself and my ego. The bigger my ambitions, the more personal each slight became. At first, I had been little more than an opportunist. My parents' and grandparents' identities were easy to access, and I could find most of the answers to security questions by asking around.

Then, I extended into community leaders who I knew a little about, such as the principal of my high school. Slowly, my circles began to widen until identity theft became a craft. At scale, my target choices were completely devoid of malice or personal retribution. I cared only about the number you represented both to the credit bureaus and to me, and that was it.

Over time, however, I began to wield my skills as a weapon. Once I was completely confident in my ability to flawlessly execute my crime, I went back to Tensas Parish for a name I'd seen every day in the summer, emblazoned on a needlessly giant mailbox purposely situated in the turn row of the cotton field along Hwy 65 in Tensas Parish, north of Newellton. Yes, a hoe field.

That name represented generations of cotton growers, and on my side of history, generations of kids and parents and grandparents out in the fields planting, chopping, picking, and stumping it. The name now belonged to an old man, a patriarch of the family and direct descendant of the original plantation owner and slaveholder.

And I took that name for myself.

He had perfect credit—820 on the beacon score. Merely shopping it around would do me no good, since perfect credit has higher automatic alerts on it. Instead, I called the three credit bureaus under the guise of raising a security alert, posing as the owner of the credit, the wealth, the field, the town, the legacy. The callback number I gave went to my own burner phone so that the bureaus would alert me each time I—or he—used these credentials to make a purchase. In other words, he couldn't buy anything without my allowance.

My abuse of his identity was a slow burn, intended to be scalding and sobering enough for him to want to change his side in history. I enslaved his identity long enough to tar its good reputation and feather it with proverbial bags of my own fortune, before discarding it alongside all the other empty, meaningless identities that disappeared into untold history.

I didn't need his money. I did it for sport. I did it for spite, though I'd never met the man. I knew what he had, where he got it from, and how I could force unconscious and unwilling reparations.

In almost any situation, I knew I could play my cards just right until any level of access and control could become my own. And any time I lost a hand, you can be sure I'd come back to win the pot.

Ridgeland, MS, set the stage for one such game. It was a fancy little money town, predominantly Caucasian, and heavily policed. These people didn't play, and all the way back in September 1999, I was wrong to think that I could creep in to defraud their business community as a minority without the least suspicion.

When I called in to "purchase" a set of tires and rims from a local tire service center, I failed to note one important detail: Black people simply did not shop in Ridgeland. Yet here I was, a young Black male attempting to pay for a customized set of rims and tires by phone under the pretense of a father placing the order for his son who would arrive to pick up the merchandise just after noon. I even requested that the rims and tires be mounted for ease of transportation.

The scam was red flagged from the moment I hung up the phone, but after seamless scams from shops just like these in Monroe and West Monroe, I had no idea. The undercover cops on the scene knew exactly when I was coming. One of them even gave me turn by turn directions, posing as a store employee. Inside, another undercover cop questioned me about the transaction, confirming that I was the imposter, then two additional undercover cops approached me from behind to arrest and take me into custody.

I gave a deep sigh and dropped my head. It hadn't been a full month from a previous arrest, yet this would become another felony in a town where I didn't know anything about anybody who could help me out. Not only was I booked for false pretense and uttering forgery, but I was also charged with possession of a controlled substance, which was none other than baking soda I stored in my travel bag, used to brush my diamond teeth.

Even the city jail was brand new, just as clean and sanitized as a hospital ward, and I sat in there a long nine days before bonding out. No bail bondsman in the area wanted to bail me out, no matter the amount. Their reasoning was that I wasn't from the local area, so I posed the liability of skipping bail and not showing up for court. It took my high-profile criminal defense attorney, Ross Barnette, Jr., Esq., vouching for me on my eighth day to get me out of jail the day following. It was my longest time in jail to that point, and I left with a sense of divine freedom and an unholy desire for vengeance.

In return for outsmarting me, once my enterprise was in motion years later, I sent five Operatives back to Ridgeland. In one vengeful sweep, they scammed that pretty little business community out of more than three hundred thousand dollars' worth of Rolex watches, diamond solitaire rings, and electronics before moving on without a single arrest. I had to blanket the city of Ridgeland, MS, with an invisible but tangible crime spree of fraud.

With every misstep, I learned to adapt. For every person or town that outsmarted me, I'd come back at them ten times smarter and harder. But it wasn't just the business community. I had to maintain my authority amongst my peers and Operatives as well. By my early twenties, I'd proven myself and felt confident that I commanded a measure of respect. But back in 2000, I was still creating that name. I had taken two thousand dollars and turned it into two hundred thousand dollars despite the setbacks of repeated gambling losses and constant legal challenges. Where I come from, that's more than most people make in twenty years of working in the cotton fields, let alone at twenty years old. That appearance of success does not come without envy from peers and jealousy from rivals. It's doubly adverse when your envious peer is *also* your jealous rival—and I had earned my share of these hybrid enemies.

Late one February evening, on a visit to St. Joseph to see my parents, I went to Bate's Store, which had been renamed to Harbor's Grocery—yes, the very store that taught me not to shoot dice with your back to the road. On this occasion, I was inside, hood fellowshipping with the homies, playing pool, and shooting the breeze.

The beloved, now late, Mel Bates-Harbor—Hood Matriarch, savvy businesswoman, owner of the store, and my own god-mother with whom I shared the birthday of October 24—always kept my parking spot reserved when I was in town. That's where I had parked my new car, which was my second Lincoln and one of six custom automobiles in my fraudulent fleet. That car, which had been acquired via identity theft and was the draw of much attention, sat out front like a trophy, announcing my presence and my clout. That night, it became the object of misdirected and ill-informed retribution.

If you remember the story of Juvy and how my pit-bull became my best friend in the absence of Marcel, you'll recall that he was serving out a prison sentence of ten years for a drug possession charge that he took in my stead at the Greyhound Bus station in Houston. That February night, his oldest brother, Lil Ed—named after his beloved and late may-oral father, Edward Brown, Sr.—directed his drunken anger and misappropriated retribution for Marcel on my vehicle, kicking heavy and deep dents in the door. He went on to make a public show of it, making sure everyone knew what he was doing and why.

When I went outside to see what all the commotion was about, there sat my customized, pearl white Lincoln Mark VIII, reflecting his rage on the driver's side. I couldn't let it stand.

I confronted Lil Ed to make sure he had targeted the right vehicle, calmly and in full witness of a growing crowd. Once confronted, I opened the trunk and reached in for a base-ball bat that I kept on hand to inspire humility in just such a circumstance. Like the unhinged version of whippins' I remember receiving as a child, I delivered the first three or four swings dictatorially before turning to engage the crowd.

This was the image I wanted to impress: I wasn't a killer, but you'd better not push me to find out what I was.

Then I beat him again until the police showed up. Before their guns were up, I landed one more exclamatory bat—one more message, that not even the police could save you if I didn't let them.

While Lil Ed was at Riverland Medical Center being examined for concussions, bruised limbs, and broken bones, I was bonding out of jail on an aggravated battery charge. Eventually, we reconciled and remain cordial friends to this day.

My calloused exterior was most vicious with my peers, most reserved with my exploits, and most noticeable in my interactions with law enforcement. On a hot August day, also in the year 2000, a Tensas Parish traffic cop spotted me doing 75 in a 55 mph zone when I knew I had a suspended license. There was no panic or worry left in me by that point. I kept the same rate of speed for another two miles while I called my parents to have them come get my car off the highway, then the bail bondsman to have him meet me at the jail.

When I did finally decide to pull over, the cop took forever to get out of his car. To alert him to my impatience, I put my car in drive, drove five feet forward, then stopped and put the car back in park. You can bet he got out of his patrol car then.

When he rattled off the typical questions about my place of departure, destination, and reasoning for my behavior, I simply answered, "You were taking so long to get out of the car, I thought you stopped me by accident. I figured you were back there figuring out how to apologize and let me go!"

The officer then instructed me to stand at the rear of my vehicle while he ran my credentials, supposing I may drive off if allowed to stay in my car. He returned with the bad news that he would have to place me under arrest. He secured the keys as well, which prevented my parents from collecting the car, but I posted bail just as soon as the paperwork was processed, collected my keys, and rode with the bail bondsman back to my vehicle.

Over the year that followed, as I realized much of my potential in fraud, I did so while carrying eight pending charges that were awaiting resolution. My probationary restrictions resided in Monroe, along with my probation officer, while my behavior that broke those conditions remained in St. Joseph and in Hammond with me. The only time I saw my probation officer would be at the revocation hearings she repeatedly called for.

One such occasion would come in October of 2001, when I was arrested due to violation reports that had been submitted to the courts. There was a *no bond* stipulation attached to the warrant, which meant I couldn't just bond out of jail as I had on all previous occasions—twelve in all, at that point. I had to appear before the judge to get a bond.

In her reports, my probation officer stated that I had failed to pay court-ordered fines and fees, left Tensas Parish without permission, and failed to report to her as directed as far back as June 19, 2000—all of which was true.

To represent me during the hearing, I retained the expert counsel and allegiance of the late criminal defense attorney, Mr. Paul Kidd, Sr., Esq. He readily dived into effective representation, and by the time of my revocation hearing the next morning, he had already worked a deal for me to pay all my previous court fines, past due probation fees, and present court costs in exchange for reinstatement of probation. Mr. Kidd wrote the court, Louisiana Probation and Parole Office, and District Attorney's Office three separate checks right there in the courtroom to cover all my legal expenses for that day, and I reimbursed him upon release.

Mr. Kidd was a master of this process, and his involvement came at a premium. He was also a well-connected man who, like most attorneys, understood and could wield the power that connection held. For each of my white-collar crimes, I could easily throw money at the problem to make it go away. I fully believed money could buy me out of any legal situation, and for a great deal of time, it did just that.

My probation officer was furious, but her powers were limited to arrests only. Anything more had to come by way of recommendation to the court via the District Attorney's Office. To get what I wanted, I gladly funneled money through the Caucasian good ol' boys club—the very same network, prejudiced perceptions, and biased laws that desperately require criminal justice and prison reform in our present day. My probation officer, on the other hand, was a Black female sitting at the intersection of double prejudices, trying to prove her rank from within that same club. She didn't understand, and perhaps still doesn't understand, that we were black chess pawns in a game masterfully designed and predetermined by the white elite. Getting the upper hand on a prominent Black male would have proved her loyalty to the force. But each time I slipped out of her hands and got away with it, without any of her colleagues calling her or keeping her in the loop, she no doubt felt herself slipping further and further down the ranks.

We were working the same system—or were being worked by the same system—and we were both determined to come out on top. Of course, there was still the fact that she was in the right. Yet none of that mattered. My attorney had built a case against her that would ultimately win and end our game for good.

For a stretch of time, whenever I got arrested, I would use one of the two identities I was living under in Hammond, which was always verifiable through the state's Office of Motor Vehicles. When I faced yet another arrest in January 2002, mere months after my victory against my parole officer, my lucky streak ran out. This time, they ran my prints through the new, digitalized National Criminal Information System (NCIS). The days of manual fingerprinting had vanished between arrests, and the technology had arrived just in time to unmask my true identity.

This discovery resulted in charges of resisting an officer by giving false information, as well as injury to public records, and once again I was locked up in unfamiliar territory with a probation hold and no way to bond out of jail. And this time, my probation officer got notice. I'm sure she was elated.

Mr. Paul Kidd, happily held on a monthly retainer, put his persuasion and connections to work while I was relocated to the St. Tammany Parish Jail in Covington, LA—a far cry from the polished cells in Ridgeland. That dungeon was so miserably cold that I couldn't sleep, and the only means of relief came through a timed, five-minute hot shower. I've never taken so many showers in a single day than when I was housed in that despicable place.

Mr. Kidd informed me that my probation officer adamantly refused to lift the hold. If I wanted out, I would have to post bail, which would trigger my probation officer to take me into her custody—though at least I would be out of that icy facility. I immediately moved to post bail. Curiously, a prison official commented that I was "wasting my money" due to an active warrant for my arrest from Concordia Parish Sheriff's Office. Mr. Kidd researched the warrant, then advised me to go over to that parish to post bail on those charges as well before my probation officer could come to get me.

I followed his advice, posted bail in Covington and was picked up and transported to Concordia Parish so that I could post bail in that parish as well. Based on the information the deputy shared on that drive, I knew the warrant had come from a frenemy and customer who had given up my name under the threat of arrest. I was disappointed, but the conditions in Concordia couldn't leave me mad for long.

See, Nellie was raised in Concordia Parish, and I made a name for myself in those streets. My reputation preceded me, and I was treated like a jailhouse celebrity as soon as the doors locked behind me. I sponsored dormitory parties for my fellow inmates every night of my stay and ordered DVDs from the outside to watch on the two weekends of my stay. I even bonded one of my new friends out of jail so they could join my criminal organization as a type of enforcer. In a weird way, I enjoyed most of my "visit." Nevertheless, two weeks there was too long, especially on top of the three that preceded it in St. Tammany Parish.

The probation hold had followed me through the system, so posting bail only moved me closer to the one person upon whom I cast all the blame for my problems: my probation officer. She had the upper hand now, and I couldn't wait to regain that control. When she finally showed up at Concordia Parish Jail in early March 2002, she transported me to the Ouachita Correctional Center with fresh, accurate charges, all under the impression that a probation hold was still in place.

As soon as we arrived, I called Mr. Kidd to let him know that I had finally made it to Monroe. We briefly discussed next steps and exchanged a few jokes, before he informed me that the probation hold had been lifted just before I called him.

Mr. Kidd had evidently called in a favor to the District Attorney and deliberately kept my probation officer out of the loop. Thanks to his efforts, I was able to bond out. I was a free man once more, and my probation officer had absolutely no idea. He had choice words to say about her, insisting that she could find out on her own about my release. I kept quiet and stayed in Monroe a couple days longer to monitor my legitimate businesses, all of which had remained productive and profitable. On the way back to Hammond, I touched down in Tensas Parish to replenish the drug sales that had waned in my absence. When I got home, I took my entire forty-member identity theft organization out to dinner, with a theme of "*we got work to do and money to make.*" I paid for the event with a stolen credit card, of course.

As Mr. Kidd had prearranged, my revocation hearing was simple. The judge gave me a verbal reprimand, issued credit for time served, and reinstated probation. I looked right at my probation officer as he spoke. She was shocked and livid at the sight of me dressed in freedom. I stared long enough to catch her attention, then winked at her as I walked out of the courtroom. I wanted her to know she was being tolerated. I was sure I had regained the upper hand for good, though in retrospect, my pretentious form of power had no real authority.

I continued to operate with unchecked arrogance throughout 2002, as it seemed there were no consequences that I couldn't evade. In October of that year, a jewelry store in Baton Rouge's Cortana Mall finally caught me in the act, and I saw when they did it. I handed the Rolex back to the cashier, shrugged, and said, "You got me!" then walked out calmly with the security guards. Despite my cool demeanor, I sat in jail a little longer than what was comfortable, given the seven hundred fifty thousand dollars I had just spent on a cocaine shipment days prior that was scheduled to arrive any day in St. Joseph. I shouldn't have been able to post bond due to the number of charges that had been filed against me, but once again I slipped through the cracks, giving me time to meet the mule and convert the shipment to its doubled profit.

Days later, I kicked off my holiday shopping spree in Tensas Parish and was promptly arrested when three John Deere sister stores—Waterproof, Newellton, and Tallulah—communicated with each other and grew wise to my crimes. But again, I bonded out, and again there was no mention of a probation hold.

A quiet voice in the back of my mind had begun to wonder whether I really was in control or if there was some alternative reason that I kept slipping under the cracks. After all, I had seen too many people recognize me, too many strange coincidences to feel completely at ease.

The more my organization grew, the less I slept and the more I worried. Whenever I was in the field of operation, my skills of practiced perception and constant presence of mind became annoyingly sensitive. I heard security code alerts where there might have been none and phones ringing by cash registers whenever I'd step near them. I'd walk into a store only to make a U-turn, sure that my profile had been shared throughout the region.

Paranoid and perturbed, I stepped back to take on the role of a Financier for the operation, doubling our order lists, expanding and alternating Field Operative shifts, and making the most of the din of holiday shopping. All my Operatives received five-thousand-dollar bonuses on top of their weekly salary. My Info Operatives each got two thousand dollars more, and my organization went on a holiday break to enjoy Christmas with our families. If I couldn't control the operation on the ground, I would ensure its continuance from a distance, sure that I had earned loyalty and security in my efforts.

In January 2003, with the year starting off just as planned, I was preparing the team to make one more round on the Christmas mess we'd made before the thirty-day window was up on the identities we'd pulled. But on a Sunday night, just after faxing my usual fifteen-thousand-dollar order to CC Man, the phone rang with disturbing news. Dee was on the other end, my cousin and one of my most trusted Field Operatives.

Instead of updating me on the high-rise he kept watch over in Baton Rouge or noting some role he had to play in our upcoming field assignments, he announced his retirement from the organization. Then he went on to shake my world at its core.

He said he had moved all of my furniture out of the stash house apartment. He had also taken the $3.1 million I had hidden in a wall inside the master bedroom closet, all converted to one-hundred-dollar bills, stashed it into bags and loaded it into his car. He advised that there was no need for me to come looking for him, because he wasn't going to be found any time soon.

I didn't believe a word he said, but I raced from Hammond up I-12, calling his cell phone frantically the whole way—all to no avail. The standard thirty-five-minute drive took twenty-five minutes. After I rushed up the stairs to the apartment, I stood there in shock and dismay. Just as he said, the living room was naked, vacant, and as lifeless as the day I toured it and signed the lease. My money was gone from the master bedroom closet. My Operative was gone—but of all people, my cousin had betrayed me. I had embraced him like a little brother, and this was a slap in the face. For days on end, it was hard to believe what had happened.

Outwardly, I brushed off his disappearance as a ten-thousand-dollar loan and five identities that he skipped town with. Inwardly, I was desperate. He left me with fifty thousand dollars in cash to cover approximately seventeen thousand dollars in personal monthly living expenses, not to mention the organizational expenses, a few costly court dates, and a pregnant girlfriend expecting to give birth at any moment.

For the rest of January, I spent most of my time in my home office trying to see where I had gone wrong in my dealings with Dee. I tried to reorganize the scale of my enterprise by establishing a commission-based pay scale instead of weekly salaries and widening our field to include Arkansas, Oklahoma, Tennessee, and Florida. But I couldn't help thinking that I was starting to reap all I'd sown.

My thoughts drifted back to my probation officer and the creeping fear that she may simply be letting out enough rope for me to hang myself. When my mom called to tell me that the probation officer had left a message for me to call her back, those fears began to materialize. I stalled on a return call until February, and when I did hear her voice on the other end, I could immediately see through any feigned concern for my welfare. We determined a meeting for February 7, 2003, with Nellie due to give birth any day.

On the way to Monroe, I recalled the events of the previous months. I thought of moments where my demeanor was unstable when out in the field, and of the way even the highest provisions couldn't keep a close relative loyal. I thought of all the ways my probation officer might be working with federal agents to outsmart me beyond what I could see or escape.

The *Catch Me If You Can* game that we'd been playing was on a shifting foundation, and if I couldn't get out of this fix, what was the point of even trying?

In Monroe, I connected with my brother Lamont first, making arrangements for him to take my truck if I were to be arrested that day. I called Mr. Kidd to inform him of my anticipations and instructed them both to move if I didn't come out of the probation and parole office in twenty minutes. In the elevator going up to my probation officer's office, I pictured prison and the thought of Nellie's impending birth.

Before I could sit down at her desk, one of the assisting officers stood up and instructed me to put my hands behind my back while my probation officer read my Miranda Rights. I asked to call my attorney, and when I reminded them of his name, the room's respect for him was palpable. They stopped the intimidation tactics immediately and gave me my call—which the officer dialed for me. Thinking it was my attorney, I had him dial my brother's cell phone number, then waited as he held the phone to my ear. I conveyed my instructions to Lamont while pretending to respond to questions from Mr. Kidd:

"Mr. Kidd, it's me...Ouachita Correctional Facility...Nellie...Mom and Dad. Thank you. Goodbye!"

Madisen Marie Williams was born into this world on February 11, 2003, weighing five and a half pounds, fully healthy and resembling both of her parents.

I missed her birth by four days.

For most of this stretch from the ages of eighteen to twenty-two, I felt invincible. I thought my crimes would carry me, my kids, and my girlfriend and new baby forever because I thought that I could continue to outwit and outsmart everyone around me.

To effectively spot and prevent identity theft, organizations have to think like criminals. Some of them, like Ridgeland and my parole officer, did. Countless others never saw me coming. If you have information, products, and people to protect, much of *America's Domestic War* explores the tactics and thought processes that carry identity theft as a crime and an industry.

SEVEN

REFOCUS

Deliver me, I pray, from the hand of my brother,
from the hand of Esau; for I fear him...
—Jacob, Genesis 32:6, NKJV

After my probation officer took me into custody on February 7, I was transported back to what had become a second home, Ouachita Parish Correctional Facility, where I was to remain until my probation revocation hearing. There were no strings to pull or bonds to post that could get me out on my impatient terms. Nellie's confidence in my impending release sustained my hope for an expedient homegoing, but I knew the odds were stacked against me.

Apparently, the Secret Service had been working an independent investigation since the previous fall, with me as their person of interest, separate from the FBI's ongoing concurrent investigation. Special Agents from the Secret Service—one of whom I vaguely remember went by the name Kirby—had even shown up at our door in Hammond trying to find me. They had gotten a hold of some check fraud or forgery, but I never stayed at the address I registered with my probation officer. Dartanyon A. Williams was always listed in Tensas Parish, while I used other names for the addresses I actually occupied.

They eventually met Nellie before meeting me. She was rightly angry, of course, by such an officious introduction to federal agents and the greater extent of my exploits. But a couple months went by between their visit with her and my probation officer picking me up, so Nellie and I had reconciled. She was sure that I would avail myself again this time, just as I had always done before. Our conversations served as an escape for my mind in place of the freedom my body craved.

At the top of every hour, starting at 9 a.m. and ending at 9 p.m., seven days a week, I would call to check in on her and the baby. After February 11 came and went, it was not lost on me that Nellie's labor had probably been induced by stress, especially since nothing else had brought labor on to that point. Madisen's birth date came after her estimated due date, and the more I thought of her tardiness the more frustrated and accusatory I became. If she'd come on time, I would have met her—could have held her in my arms.

In reality, I only hoped to shift the blame for my absence off of my shoulders. I wanted to believe that being around beyond her due date had been enough, but I knew that wasn't true. Nellie had given birth to a beautiful baby girl—and I had left them to begin their life together alone. The struggle and stress that I knew they were stepping into compounded my guilt as I reflected on my inexcusable absences at the births of both Emoni and Darquise as well.

Pity parties wouldn't get me home to them, though, and I had to move my thoughts away from guilt and toward life outside those concrete walls.

As the mastermind of my own identity theft organization, I enjoyed being in control. I relished in the power and influence I had over Operatives twice my age. I carried a commanding presence and dictated orders with ease. I was in control. If money couldn't pry open a door, my mouth usually could. I was the man with the master plan. Underlying those gratifying strengths, I also carried a burden of great pressure. The constant threat of capture paled in comparison—and possibly contributed to—the constant threat of depression.

I had few fears around botched missions themselves, but rather about what incarceration would mean. The possibility of losing control over the operation meant a loss of power, and with a loss of power came a loss of control over *myself* in ways that kept me up at night.

All that power had come at a price. For years, I might expect a combined four hours of sleep in any twenty-four-hour period, spread across naps and quick hits of REM sleep manufacturing the energy I needed to keep going. I constantly obsessed over the structure of my organization, always manipulating numbers, routes, and regions. I pored over ways to perfect my craft while navigating the countless liabilities I carried. With forty people relying on me, not counting Nellie and the kids, family members, and false friends, it wasn't just a game anymore. I felt the full weight of responsibility, with so many relying on my intelligence and the moves I would make.

Thinking my way out of a situation had been thrilling when it was just me—but in order to keep real control, I had to think for the next man, too. Each Operative represented a financial obligation and a potential criminal liability. If one person got caught, how would that come back on the rest of us? What procedures would mitigate the fallout? What kept those people from ratting out the others? What plans had I made in case of failure? What if I can't get out of jail for Nellie and my children.

I never took a hit off the cocaine I was dealing, nor a puff or drag off the marijuana I was selling, and I didn't have to. Power itself was addictive enough, tantalizing me with its highs and then dropping me to the lowest lows. Sitting in Ouachita Parish Correctional Facility, without any adrenaline in the chase and rapidly losing control of my environment, I could feel the threat of depression creeping up on me, though I didn't have a name for it at the time. This was a mental disorder masquerading itself as mental organization.

I didn't know what insomnia was or what chemical imbalances looked like under normal circumstances, let alone the extremes I'd created. I was barely twenty-three, with years of cognitive development expedited toward this rat-race to the top—all restricting the personal and emotional growth that my mind and heart quietly craved. My development was arrested long before restraints were clapped on my wrists and ankles. I had shackled my emotions, restricting them as the greatest liability in my pursuit of power.

My parents raised me as a Southern Baptist, but my religion was one of self, as much as my inflated ego could comprehend. Ignorant of the fact that Yahweh could do exceedingly and abundantly more for me in an instant than man or money could accomplish in a lifetime, I turned to self yet again to soothe my internal wounds.

I had to regain freedom. I had to keep control.

Approximately one week after that arrest, Mr. Kidd came to visit on a Sunday afternoon. He was dressed in casual attire, smoking some of his favorite cherry tobacco while we spoke in hushed tones about the obstacles ahead. He had kept our phone calls limited, out of a healthy paranoia that our attorney/client privilege was never fully protected as long as conversations were being monitored and recorded on jailhouse phones. During our visit, he grew candid about the uphill battle we faced.

My probation officer and the state prosecutor had collaborated to have all five years of my probation revoked. There were no plea deals on the table to exchange for my admission of guilt, nor was Mr. Kidd interested in any plea deals if they'd been an option. Instead, he laid out our defense in a manner similar to David's selection of his five smooth stones, hoping to take down Goliath via an attack on my inexperienced probation officer. He believed she had been fumbling with bias and prejudice from the first day she was assigned to my case. He was confident that the law was on our side and the state would have to take the defensive position to carry my probation revocation.

Mr. Kidd determined that my fees and fines were a cornerstone of the case against me, so I orchestrated payment to eliminate that angle. He intended to argue that my probation officer's proposed violations were rooted in vindictiveness, and that the only time she had ever paid my case any attention at all was when an arrest afforded her the opportunity to tighten the proverbial noose she had placed around my neck. By paying the court fines and probation fees before the revocation hearing, Mr. Kidd believed he'd given our defense a little more breathing room.

There was nothing more to do but wait.

For two weeks, I sat in Ouachita Correctional Facility, pondering worst case scenarios and thinking about the moves I could make to keep my identity theft operations going. I had to figure out how to keep a steady flow of income to support my family if I had to serve some real time. There was no worthy successor to manage my organization—and I wasn't looking for a genius. I only needed someone with a bit of uncommon intelligence who wasn't afraid to think outside the box just a little. Unfortunately, I had deliberately kept my peers ignorant of the manufacturing process of identity theft in order to avoid undesirable competition within the organization. I also kept specific information confidential in order to discourage compromise. One cannot tell what one does not know.

The very measures that I took to protect my criminal interests ultimately handicapped my criminal enterprise. I built my house on shifting sand, and the foundations were beginning to erode.

On February 28, 2003, the Honorable Judge Benjamin Jones presided over my revocation hearing, with police escorts by my side and Mr. Kidd ready and waiting. He assured me that he had our case under control, and I only needed to keep my mouth shut and let him do the talking. My probation officer was next, and she entered the room with an air of disgust. When we made eye contact, I could see the glint of vengeance that I'd felt in my own eyes so many times before. I could see a fresh piece of gum tucked into her mouth when she walked over to me and crooned, "Today, you can expect to be sentenced to five years in jail."

I politely responded, "Yes, ma'am," and waited for the proceedings to begin.

The state began by presenting its case, laying out all violations for which my probation should be revoked, then pointing out that I was not current of the payments for my court fines and probation fees, showing my disrespect for the court and total disregard for the guidelines of my probationary sentence.

When the Assistant District Attorney rested, Mr. Kidd took the stage with the wisdom of a seasoned veteran. He did not argue against that which he could not disprove. However, he reminded the court that my recent arrests were only allegations for which I had not been convicted. Turning to the issues of non-payment, Mr. Kidd called my probation officer to the stand. She was ill-prepared for his direct examination and nervously struggled to read from outdated documents. Mr. Kidd interrupted her, of course, handing Judge Jones up-to-date

THE MASTER IDENTITY THIEF

receipts verifying proof of payment in full. After what had to be the longest twenty minutes of her life, Mr. Kidd thanked and excused her from the witness stand. Admittedly, I felt sorry for her as the disdain and disgust on her face dissolved into chagrin.

The court wasted no time making its ruling. Judge Jones began his statements by declaring that the state had done a poor job in supervising my probation, and that such negligence may be partly responsible for what he deemed "questionable behavior" on my part. He gave me a lecture about the many chances I had received and assured me that if I continued down the criminal's path, one day I would certainly find what I was looking for: a lengthy prison sentence or untimely death.

He did agree that I was in violation of probation on a few minor technicalities. My probation was being revoked, and I would have to serve additional time in jail. Instead of five years, however, I was sentenced to ninety days in the parish jail. According to Louisiana's good time laws at the time, I was to receive two days' credit for every one day served, which meant that I would only have to serve forty-five days before being free to go without further reports to my apparently vindictive probation officer.

On the record, we had lost, but everyone knew we had won.

After Judge Jones concluded, Mr. Kidd winked at me with a slight smile and told me to come see him after I was released, while my former probation officer stormed out of the courtroom just as soon as the prosecutor called the next case.

I returned to the parish jail ecstatic about my impending release. Without a shadow of a doubt, I only had twenty-four more days left before I would get to hold my newly born Madisen. I rushed straight to the payphone to tell Nellie the good news. Between her enduring optimism (and the loose lips of Lamont, who happily rushed to tell her before I could), she was neither shocked nor surprised.

Over the next couple of weeks, I envisioned the different ways in which I would motivate the commission of identity theft to quickly recover from my absence as well as Dee's betrayal and theft. I had rebuilt my coffers to a little more than one hundred thousand dollars, a few multithousand-dollar IOUs to be collected, and enough street credibility to rival any 850 beacon score. My remaining resources would be deferred to the *Hit 'em Hard to Theft Tour*, celebrating the end of my forced leave of absence as well as the loss of my probationary leash. I was determined to go on a permanent paid vacation as the sole Superintending Financier of a thriving identity theft organization.

I drew mind maps of merchant itineraries and mentally nominated selective candidates to join my new line up of Field Operatives. The Operatives I had been running for the past year had become familiar faces to the merchants and security forces within the boundaries of my operation. It was time to bring in new faces to our familiar places, while my veteran Field Operatives would expand their horizons on field trips to Arkansas, Oklahoma, Tennessee, Alabama, and Georgia.

On the morning of my release date from Ouachita Correctional Facility, I was...not free to go hold my baby girl or start a new life with Nellie.

Instead, I was taken into custody and chauffeured by two US Marshals to the Chalmette Parish Prison, where I was to be held throughout the pre-trial proceedings of my now federal case. Federal charges—apparently connected with my identity theft activity—were new territory for me. I had Nellie reach out to Mr. Gary Jordan, the notable criminal defense attorney I previously retained for white-collar crimes in the Hammond area, to inform him of my transfer. He met me at my arraignment at the Hale Boggs federal courthouse in New Orleans and, through the thick glass dividers of the visiting booth, advised that bond would be highly unlikely.

In federal court, the bond hearing and proceedings are vastly different from state court. There, the defendant must plead and prove his case to secure pre-trial bond, while the US Attorney's Office seeks detention and argues to prove to the US Magistrate that the defendant is either or both a flight risk and danger to society. The US Attorney's Office doesn't always oppose bail for the defendant. In rare instances with special conditions, the government doesn't oppose at all.

Watching Mr. Jordan argue with the Asst. US Attorney about my freedom was more melodramatic than I ever expected it to be. He pulled no punches in his attempt to secure a bond for me, informing the court that I was a business owner and father of three, one of whom had been born while I was serving out a probationary sentence. The Asst. US Attorney rightfully reasoned that I was a danger to society, though I felt that his assertion that I was a flight risk was contradicted by the many court appearances I made without fail. Still, he only had to show the court that my historical culpability gave merit to his reasoning. It was not hard for the US Magistrate to deduce that my criminal career would only find seasonal cessation, not permanent retirement, in incarceration. What started off as a fighting chance ended as a crushing defeat in denial of bail.

Prolonged detainment meant that Nellie would have to rise to the unwanted, unwelcome challenges of being a single mother—as a rookie mom and senior in college. My record in fatherhood was continuing to spiral. Previously only a provider and occasional visitor for Emoni and Darquise, now I would be a total stranger and a limited provider to Madisen. *How was I going to tell Nellie that I wasn't coming home?*

Mr. Jordan made it clear to me that I was still being investigated by the FBI, which made me too paranoid to move on my plans to quarterback more identity theft. Nellie would have to wisely manage the money I had given her access to, or otherwise secure gainful employment. I never wanted her to work at all, especially while she was in college. Her work ethic never wavered, though, and her industrious personality would ultimately keep *me* afloat.

When I did finally make it to the phone to call Nellie, she accepted the collect call with her usual enthusiasm, happy to hear the voice of the man who would soon be reunited with his family.

It would take three timed collect calls for us to console each other and make plans for her future.

I tried to hold it together, to be enthusiastic and uncover the bright spot in the darkness, but her silence was too heavy to bear. The tears came freely in unintelligible sobs as we grieved together across the miles my crimes had put between us. Eventually, we decided that she and Madisen would move back to Ferriday for her mother to help, then I returned to my bunk and strained out a prayer that seemed to bounce off the ceiling.

Looking for any hope, anything solid in this world to grab onto, I reached for a prison Bible, opened up to Genesis, and read of the plights and exploits of Jacob and Esau until I fell asleep.

To adjust to life without income—let alone the income I was used to—I had to make some changes. I eliminated four thousand dollars' worth of bills by (legally) selling the Cadillac truck, car, and Nissan 350z. I bought my way out of three different upscale apartment leases in Baton Rouge. One of my legitimate businesses cost more than it made, so I advised my brother to sell it and one other before they went under. I retained full ownership of the barbershop that took care of itself and gave my brother whatever pieces of jewelry I didn't arrange to be sold as his compensation for mediating so many transactions. Lamont also filtered funds to Nellie, Emoni, and Darquise, and my aging grandmothers in the hopes that I could provide for them as long as possible.

With forty organizational members left out in the cold, I arranged for their care as well. I contacted my most loyal and lucrative Field Operative to arrange for him to come visit me immediately, and I entrusted him with instructions to divide the most recent order from CC Man amongst himself and the others. They were now on their own, free to do whatever they

desired with the multiple thousands of dollars' worth of sto-
len identities and credit cards that I was too scared to even
orchestrate. He understood, a bit too happily. Later, he would
get too comfortable with his OnStar GPS-equipped Cadillac
Deville sedan and would find himself arrested in Kansas.

As I began to shed my connections with the outside crim-
inal world, I had to come to terms with the news Mr. Jordan
brought to me. The FBI wanted to host a debriefing, with me as
the suspect of honor, alongside a number of law enforcement
agencies from around the state, including the Secret Service.
Knowing that I didn't have much room to bargain since I was
guilty of every complaint I was being held on, I accepted the
invitation on the condition that my own criminal activities
would be our only subject, and that any information that I
provided would protect me from self-incrimination. Special
Agent Dan Evans and his federal organization agreed to my
conditions and returned with a proposed date, time, and place
to hold the debriefing.

I spent the next few days imagining a smoky room with a
hanging light, being bombarded with questions, and men in
black suits, white shirts, and black ties interrogating me as a
menace to society.

When the day came, I was surprised to see that the mov-
ies had misrepresented reality. While the building was as
grand and intimidating as all other federal buildings, I was
taken to an office instead of a bare interrogation room. We
sat together—Mr. Jordan, the Asst. US Attorney, and an audi-
ence of plainclothes FBI agents, Secret Service agents, and all
kinds of other agents seeming to be from any and everywhere.

The Asst. US Attorney offered me a drink as soon as I arrived. I declined the club soda but did request that my handcuffs be removed. I took deep breaths and signed the proffer agreement with a steady hand, though my foot tapped out a relentless, anxious beat. Then Special Agent in Charge Dan Evans suggested I begin my story, and I did. Starting with the theft of my parents' identities, I released my burden of secrecy by sharing my exploits with the room.

Again, to my surprise, the special agents leaned in, listening intently and recording notes and audio of my explanations. The paranoia and anxiety that had come with wondering how much the FBI knew began to alleviate as I told them as much as I could remember, being as truthful as possible. In fact, my attorney soon called a "time out" to speak with me privately. I was still encouraged to be forthcoming, but he had noticed the intrigued and captivated audience as well.

The FBI had to have been monitoring me from a distance. They didn't know as much as I thought they knew, nor did they pretend to. They were genuinely interested in what I'd been able to accomplish. I was teaching the federal government Identity Theft 201 as an expert witness to the technical crimes I committed.

We all held to our bargain—me a little more confident knowing what side of the scales of justice I'd fallen on—and Special Agent Evans interjected when another agent asked who was printing my checks. He reminded his colleagues that we were there to discuss "the how" of my criminal activities only, with no others to be named. (No lie, I did briefly consider volunteering my cousin up to bring him off the joyride

I unwillingly funded. The only thing that stopped me was the potential that he might tell on too many others. I wish I could say he was spared by forgiveness or friendship. It was only loyalty to my organization.)

After I candidly confessed to all my known, and some unknown, white-collar crimes under the protections of a proffer agreement, Mr. Jordan immediately entered in plea negotiations. A couple weeks after the debriefing, the US Attorney's Office consolidated my pending state charges into one count of "Conspiracy to Commit Identity Theft" under a federal indictment. After my release from prison, I would be required to pay full restitution to the merchant victims who netted a lost as a result of my identity theft crimes—a total of about thirty thousand dollars for the crimes that they tracked—and would be placed on three years of supervised probation. Since I was facing five years for the state charges in St. Tammany Parish alone, not to mention Ferriday, Metairie, and Baton Rouge, this was a deal for real that took little convincing for me to agree.

While my case ran its course, I spent my days doing calisthenics and my nights reading the Bible. Outside of prison, I never took the time to watch fifteen second commercials on TV, much less whole programs. But within those walls, the cadence of regularly scheduled programming helps time go by and provides a bit of structure to mundane days. TV choices for the group would vary throughout the day, with the exception of three types of programs: nightly news, sports events, and *Days of Our Lives*. If you mess with a prison dorm's soap operas, you're in tedious territory. ABC's late Peter Jennings provided my personal programming of choice.

Other than TV privileges, access to the payphones mounted to the walls, time at the commissary, prison mail, and visits from family members are the most hallowed rites in prison. The telephone was my evening treasure, just after the news, and my family accepted those collect calls whenever I called.

When Nellie returned to Hammond after maternity leave, I grew increasingly anxious about her and Madisen living by themselves. Lamont and his family had recently finalized a permanent move to Baton Rouge, and I arranged for them to take Nellie and the baby in. I assumed visitation would be too hard on the both of us, but after seeing my fellow inmates return from their weekly visits with enough verve to endure another week of being separated from their family and friends, I eventually got with the program. Every day, Nellie took Madisen to daycare then commuted to Hammond to finish school, and on Fridays she would travel to visit me in Chalmette.

The staff at Chalmette Parish Prison were professional, not prone to intentionally make life harder. Federal inmates were segregated from state inmates, as well, which grants a form of status to the former. State inmates often see the federal offenders as the class of criminal they aspire to be, holding them in higher esteem. Although I enjoyed the pseudo-admiration of the state inmates, I couldn't help but think that if I were a state inmate, I'd at least be out of jail and free on bond.

Still, the segregation of federal inmates put me in the company of people who were more versed in federal criminal law than most university law professors, all learned and earned through experience, of course. Federal criminal code and sentencing guidelines form a labyrinth of technicalities that require a certain level of expertise on both sides of the law to navigate, interpret, and apply. This is why most criminal defense attorneys don't practice federal law. My cellmate, Leon Duncan, was a former New Orleans police officer serving a twenty-four-year sentence for his part in fellow officer Len Davis's illegal enterprise that allegedly protected, enabled, aided, abetted, and strong-armed inner-city drug dealers.[20]

At that time, Mr. Duncan had already been incarcerated for six years and seemed to have used most of his time becoming intimately acquainted with federal law. As a respected convict with senior status, he taught me not only about my case, but about the first principles and key essentials to survival in federal prison, where the inmate population is segmented based on gang affiliation.

Mr. Duncan was also a spiritual man. He did not possess a deep knowledge of the Bible, but he knew the difference between fundamental truth and denominational fallacy. Together, Mr. Duncan and I read and discussed the Bible in ways that I had never attempted to at Guildfield Baptist Church. The more open I was to his spiritual direction, the more I discovered just how sinful I really was. I did not fully understand the doctrine of repentance just yet, but I knew that I needed to be saved and forgiven of my sins.

---

20 *Times-Picayune* Staff, "Len Davis, eight other New Orleans police officers, charged in drug sting," *Times-Picayune*, December 4, 1994. https://www.nola.com/news/crime_police/article_e41852b8-2256-550f-a3e0-3ca63fd5e8e2.html

My eyes were ever on the material prize, however, and as I struggled to understand my childhood's Biblical application in adult life, old practiced patterns began to take over. Like a reconnaissance mission, I took note of the significance the text seemed to place on numbers. I saw those numbers as a business in disguise that I could claim by faith. Gradually, I went from studying the Bible for understanding, to reading it out of greed. Eventually I phoned home to convey anointed lottery number picks to trusted family members, asking them to play the Powerball on my behalf. Of course, I did not let anyone know the source of my sequences. Eventually, after reading the gospel account of the Roman soldiers gambling portions of Yahshua's tunic, I permanently, dejectedly retired my efforts at Biblical Powerball without having won a single dollar.

I did want to be spiritually and physically free. I did want to find peace. But allowing my spirit to break enough to sever the bonds would be another question entirely.

When the US Attorney's Office finally adopted all my pending state charges, I was officially indicted on one count of conspiracy to commit identity theft and was scheduled to plead guilty at my pre-sentencing hearing. Well in advance of my scheduled court date, Mr. Jordan brought the prepared plea agreement for me to sign. The conditions were exactly as he had previously negotiated and advised, and I signed it no sooner than he finished explaining its contents. I was ready to conclude this phase of my case and move on to the next.

I appeared in court on May 21, 2003, to change my plea to guilty, and sentencing judge Madam Mary Ann Via Lemon ordered that a pre-sentencing investigation be conducted by the US Probation Office—a condensed bibliography of the defendant's life happenings and history. It is generally prepared after a defendant pleads guilty or is found guilty at trial, and typically takes three or four months to complete.

My pre-plea negotiations had situated my guideline recommendations to a prison sentence of eighteen to twenty-four months, so I wasn't overly concerned with the results of the report. I spent the next few months studying, exercising, and learning how to cut hair using my fellow inmates as practice. On October 1, 2003, I was officially sentenced to serve eighteen months, with the restitution requirement and probationary period standing as well.

While Judge Lemon read this announcement, my small family reunion of supporters sat silently by my side. The only sounds I heard came from Madisen's babbled pleas for leniency on behalf of her dad, while I stood shackled near her and unable to respond.

My parents, siblings, and Nellie and her parents had all planned to come, but I was surprised to turn toward Madisen's cries and see she was in my grandmother's lap.

Ida Turner, the grandma who prayed for me nightly, had made the effort to come. She's the grandma whose lawn I mowed for free, though I also stole candy from her purse or her corner store. She's the grandma whose identity I turned to after stealing my parents'—both hers and her husband's. Yet she's also the type of grandma whose kids can do no wrong. You could burn down the house and still be her baby. And there she was, sitting in the courtroom, holding the baby I'd never held, listening to my wrongs, and never failing to believe in me.

Maybe it's because I was the worst of all the grandkids, but I was her favorite. I tried to return the love by taking care of both of my grandmas in their old age. I left provisions for their monthly medication and tried to stay in touch—or at least asked my mom and dad how they were doing. I was still painfully naïve at the time, thinking money was the answer.

Looking back on that moment, I can still see her arms around Madisen's waist, those chunky baby thighs straining to stand on the aging foundation of her great-grandmother's lap.

All that love and wisdom Ida Turner had stored up in her bones was ready to be passed on to my Madisen—and there I was, the prodigal son and absent father, a collapsing bridge between the two.

The closure that sentencing brought meant it was time for me to relocate to a federal facility. The Federal Bureau of Prisons designated me to the low security federal correctional institution located in Texarkana, TX, which was considered to be one of the premier institutions in the entire bureau. Arguably, it had to have had the best food that could be eaten behind prison walls. Even the staff members ate inmates' cooking. For all its pleasantries, the differences between jail and prison are as vast and complex as the differences between an inmate and a convict.

Inmates do time in local jails with no respect for staff or regard for their fellow inmates, unconsciously inviting unwanted corrective attention from staff and inmates alike. Conversely, a convict won't make those "fresh fish" mistakes. Convicts know the difference between a right and a privilege in a prison setting and have learned to do their time respectfully and peacefully without making anyone else's time harder.

Mr. Leon Duncan's etiquette advice made my transfer from the parish jail to federal prison a smooth one, without the usual exploitation from the vultures of prison politics. Within the first week of my arrival, I began looking for someone to study the Bible with. I was introduced to Brother Sedrick Pierre, who organized a Messianic study group and welcomed me with open arms.

This was no ordinary gathering of religious fakes and spiritual frauds. It was too deep for those hoping to play church, while other faith groups decried us as sanctimonious. But Bro. Pierre had brought together a group that was truly dedicated to making a 180-degree change in their lives. In my heart, I felt ready for that total transformation in my own life, and after joining I prayed for strength where I lacked effort.

It was in this group that I found a love and loyalty of brotherhood that continues to create eternal relationships to this day. It was in these foundations that I would find strength when all else eventually crumbled away.

December 2003 was filled with new experiences and new horizons. For Nellie, it meant graduating from South Eastern

University. For me, it meant holding Madisen in my arms for the first time ever.

Back at the parish jail, federal inmates were not allowed contact visits. I had only seen my baby through two-inch-thick glass, using phone receivers to communicate with Nellie. Madisen and I made up games through the glass, like "touch-4-touch," but nothing can compare to holding your baby in your arms.

Madisen was nearing her first birthday by that point—plenty old enough to have opinions on who holds her. During our first several contact visits, she treated me like a stranger. My constant solicitations for her attention only worked if I waved around something that piqued her curiosity or pleased her palate. The vending machine served both needs, and she loved wiggling her fingers in the coin return slot to get the change then retrieving the purchased item from the drawer. In all the time I spent dreaming of the day I could hold my baby, never did I imagine a vending machine facilitating our bonding experience. But it's what we had, and we made it work. We spent a considerable amount of time at that vending machine, much to the annoyance of the line of other prisoners and their guests.

With a bachelor of science degree in sociology, it was time for Nellie to choose a career path. Of all the professions, job offers, and employment opportunities that were available to her, she chose a career in law enforcement. As I completed my remaining sentence, Nellie plunged into the public service of protecting society from the very criminal she loved so dearly. She became a deputy of the East Baton Rouge Parish Sheriff's

Office, and I gave no objection. I never even asked Nellie why she decided to be a cop, though I am sure she saw it as a way of helping me stay out of trouble without admitting it.

In fact, I also believed Nellie's occupation would help to dissuade any unchecked criminal desire in me. I welcomed it. My hope for change was honest, sincere, and met by constant efforts to align my heart and my will. One day, after reading some of the book of Ecclesiastes, in genuflection right there beside my bunk in the noon hour, I made a vow to God that I would never return to the crimes I'd relied on for so long. I sealed my vow with a wish for punishments three-fold what I'd already endured.

By January 2004, the money I had left for the care of Nellie, Madisen, Darquise, Emoni, and both my grandmothers was rapidly depleting. Nellie was proactive and secured the fruit of honest gain to provide financial insurance for her and Madisen. We also arranged for her to move from Lamont's house to join up with my sister Samantha, who had moved from Houston to Baton Rouge, to be strategic with her finances. Whatever money Nellie wasn't saving or spending on bills, she sent to me to make sure I never went without anything I needed or wanted.

In federal prison, a man can survive off of five to fifty dollars a month if he had to. You're not even allowed to spend more than three hundred in any given month. Nellie spoiled me by sending four to six hundred dollars a month for my discretionary commissary purchases. This was an absurd cost of living and had more to do with upholding an image than with need or necessities.

Once a month, she and Madisen traveled six hours one way to come see me. While counting the days between visits, I studied with my Messianic Brothers under the tutelage of Bro. Pierre five days out of the week. His unusual anointing and impeccable character commanded deep respect from every inmate and all of the prison staff. Under his direction, I was introduced to the deeper doctrines of the Bible. I even got involved in the prison's sports program, ultimately coaching an A-league prison basketball team with whom I won the championship. My six-month stint at FCI-Texarkana endured without incident, injury, or loss of any kind.

On the morning of May 21, 2004, I walked through the front doors of the prison and straight into Nellie's warm and welcoming embrace. Together, they had been waiting for me in the parking lot, with Madisen asleep in her car seat, exhausted by the trip. I couldn't help but wake her up.

The idyllic landscapes that flew by on our way home from Texas reminded me of the fields and farms of my hometown in Tensas Parish. I had a new appreciation for the sights and sounds and smells that I'd been deprived of in prison, and I was determined to savor it all.

In a publicized move to demonstrate the genuineness of my repentance, I returned to St. Joseph to have the *Tensas Gazette* newspaper publish the public apology I authored while in prison: "Twice Pardoned: A Public Apology and Plea for Forgiveness." It featured a picture of me on the steps at Guildfield Baptist Church, head bowed in humility in light of my past behavior. The publication was bold, and I felt secure enough in my convictions to live up to its expectations.

Going into this sentence, I was weary of criminality, and my desire for reform was genuine. People in the community called my parents after that publication, praising the change it reflected. Finally, I had done something they could be proud of.

But the FBI's lack of understanding stayed in the back of my mind. I had figured something out that the experts knew nothing of. In chapter 2 of *America's Domestic War*, I explain some of the things they were curious to know, and why that bit of power would draw me back in deeper than I'd ever planned to go.

EIGHT

GOOD INTENTIONS

Do not merely listen to the word, and so
deceive yourselves. Do what it says.
—The Apostle James, James 1:22 (NKJV)

S ix hours after we left Texarkana, Nellie pulled up to a three-bedroom house in Baton Rouge that she leased two months prior. Though we had talked about it on visits and calls, she managed to withhold the more significant details of this beautiful residential trophy and symbol of her independence. The interior decor resembled the luxury we lived in before my federal troubles, but this time with more of a feminine appeal than a masculine overtone. I was moved at the sight of approximately two thousand square feet of responsibility as she gave me the tour of our new home. I always knew she was capable, though I wanted to believe she still needed my assistance. Nellie rose to meet the challenges of single mother-hood that I'd left her with in ways I hadn't imagined.

One of the conditions of my supervised probation was to acquire and maintain gainful employment, and *daddy daycare* was not the job for me. I couldn't find the relief of an occupation soon enough. I had taken and taught parenting class in prison, but nothing prepared me to be home alone with a toddler nearing terrible twos. Madisen was fourteen months old now and it seemed she could do any and everything she wanted except cook on the stovetop. By the end of the day, I praised Nellie for her patience, tolerance, and seeming ease of management with Madisen. Meanwhile, my parental gover-nance relied on popsicles and gummy bears to bring this tiny dictator into compliance.

She even seemed to dominate her K9 brother, Juvy, though he weighed sixty pounds more than she did. Remember, Juvy was an eighty-pound, pure white, American Standford pit bull. Both his ears and tail were clipped—aesthetic modifi-cations that made him appear to be more intimidating than he actually was. He and Madisen got along so perfectly that she could stick her hands in Juvy's automatic feeder as he was eating—an innocuous risk that I supervised, teaching Juvy to remain submissive and obedient to Madisen at all times. I think Madisen enjoyed Juvy's company more than he enjoyed hers, yet he would yawn and willingly comply whenever she would pull on his ears and tail, saying, "C'mon Duvy!"

Every morning, I let Juvy out the backdoor to relieve him-self during the normal morning routine I kept with Madisen. One day, Madisen signaled to use the potty at the same time

Juvy signaled to go outside. I put Madisen on the potty first, thinking she would be content listening to the potty-training music for a moment, then I let Juvy out the door. When I made it back to Madisen, in less than a minute she had moved her bottom from the potty to carpeted floor, defecating in a tiny little squat position. I saw this as a deliberate act of defiance against my authority that I immediately spanked her into humility, then remembered Juvy was probably sitting at the door.

When I went to let my best friend back in, he wasn't there. Something was wrong.

Madisen and I immediately started our search for Juvy, driving slowly through the Shenandoah Subdivision. I yelled Juvy's name in a panic, up and down the neighborhood streets, while a forgiving Madisen stood in the passenger seat unrestrained and mimicking an innocent "Duvy!, Duvy!" out the passenger side window.

With the out of sight, out of mind innocence of a little child, Madisen was completely unaware that her Duvy had just been dognapped. We never found him.

My entire family was devastated by the news of Juvy's disappearance. Although Juvy had identifiable tattoos in both ears and on his inner thigh, to this very day I regret not taking the time to get the "locator chip" planted beneath his skin that would have led me to his location and abductor. I never saw Juvy again, and I often wonder if he was taken to undesirable conditions.

Juvy had been an icon of an era in my life. He represented the connection between my family and Nellie's. He represented my organization and its structure. He was the Spuds MacKenzie of his time, well-manicured, trained to listen to commands, and charming to all he met. And he was the first child Nellie and I had together.

Juvy represented everything that life had been before serving my white-collar sentence.

We were together once again, and now we were a new family. Nothing could be the same. I wanted to be proud of Nellie for holding it together while I was gone, and I was. But her independence highlighted the disparity that my absence had caused. She did so well that, upon my return, I felt like I wasn't needed.

I wasn't the breadwinner. I didn't have the same routines with Madisen that she had. I wasn't even on the lease. I felt like I had little leverage in the economy of our home, and now Juvy was gone on top of it all.

There was nothing left to do but start over.

In September 2004, I landed my first real job ever with the Wal-Mart Distribution Center in the town of Robert, Louisiana. Thanks to my brother Lamont, who had worked there for five months already, Wal-Mart took a chance on me as a convicted felon. To this day, I venture that Wal-Mart remains the largest, most considerate and forgiving employer of convicted felons.

I was hired as an order-filler, working ten-hour shifts with a starting pay of $13.50 an hour. It wasn't the hoe fields, but it wasn't a trip to the Bahamas, either. It certainly didn't carry the fast-paced appeal of my former enterprise. There were two role options: put on a headset and listen to the automated orders from a computer in a warehouse-like environment or put on a sub-zero suit and fill the orders from the freezer.

Before working at the Wal-Mart Distribution Center, I had never even heard of the term logistics, although my identity theft operation was logistical, but by the time I left I figured they invented it, or at least could be credited with perfecting its science. Although youthful agility and the weights I lifted in federal prison had prepared me for the basic job description, stacking boxes was not for me. There was a rhythm and strategy to it—big boxes then the small ones, stack them to a certain height, keep them together to be Saran wrapped so the forklifts could pick them up. No matter what I did, my stacks would not stay up. Given the choice between constant fumbling in the freezer and the droning boredom of the computers, I opted to quit. I claimed the job was too strenuous, though it was only my need for control that was taking a hit, and I left within thirty days.

Lamont was incensed. Nellie didn't know. She was working twelve-hour shifts as a sheriff's deputy, sometimes pulling double shifts, and the least I could do was meet her half-way in contributing to the maintenance of our home. Still, I convinced myself that there were other ways to make these provisions without having to commit myself to physical labor. This was my first step backward, as I returned to living a lie.

I managed to keep Nellie in the dark until she retrieved a letter from the mailbox that verified I was no longer an employee of the company. Rightly exasperated, she began to interrogate me about the last two weeks when I told her I was at work. In fact, I did *go* to work. Once I got there, I simply slept in the car in the parking lot until boredom drove me to the shopping mall in Hammond or back to Baton Rouge to drive around until "clocking out."

These seeds of dishonesty caused her to question my morals, motives, and commitment to change. She saw what I could not. The demons of my past were working in collaboration with the aspirations I still harbored for the future. As long as I lied to myself and my family about who I was, what I was doing, and why I was doing it, a return to the captivity of crime and imprisonment of sin were inevitable.

At Nellie's discovery of my unemployment, I resumed the daily duty of attending to Madisen—before and after daycare, rather than the whole day through. Whereas before I couldn't be paid to babysit Madisen, now I actually looked forward to picking my baby up from daycare. At promptly three o'clock every day, I met her at the daycare and presented her with a miniature bag of Skittles. She snatched that candy out of my hand as if I owed them to her, and not a day went by without her trying to direct me toward McDonald's golden arches for french "fies." When Nellie had prepared home-cooked meals on her off days, we'd take an alternate route to avoid the *fies*.

Throughout the day, I had too much time on my hands, often finding myself drifting away to thoughts of *what if?* I needed to be busy, not to mention I needed to be employed for probationary reasons. So I turned to my next door neighbor Rob for help.

Rob and I were in a neighborhood Bible study group together. He was a veteran employee for Shell Chemical in Geismar, and he knew several independent contractors that worked within the plant. He was a "Salt of the Earth" kind of person, and in November, within days after I asked him for job assistance, I was hired by Basic Industries of Baton Rouge.

My role at Basic Industries was to assist in the construction of scaffolds within and throughout the Shell Chemical plant. Although I had to work in the elements and occasionally endure the biting chill of cold weather, I found I actually liked building and disassembling scaffolds. I started at ten dollars an hour, on four, ten-hour shifts from Monday to Thursday, with the option of overtime or to work plant turnarounds. It was a good job—I was getting paid to do something I at least didn't hate.

Being part of the working class gave me a sense of pride, and for a moment I actually felt good about doing the right thing. As I worked with the carpenters performing their various duties around the scaffolding, I built a camaraderie with my coworkers. The easy conversations that I employed in the field I could now use to get to know the people I saw day in and day out. Though I stood out from the crowd of blue-collar plant workers with my dental jewelry and demeanor, my character and conversation convinced my peers and superiors that I was not the drug dealer they undoubtedly took me to be. Soon, I stood out not for my dental jewelry but as a quick learner with a commendable work ethic and safe practices.

Within weeks, I was given a two dollar pay increase and began to share in the work assignments of the carpenters. My supervisor began training me for a carpenter position, assuming I continued to show an industrious work ethic. Like Wal-Mart, Rob and Basic Industries had given me yet another chance that I did not want to give myself.

There was no pretense in my conversation, no con in my approach. Still, as time went on, the tasks grew rote and conversations grew stale. The older carpenters didn't share in my interests or hold the same level of discussion that I was used to, which was fine for a time. It became clear that my four-hundred-dollar checks were sufficient for their careers, while I was merely taking it to appease my probation officer. My job satisfaction was merely tolerance, and it would soon run out.

In an attempt to foster the repentance I so deeply wanted to model, I decided forgiveness had to be part of that journey. So I called my cousin Dee's mom to let her know that I harbored no ill-feelings toward her son. I explained that the change I sought in my life necessitated a change in my attitude towards my frenemies as well. She had read the news article with my public apology and pleas for forgiveness, and she took my contact number to forward to Dee.

He must have been anxiously awaiting that first move toward reconciliation, because within minutes after speaking to his mom, he called me excited about the idea of forgiveness. He did not then know that my forgiveness would be conditional, dependent upon his repayment of the money he had stolen.

I still did not fully trust Dee, so I arranged to meet him in a Wal-Mart parking lot, where I knew that our reunion would be under video surveillance if he happened to have more treacherous tricks up his sleeve.

I pulled up after a day of building scaffolds. He stepped out of his customized GMC Denali, decked and dazzling with platinum jewelry on both wrists and around his neck and diamonds in both of his ears. Everything about his swagger and appearance reflected the image I portrayed only months before. He was showing me that he could live as I once lived, even if his lifestyle came at my expense.

Feeling a sting of regret at the life I lost, and not a little anger at what he took from me, I seized on my opportunity. He so daringly made it known that he wasn't living in poverty, so I could make known the conditions of my forgiveness. I advised Dee that I expected him to repay me at least the one hundred thousand of the $3.1 million he had stolen, in ten-thousand-dollar increments, starting as soon as possible. The sooner he settled the debt, the sooner the deed could be forgiven.

I knew that I was shooting for the stars and wasn't in a very good position to make demands. Even before being arrested, I cut my losses as part of the game and accepted the fact that I had gotten too comfortable in crime. But a scaffolding salary was not cutting it, not only monetarily but internally. I was craving that hit of power that had sustained me for so long, and Dee provided the opportunity to get something for nothing.

He hadn't stopped playing the game, either. He saw my conditions as an opportunity to advance his lingering interest in identity theft. He agreed to give me ten thousand dollars once every two weeks, but only if I were to help him start up his own identity theft organization. I agreed to give him what he wanted in order to get what I wanted, but it would have required contact with CC Man, whom I had not spoken to since February 2003. After he gave me the first installment, I failed to deliver; Dee began to spoon feed me two thousand dollars here and there, supposing I was entirely dependent on his generosity and would eventually come around to accommodate his expectations.

My days at work became increasingly long, and I pondered the potential of using Dee to relaunch my identity theft operation. I had a taste of the old life and was done with the new. I was not without friends or a future. Rob had gone out on a limb for me, and my supervisor seemed to look forward to what I could bring to the job. Still, it wasn't enough. The job quickly became a front to the developing interest of my heart. I could mindlessly perform my tasks while waiting for an opportunity to spring back into motion.

My descent happened so slowly, so justifiably in my mind, that I hadn't seen it coming.

We often find what we're looking for, and soon an old acquaintance named Mike reached out to me. He had someone I needed to meet. We had a great deal in common—this person was an expert in white-collar crimes who had also been to federal prison. Mike gave sinfully satisfactory answers to my every question about this individual's abilities.

The very next day, I drove to the corner of College Drive and Corporate Boulevard in Baton Rouge, to a Ruby Tuesday's that's no longer there. Waiting for me were Mike and a clean-cut fella who introduced himself as Johnathan. Over steaks and baked potatoes, Johnathan and I discussed the ins and outs of identity theft and credit card fraud, while Mike enjoyed his meal and the music of mayhem in the making.

> Good intentions are rarely enough to carry us. My whole life, I've had every opportunity to thrive under "normal" circumstances yet found myself bored by them. From the Sunday School room to landscaping, to scholarly pursuits and employment opportunities, nothing could fill that void I thought could be answered with criminal activity. For more on the mind of the identity thief, see *America's Domestic War*, chapter 4.

NINE

360 DEGREE REPENTANCE

As a dog returns to his own vomit,
so a fool returns to his folly.
—King Solomon, Proverbs 26:11(NKJV)

Johnathan knew things about credit card fraud only myself and the credit card companies knew, and I relayed aspects of identity theft he had not yet begun to fathom. What had begun as idle, bored thoughts of identity theft while working with scaffolding became tangible in this connection. We were the missing pieces to each other's criminal aspirations.

Unlike long-distance CC Man, Johnathan lived in Baton Rouge—a detail Mike had kept to himself until his interests had been clarified and confirmed. In return for this dream connection, Mike wanted an introduction to one of my old drug suppliers in Houston. A simple enough request that removed

Mike as mediator and left Johnathan and I with direct access to each other.

Outside of work, all of my spare time went to devising a new plot. Dee's sporadic payments would fund our venture. Johnathan would be my master Printer—a computer wiz who knew how to replicate cards and IDs of any kind. We didn't have to stay in the game forever. Just long enough to make a quick mil' and get right back out.

Before, it had taken about a year to reach seven figures. With more lived experience, Johnathan's expertise, and a solid plan, I was ready to hit that target in six months.

I even had a story ready for Nellie.

My custom dental work needed to come out, and I could take thirty days' medical leave to do it. It wouldn't raise any red flags for probation, either. After that month, I would prevaricate and explain that they replaced my role and let me go. With legitimate businesses in my background, I could simply divert my visible energy to some kind of above-board business venture. That would keep the probation requirements at bay, and my underhanded earnings could fund my entrepreneurial calling long into the future. I knew working for someone else was never going to last. It's not in my nature.

Still, I was bringing the cat and mouse game right into my home—could I get away with this right under Nellie's nose, as a deputy sheriff and the mother of my youngest child? The thrill was bigger than anything I chased before, and it pulled me completely under before I realized what happened.

Johnathan and I established a joint venture agreement, which gave me a closer connection to the work than my transaction-based relationship with CC Man. I needed to understand how the work was done instead of simply collecting and moving information, so I sat beside him as he expertly navigated the internet to order equipment, and I learned our sources, costs, and logistics firsthand. I learned how a duplicate driver's license was manufactured and encoded. Together, we ordered the best equipment and divided overnight deliveries between various addresses. I made sure to have three of everything to secure backup equipment—scanners, encoders, decoders, embosser, printers with built-in laminators, high-resolution digital cameras, photo editing software, false fingerprint gloves, skimmers, copy machines, and everything else needed to return in full force. We set up the laboratory in an apartment we had specifically rented for that purpose. Only Johnathan and I knew the location, and in the evenings and on the weekends, he taught me how to master the equipment, one piece at a time.

The only thing left was to locate new Info Operatives and Field Operatives.

I immediately canceled out Dee as a potential Operative. He felt as if he should be an organizational Financier with his own identity theft operation anyway, and who was I to dash his dream?

I was off the list as well—it'd be stupid to explore the field while on the Feds' watch list for technical financial crimes. For every identity-related crime that hit the federal radar, my name would be checked as a possibility. This operation would have to be completely secure, so I had to make sure they could rule me out right away. A good friend we'll call Kenisha was the answer.

I had long since graduated from fishing through mail and hefting boxes of receipts out of hotel storage rooms. Employees in restaurants, car dealerships, tax prep offices, and hospitals had direct access to endless amounts of thorough card info and personal data. More importantly, they were often paid little enough by their respective employers to find the extra cash I offered appealing, in spite of the shady implications.

Kenisha lived and worked in mournful Monroe at the privately owned, prestigious St. Francis Medical Center. Not only did she have access to plenty of identities, but they belonged to some of the wealthiest people in Northeast Louisiana. I coached her on filtering through the system to gain seamless access to the most lucrative information, though I didn't elaborate on where the information went after she turned it over to me. The less she knew, the less she'd have to tell the police if and when they came knocking.

In December 2004, the season for fraud was upon us, and Kenisha was ready for some beta field testing. I used the busyness of the season to work out her fear and nervousness that no doubt would have drawn suspicion in a normal sales transaction. Retailers are so focused on getting out of the red that between Black Friday and Christmas they don't stop to validate IDs and legitimize transactions. Self-checkout terminals breeds fraud. Security alerts are lax as long as nothing is glaringly fraudulent, so the holly jolly season keeps loss prevention at bay.

Though I needed most of my Field Operatives to be fresh-faced and free from retailer suspicion, I did reach back out to my car sales friend Chris to have him pull copies of credit profiles for us. My operation had to function with zero deficiencies in order to grow at the pace I needed. Meanwhile, Johnathan busied himself training two other promising prospects for any future fraudulent explorations.

Word of our discount distribution spread, and the orders started to pour in. To make up for the days where I had begun to miss work, I took orders for big-ticket items that sold for four thousand dollars or more at resale value on the black market. I wrote up weekend merchant itineraries for retailers who had never been my targeted victims before. Kenisha accommodated the wish lists, and I established a financially solvent clientele through trusted mediators in order to keep my identity hidden.

By the time December ended, things were so good that Kenisha and I both were ready to quit our jobs. I held off on that piece of the plan for a while longer and kept both Nellie and my probation officer in the dark about my developing and evolving criminal enterprises by working forty hours a week. Whenever I produced the extra cash that I conveniently pulled from the profits of my identity theft operation, I credited it to overtime hours that I hadn't worked for Basic Industries, Inc.

Once I started back down the criminal path, I found it was worn and familiar. I slipped back into all the old steps that had already led to prison once, with the sole exception of gambling.

I even found myself tossing thousands here and there toward Mike and his newfound connections with my longstanding suppliers. My street credibility was high and old drug associates contacted me when they needed a reliable source. I knew the cost of the product and had calculated interest in "orders." Without being the point person for acquisitions and deliveries, my risk was lower than it had been before, and the connection I provided for Mike had given me the benefit of tagging along on a deal now and then. No traveling to Houston, no mediating deliveries. I just put my money on the backend of Mike's orders and for a season, my run was good and golden.

With the worn Bible that carried me through my eighteen-month sentence now collecting dust on the shelf, I deliberately forgot about my vow to renew my life—including the consequences I promised to be held to. In February 2005, I quit working for Basic Industries, Inc., with the predetermined excuse of major cosmetic dental surgery to remove the diamonds and platinum from my mouth. And, as expected, both Nellie and my probation officer found the story believable enough to go along with it.

In addition to strategic drug dealing, I took orders for the standard lot of electronics, guns, jewelry, and police commission badges and military IDs. Rival drug dealers might order IDs to orchestrate and warrant an illegal search of their competitors' stash houses. My other customers from Chicago, New York, and Houston were notorious for purchasing fraudulent search warrants and law enforcement credentials. On several occasions my Field Operatives flanked a supposed high-earning pseudo-celebrity as their "police escort" to validate the identity thief's scam and gain exclusive shopping access and excess without raising suspicion. The bigger the lie, the easier it was to sell.

Far beyond Christmas shopping, I armed the hood, gun fanatics, fools, and collectors alike without a second thought to the consequences. If anyone wanted a fully automatic weapon without attaching it to their name, I gave them access as long as they paid the price. I carried on toward my objectives and never looked back to see the chaos left in my wake.

My real bread and butter—the reason I was comfortable quitting work—came through a venture I had been working on for months, using Johnathan's printing abilities to perfect it: the new grand theft auto.

For years, my own fleet had been stocked by ill-gotten gain, combining stolen identities and woven stories in order to convince desperate salesmen to sign off on dubious deals. By the time I was twenty-four and working with Johnathan's printing press at full scale operation, my initial scams became rudimentary in comparison.

I could still secure a car for a buyer, just as I secured the four wheelers and Lincoln and so many others. But that was only the first step in the larger scheme. The next step was to authenticate the vehicle with a clean registration and full insurance coverage. To do this, we simply took advantage of the paper chasing and communication gaps that exist around vehicle ownership and between respective regulatory agencies. Not only did I pull in hundreds of thousands of dollars from this scam in the last quarter of 2004 and first quarter of 2005, but I earned as much or more through consulting services to teach this method to others.

Car thieves who had played the *Gone in 60 Seconds* story out in their own hectic, high-risk lives paid upwards of fifty thousand dollars to learn my calculated efforts, high-yield methods. They flew in from all over and on occasion, but only by special request, I went to their domains. I not only taught them the strategy but I coached them through their first time engagement to ensure a smooth, hands-on educational experience.

No one had hacked the grand theft auto process to this extent before, and to my knowledge no one has surpassed it since. After all, it flew so completely under the legal radar, why would anyone reinvent the proverbial (stolen) wheel?

My complete dedication to self was made clear on February 12, 2005, when my little Madisen turned two years old. This was not only my first opportunity to attend one of her two birthday parties, but it was also the unfortunate timing of a vehicle delivery.

Hours before her birthday party at my parents' home in St. Joseph, without a second thought for time, I left to drive four hours to my buyer's drop point and collect the thirty thousand dollars that was owed to me for my efforts.

Everything that I aspired to gain less than two years prior, while sitting in federal prison, had been mine. I had a beautiful baby girl to care for in a free society. I had three- and four-year-old Darquise and Emoni to build a relationship with. For a time, Nellie and I were finally beginning to walk in the same direction. I had been showered with blessings of friends and employers looking out for my bright future, filled with the promises of redemption and righteousness.

And I was willing to let all of it go in favor of old patterns and familiar highs.

I did make it back from my drop point to slide into Madisen's birthday party, self-satisfied with my ability to keep this second life of selfish recidivism intact. Less than one month later, my tunnel vision for the almighty dollar and disregard for relationships would come full circle to finally take me down.

As 1 Corinthians 15:33 warns, *bad company corrupts good habits*. I knew what I was getting into when I sought the company of Mike and Johnathan, and they knew what they would get with me. You become the company you keep, and I chose to associate myself with familiar spirits rather than the waiting arms of people who wanted more for me than I aspired to for myself.

Chapters 5 and 7 of *America's Domestic War* delve into the chaos this corruption created, the extent to which undoubtedly carries on today in echoes of vehicular identity theft, and the violence perpetrated by illegal guns that continue to move in similar ways.

 זהוה

ᗑᎩᏍᎧ

YHWH

יהוה

TEN

BLINDERS UP

Pride goes before destruction, and a
haughty spirit before a fall.
—King Solomon, Proverbs 16:18 (NKJV)

wasn't being reckless.

I stopped gambling with my back to the road. Stopped gambling at all. I stopped riding with drug merch in the car. I stopped racking up incriminating arrests—I got out of the field and off the precarious path of the merchant itinerary. I thought I learned all my lessons.

In that world, there are certain things you can guard against, and others you cannot. When loyalty is valued above all else, and you find someone you can trust with hundreds of thousands of dollars in cash, with entire cocaine shipments, with intimacy... how can you guard against their sudden, abject betrayal?

Throughout my relationship with Nellie, there were other women. Friends with benefits, *side and simultaneous pieces*, what have you. In this scenario, I was good friends and partners with this woman named Genette, who I trusted implicitly with criminal dealings. When Genette got snagged by the federal government with some of my cocaine, she took the latter of two options presented to her by the DEA: go to jail indefinitely or help us get your supplier. I reason that fear of the unknown overtook her. The walls were closing in, with pressure from a designed and deliberate exploitation of her ignorance, by professionals who were specially trained for such a task. Her cooperation may have been willing, but it was neither ready nor voluntary.

In any case, to seal the deal and ultimately face lesser consequences, she had to give me up to the authorities, and give me up she did.

In a sting operation complete with body mics, she secured enough recorded conversation to earn me a "two-count conspiracy to sell 500 grams or more of cocaine" charge.[21]

When the unmarked cars started to swarm from all directions into the front parking lot of the Jefferson Lakes Apartment complex in Baton Rouge, I recognized the betrayal for what it was, and I ran.

I could have been running for the means I needed to secure before going to prison.

---

21 For perspective, five hundred grams is equivalent to half a kilogram. The largest cocaine bust in US history was more than fifteen thousand kilos, and it came in via a JP Morgan Chase cargo ship. https://www.cbsnews.com/amp/news/ship-seized-in-1-3-billion-cocaine-bust-is-owned-by-jp-morgan-chase/

I could have been running for the last vestiges of a life of freedom.

I could have been running for all the times I should have run before—for the twenty-four-year-old me who had a legitimate life right at my fingertips, for the eighteen-year-old me with a computer in my right arm and a K9 gnawing on my left leg. For the fifteen-year-old me who could have run in my father's footsteps.

But there was only one thought that stayed with me, step for step:

My family.

Nellie. Darquise. Emoni. Madisen.

My family. My woman. My children.

My family.

I couldn't live on the run forever. Somewhere inside, I always knew I would have to give account for it all, and as I ran across the apartment complex parking lot and hopped a fence, I thought, *This must be it.* But I also couldn't get caught without making sure that Nellie and my kids were taken care of, my family was safe. So I kept running across the street, through an open field, and to a canal.

The thing is, I had two suitcases full of cocaine in the attic back at the home Nellie had secured and situated for us. For all the times I felt betrayed by those close to me, I still chose to keep a stash of drugs in the attic of the home where my baby girl went to sleep at night. I needed to make that right— needed someone to pick me up and get me to a secure location, where I could sort everything out before any authorities got to our home. Before turning myself in.

I had two burner phones in my pocket, so I put their antennas in my mouth and started swimming across the canal with my head above water, like the alligator carrying the gingerbread man to his demise.

On the other side of the canal, the trail cooled for my pursuers. Soaking wet, I slipped into a BREC park to make my calls and drop the phones into garbage cans while I kept moving. One contact was a close friend named Keith who booked a hotel room at an Extended Stay on Corporate Blvd, and another contact was a trusted ally named Marcus. He booked me a separate room at the Home Suites by Hilton, just up the road, under a name that was completely disconnected from the situation.

Before discarding the phones, I set a transport up to come get me, in proximity of the park where the burner phones met their end.

In the back of the car on the way to the hotel, I used my transporter's phone to make one more desperate call to someone who could get the attic clear, not knowing whether I would be able to turn myself in at my leisure or whether the unmarked cars that sent me running would catch up to me once more.

Things were happening fast, real fast. But even under those dire circumstances of uncertainty things were still happening in my favor. I wound up with a full ten days to maneuver as much as possible. I met with Johnathan to help him continue our venture in my absence. I let Mike know that I was compromised and by whom. I shut down the drug contacts and reignited my relationship with my attorneys.

The worst call of them all was the one I had to make to Nellie.

She found out before I got to her, when her supervisor informed her at the station that she was part of the DEA's investigation due to her proximity to me. The kilos of cocaine were out just before the DEA made it to the house, fortunately while Madisen was in daycare and Nellie was still at work. That might have softened the blow, but it didn't stop the emotional bleed. Nellie was absolutely devastated, and rightly so.

All of my vehicles with Nellie's name on them were confiscated. Everything about our relationship called her into question, even though she believed I was on medical leave for dental work intended to create the outward appearance of what she thought was an inward change.

Short-sighted by sin and narrow-minded by selfishness, I wanted to believe I was an island. I wanted to be in control of me and me alone, directing my paths and letting everyone else fend for themselves. Nothing could be further from the truth.

With as many provisions made as possible and a self-surrender deal in place with my attorney, I walked into the DEA's office located on North Acadian Thruway knowing I wouldn't walk out the same way I walked in.

Without me, Nellie set up a beautiful home and settled into a reliable job. And in less than a year, I betrayed every ounce of trust left and tore that life apart. Madisen had just turned two, Darquise was three, and Emoni was four, and now their dad was abandoning them—again. Their psychological and emotional pain would completely overshadow any physical or legal trouble I was in.

In the holding cell the evening after my surrender, I tucked into a corner to escape the walls that closed in around me for the first time in years. Unlike that first time behind bars, there were no calls I could make to get me out. No parental bond to post or attorney strings to pull. I would spend the next six serious years learning the fundamental, near fatal difference between repenting from the cause of sin and simply regretting the consequences of crime.

Six years for a single drug-related offense.

After years of building a white-collar case against me, the system still could not fathom my catastrophic capability and approximated my exposure to a year and a half of prison time in response. But one instance of a non-violent blue-collar street crime merited an easy six-year sentence. Like the old jailer back at Ouachita Correctional Center had predicted, I finally hit the lottery.

Through our broken, shortsighted, legal system, it was time to give account. Satan had to be smiling at the mockery I made of my public apology and a plea for forgiveness. Not long before, I was held as a model of repentance. Now, I rightly should become the deserved target of ridicule. I had embarrassed my family and all of heaven. My broken vow demanded three-fold retribution, and I had to pay up, exactly that.

It would take most of those six years to learn that both heaven and my family had nothing but grace waiting for me. But I would have to find some grace for myself first.

My despair in that cell was so much heavier because, for the first time, I realized just how deep and wide my actions affected the people around me. The choices I made had always been for my own benefit, no matter how much I said I wanted to provide for Nellie or my kids or my Operatives. It was about me.

More than my provision for them, I left them to pay consequences in as much or greater magnitude to what I would pay. I deprived my kids of their dad, Nellie of the life she built, and countless victims of their security. There is no follow-up chapter or side note for a moment like that. Only deep and sincere regret and apology.

HWH

ELEVEN

DARKEST BEFORE DAWN

*If we say that we have fellowship with Him, and walk
in darkness, we lie and do not practice the truth.*
—The Apostle John, 1 John 1:6 (NKJV)

My return to penal residency felt surreal. Greed and misplaced trust had blinded me, and that single drug charge slipped past my carefully concealed fraudulent exploits to bring the whole production to a grinding halt.

Nothing about prison life is desirable. Nothing! Take privacy, for example. There is none. Everything, including toilet and shower time, is open for both staff and inmate to gaze at will. But privately owned and poorly funded parish prisons tend to exaggerate their disciplinary responsibilities to miserable levels.

The food tastes like roadkill, designed to force an influx of purchased items from the prison commissary. It's colder than any hospital, year 'round, under the notion of keeping germs down, conveniently underscoring the overall punitive, disciplinary design of the place. Medical and dental services are horrendous. In prison, ibuprofen is the cure for AIDS and cancer as much as aches and pains—an industry-wide panacea for whatever ailment a prisoner might be suffering from. The further away from federal prisons you get, I've found, the worse the conditions tend to be.

Whether it's state or federal prison, Dorothy's wisdom holds true: there's no place like home. Unlike Dorothy, however, the storm brewing around my return to penal confinement was far from a bad dream. My Oz was akin to HBO's production more than clicked heels and happy songs. This was my life now, and I had no directorial control over this reality.

In West Baton Rouge, where I was first transported, the facility housed around sixty prisoners in one open dormitory. I often wondered how the report would read if noise meters were part of prison surveillance. There was one TV to be scheduled out by the group, access to a communal payphone, and seemingly endless rounds of dominoes and card games running in shared spaces.

In spite of the forced community, I felt complete isolation. I had no interest in pastime games. I barely used the phone for fear of federal surveillance. I avoided visits with my family—especially with my children. I was sure it would be too much for Madisen and Emoni to be there once more in that restricted context after only a few short months with them.

Put simply, in America, prison is not designed for rehabilitation, but to mentally break the prisoner down by way of attrition. And it works, almost all of the time.

As I found myself sinking into that place of broken despair, I finally gave in—not to the creeping depression, but to the fatherly desire to see my children. In May of 2005, it was reported that Madisen, in particular, wouldn't stop asking about me. At my request Nellie brought her to a thirty-minute visitation.

Seeing Madisen's face, her baby hands trying to push through the glass to get to me—that shook me back to life. Prison might be bleak, but it wasn't going to last forever. On the other side, I had family waiting for me. I had a home to go to.

Everything that was numb and empty in me filled back up and spilled over in the one or two tears I could let drop on the way back to the dorm. Since I couldn't go back to the den of wolves crying in a display of weakness and defeat, I concealed my anguish with a smile that I had not felt in months.

There were many months left to endure, but the waiting game was one I finally believed I could play.

Back in the dorm with a fresh perspective, I slowly began to reconnect to my environment as a quiet observer. Thinking about how my children could bring me back, I began to watch the people I lived with under a different lens. I watched how they lived and what they responded to. What did they have to live for? I started stereotyping my fellow inmates and studied their behavior patterns using my own system of analysis as a seasoned convict.

I thought back to my limited options as a teenager and the decisions that I made to create something new—both opportunities and limitations. I began to wonder what they had been exposed to in their own lives. I realized that most of the people around me never had access to the privileges that I had come to acquire, and in some ways, they did not have the "privilege" that I was attempting to escape all those years ago. They certainly didn't seem to have the wisdom gained from experience, and most had no clear path out of their glaring ignorance. Most notably, they rarely had the model of forgiveness my parents held up for me.

In response to this realization, I determined to continue to educate myself despite being a POW in America's misguided war on drugs. Through observation and whatever means I could access, I would not let my time or opportunity be another political casualty to this war that defines America as a nation of mass incarceration.

Less than six months after returning to custody, on August 29, 2005, Hurricane Katrina slammed into south Louisiana as a catastrophic Category 5 hurricane, leaving her footprints of devastation and destruction forever. Before anyone could catch their breath, she was followed by the monstrous Hurricane Rita, like Atlantic salt in the wound. Life in south Louisiana was confused and chaotic. The Big Easy was under water, along with its surrounding suburbs and exurbs. Families were scattered, lives were lost, and hope could barely glimmer through the muddy waters, debris, and detritus.

Among the near-million people rescued, refuged, and relocated were thousands of hurricane-impacted inmates spread across penal institutions throughout the state of Louisiana. Small parish prisons like West Baton Rouge Parish Prison, where I began my six-year sentence, and Tangipahoa Parish Jail in Amite—an hour north of New Orleans and where I was transferred just after Katrina to complete my dental work— shared in the division of some seven thousand displaced New Orleans Parish prisoners.

The picture of a rural prison is subpar from the beginning. Factor in overpopulation, and the conditions become dismal. Two-man cells shift and make limited room for a third. Tangipahoa's small twenty-four inmate dorms crammed thirty-six to forty people into limited spaces, and sometimes more. Air circulation changes and the systems destabilize to freeze some rooms out and turn others into saunas. Noise levels rise so much so that you can't hear yourself think, personalities clash and inevitable chaos emerges, and you're all left to figure things out on your own and maintain your own sanity. This gumbo of commotion and confusion yields an environment that backwoods Amite had neither the acumen nor the manpower, never mind the funding, to adequately engage crisis management.

I remained an observer during my transition from West Baton Rouge to Tangipahoa—my first priority was to finish the dental work I'd begun pre-incarceration. The temporary crowns that replaced the diamonds, platinum, and erosions were long since due for replacement with permanent veneers.

Still a federal inmate, I had the benefit of US Marshal-enforced segregation from the general population of parish and state inmates, which granted me some distance, as long as I knew and respected my limits. From my somewhat privileged firsthand vantage point, I witnessed malfeasant incompetence and a malignant ineptitude among the senior ranking officials at Tangipahoa Parish Jail.[22] While I was never beaten by inmates or staff, it was a regular occurrence for my fellow inmates, especially outside of federal segregation, in complete disregard for any of their constitutional rights. The good ol' boys ran the show, and as long as they didn't draw attention to the US Marshals, no one who could keep them accountable was paying attention.

No one wants to live like that, but not everyone has the experience and initiative to do something about it. To live in an organized manner in such an uncontrolled environment, we needed to create order from within. After a couple months of observation, I was ready to communicate with my fellow inmates. Our limited space and dangerous, unpredictable dynamics demanded some decency. As one of a few pretrial federal inmates who had been to federal prison beyond the parish walls, I had the experience and ability to bring calm and comfort into our chaos.

One morning, trying to read a book from the intended peace of my shared room, I couldn't even hear myself think. It was time.

---

22 You might remember this Parish name from the 2009 newsworthy case of a justice of the peace refusing to marry an interracial couple—one of whom hailed from Hammond. That should tell you what you need to know about some of the officials in this region. https://www.theroot.com/keith-bardwell-defends-denied-interracial-marriage-1790870478

I went out to find one of the bigger homies in the dorm to help me call attention to the room. He had my back as I walked over to turn the TV down in the middle of the show and paused the games and the phone calls to ask for five minutes of everyone's time. With a quick window to make my case, I introduced myself. I explained where I had been and why I was there. I explained my hope for our continued peaceable existence. I invited each dorm member to a Bible study each morning before chow.

With their attention and trust both building, I went on to explain how our new living arrangement would work.

I proposed a TV schedule that respected the group's standard news and *Young & the Restless* spots, a phone schedule that could accommodate everyone, and a game-playing schedule that we could—and would—all abide by.

After five minutes, and at 5'7" and 150 lbs., I became the littlest Big Homie and our living arrangements became much more tolerable.

As the days went on, after noon-chow I led daily conversations about the activities to come. We voted by show of hands. Any dissent was discussed, and participation was in everyone's favor. No one wants to be transferred to federal prison without understanding how to identify and avoid invisible lines of demarcation. I held that wisdom for them and exchanged it for a peaceable living environment.

Report about my dorm's civility quickly spread throughout the prison. I gained a reputation as someone who had some sense. Fellow inmates started asking me to write letters to their lawyers, their judges, their girlfriends. They would come to me with questions about federal code and their ongoing criminal proceedings. I wrote petitions for leniency, termination letters for attorneys, and Dear Jane letters to soon-to-be ex-girlfriends.

With a more stable rhythm to my days, I felt more comfortable on the phone again and regained connection with my family.

My grandma Ida Turner was nearing the end of her days at that point, going to dialysis three times a week and becoming weaker by the visit. Rather than calling my dad to ask how grandma was doing, I made more calls directly to her. Over time, her jokes and lighthearted spirit began to dim, and I began to fear calling home.

In one of our last conversations, trying to glean whatever wisdom I could from her before she took it along with her to meet the Ancient of Days, I asked her how she learned to pray.

She told me, "There's no certain set way how to pray, baby. But if you want to learn from a praying man, study the book of Psalms. There's no more effective way to pray than to send God's word back up to him."

A lightbulb went off for me then as I finally realized why my prayers had been bouncing off the bunks. I had to learn to let go of conventions and step into a deeper, meditative sense of communication with the God I wanted to serve. The God of my parents, who held me in such deep regard that forgiveness was never out of reach. The God of my grandma, who never wavered in her belief in me—reminding everyone to put me in her obituary as her favorite grandchild. (An awkward moment in a family with dozens of grandkids, especially when everyone knows the trouble you caused.)

The same God who had faith in Jacob gave them faith in me. To know what I did, what I continued to do, and to love me just the same.

I continued to pursue the faith that they modeled to me, reaching for it and hoping to make their belief my own. At least half of the dorm inmates attended morning Bible study with me, and the ones who didn't attend group study would come into my cell privately, like when Nicodemus sought the counsel of Yahshua by night for fear of what others might think of his acquaintance with The Messiah.[23] During those one-on-one sessions, I began to see just how dark and hard our hearts could be, though never beyond the power and persuasion of true redemption.

Federal inmates in other parts of the prison started submitting "inmate request" forms to be relocated to the dorm in which I was being warehoused. These repeated requests brought about unwanted attention from prison staff, raising unnecessary suspicion and causing the dorm to be the target of random shakedowns and repeat harassment in search of contraband. Initially, the searches were futile. Eventually, my dorm became contraband central.

Prison staff were intrigued with me, but I deliberately kept little to no interaction with male staffers. Female staffers, on the other hand, are often intrigued by the masculinity of an inmate. Silent admiration and subtle flirtation, if entertained and cultivated, leads to favorable interactions.

23 John 3:2.

There is an aura about the criminal element of a man that is attractive and appealing to some women, underscored when you want the movie bad guy to get away, just that one time— every time. The notion that "all the good men are in prison" takes root after enough interaction and can grow out of control if she dares to let the inmate know how she's feeling. Sympathy is the first cue. Once this emotion is tapped into, a man can exploit it to affect the most advantageous opportunity.

Deputy Camillia, an African American woman in her mid to late fifties, posed such an opportunity.

Camillia was obviously single and lonely in life, with only an adult daughter who lived in California, I learned. She was a sweet lady, reticent and reserved, quiet in spirit, and beautiful in personality. It was from her that I learned just how much women enjoy compliments and appreciate acknowledgments. I sensed her weaknesses and recognized her lenience and consideration. And I pursued the former for the sake of the latter.

She wanted to find intellectual stimulation in rote day to day work. She wanted her femininity actuated and validated. She wanted to be acknowledged. Over time, I gained her trust through respectful flattery and exploitation of these clear needs. I complimented her as often as her work shift allowed. In time, we would pass shorthand notes expressing mutual admiration. On random and special occasions, she would mail me a card containing money orders to add to my commissary account, though the cards had no return address on them to keep her identity concealed from fellow staffers.

Though I had regained a sense of self since that low point in West Baton Rouge, it was undoubtedly my most familiar self that I engaged. The same calculated conversations and personality persuasion that gave me access to fraudulent purchases, I maximized in our limited interactions during escorted walks to and from medical, attorney, or family visits that she and I orchestrated. I passed her handwritten love notes, produced by the same studied deception that I had used to take on another persona in a transaction. She fell in love with the man I introduced to her via the costume of my orange prison jumpsuit just as much as any forged police badge had fooled a cashier or gatekeeper in the field.

In my last note to her, I requested the phone number to the prison along with her cell phone so I could call her directly. Without hesitation, she did as I asked. Every day or night that she worked, she would bring her cell phone to me, and we would talk on the prison phone for the majority of her night shifts—not so much during her day shifts because of the business of daily prison operations.

From our conversations, I learned that she didn't enjoy her job but enjoyed coming to work to see me. I learned that she sympathized for all inmates, more so female inmates, but especially for me. I rehearsed thoughts and theories in my mind of how this sympathy could come to benefit me. By sheer deceit and determination, I studied her responses and reactions to varying requests, trying to gauge where she would draw the boundary line.

She had no boundaries.

Gradually, I had her bring me all kinds of contraband into the prison. We began with dental floss, fingernail clippers, chewing gum, specific ink pens, and other everyday items that were not permissible per prison policy. After about a month of using her cell phone, I told her that I needed my own untraceable prepaid phone so we could talk whenever we wanted to. She was ecstatic about talking to me anytime she wanted to, including on her off days, so she delivered me a prepaid AT&T Go-Phone the very next day, fully charged and ready to receive and place calls.

Deputy Camillia had become my friend, but she was also an asset with access that I did not have as an inmate. In prison, an unauthorized cell phone is a luxury that every prisoner wants but cannot afford. With a cell phone, you can better manage family and business affairs, place unmonitored calls, and stay relevant in an outside reality that all too easily and quickly forgets about you.

The cell phone became more of a distraction for me than anything, as I became inundated with constant requests by fellow inmates to make "important" calls to family members, friends, doctors, lawyers, girlfriends, and more. A cell phone in prison is the closest thing to freedom a prisoner can get. As long as you stay tucked under a cover out of sight of monitoring guards, no one knows you're tasting freedom through forbidden fruit. And, as I soon came to realize, that taste of freedom is as valuable as gold.

A new federal offender assigned to my dorm—an Asian man named Tim—made his welcome by heading straight to the payphone, where he spent the next two to three hours making back to back calls. He was fresh off the streets and evidently trying to tie up loose ends, getting frustrated in the process. Once he finally went to his assigned cell, I introduced myself and discretely offered him access to my cell phone if needed. Instead of accepting my offer, he countered with a purchase offer of one thousand dollars. He assured me that he could either have the money put on my commissary account or sent to whomsoever I desired.

With the lightbulb going off in my mind, I finally realized the potential in my relationship with Deputy Camillia. I saw the bigger picture. With access, federal inmates would buy prepaid cell phones at a premium. I couldn't sell my one and only cell phone without making arrangements for its replacement, so I let him use my cell phone through the night while I devised a new black market for Tangipahoa Parish Jail.

My plan consisted of four key individuals: myself, Camillia, a state inmate trustee named Tyrone who had liberty to move around freely in the prison, and a trusted friend of mine in the free world, Monte.

To begin, Monte, my trusted friend and accomplice in the free world, would purchase ten AT&T prepaid Go-Phones at twenty dollars each. All of them would be activated with fifteen dollar Pay-As-You-Go phone cards, bringing the total investment per phone to thirty-five dollars. Monte would then put all the phones in a single 10x12, three-day priority postal envelope, with every phone powered off and attached to a measured layer of cardboard so that nothing shifted around.

Once purchased and packaged, Monte would meet Deputy Camillia at the Super Wal-Mart in Amite, near the jail. She would then take delivery of the sealed envelope directly and deliver it to me as part of routine nighttime mail distribution, often left over from lazy staffers on the day shift.

She never questioned or knew the contents of the priority envelope, and we did this only on the night shift, when prison operations were more relaxed. Tyrone, a fellow state inmate and trustworthy trustee that had the liberty to move all over the jail without a guard escort, got word to the other federal dorms that cell phones were for sale. If interested, they were to meet me at the prison-wide church activities on Tuesday and Thursday night of every week, hosted by various churches from Amite and Hammond.

Before the church services started, I would gauge the interest of prospective buyers, then slide them a piece of paper with Monte's alias and contact number. Payment arrangements were made between their outside support people and Monte directly. I listed the cell phones for a non-negotiable five hundred and fifty dollars, using the fifty dollars to pay Tyrone for delivering the cell phone to buyers once Monte had secured payment on the outside. With this nearly foolproof plan, I sold an average of ten Go-Phones a week, consistently for almost three months straight—until word got around.

One indicator to prison staff that something wasn't right was that federal inmates were no longer purchasing prepaid phone cards from the jail commissary. Another tell-tale sign was the increase in AA battery purchases, which were used by MacGyver-inmates to make battery packs to charge the cell phones with.

Prison officials caught onto the increased battery purchases first and eventually took them off the commissary completely. The word was out, and it was loud. I sent a message around the dorms to be on high alert—a prison shakedown was brewing. Getting caught with a cell phone meant getting rebooked on a new charge. No one wanted to get caught with any kind of contraband, let alone a cell phone.

When the inevitable prison-wide shakedown eventually came, not a single phone was found on any federal inmate, in their property, or in their cells. There were phones stashed behind the mounted dorm TV, behind the commode, in the shower, under steps, under the table...but we couldn't be charged with "Introducing Contraband into a Penal Institution" if it wasn't found in our possession or amidst our property. This made the prison officials twice as mad.

Even without evidence, my name was evidently first on the hit list, and I was relocated to punitive segregation—a.k.a., the hole—and placed under administrative investigation for thirty days.

The "hole" is the inner prison within the prison, calling to mind the space Paul and Silas praised their way out of.[24] No phone. No TV. No commissary. Nothing but prison food three times a day, like living in a dungeon for thirty seemingly impossible days. I did have access to Tyrone though, who delivered food to the hole, and I had anticipated something like this happening.

When things were good and golden, I actually had two priority envelopes delivered to Deputy Camillia for every order, totaling twenty phones, with batteries, in anticipation of a cell

---

24 Acts 16:24

YHWH

phone drought after a shakedown. Tyrone then hid the extra priority envelopes somewhere in the jail's kitchen, which he had regular access to as a prison cook and food deliverer. The prison guards had found over one hundred cell phones as a result of the prison-wide search and seizure, but I had exactly eighteen priority envelopes with eighty more cell phones and hundreds of batteries ready for sale.

Tyrone's first order of business was to bring me one of those phones so I could make contact with Camillia and the outside world. His next order of business was to get Tim a replacement phone back in the dormitory. After Tim got his phone, I directed Tyrone to deliver one complimentary replacement phone to each of the federal dormitories who had lost theirs. Giving away eight phones for free would help me to sell the remaining seventy-one much faster.

To offset the giveaways, I simply increased the price of the phones to seven hundred fifty dollars. They sold even faster than the previous batches. In three weeks, I sold seventy phones and let Tyrone have one for free—which I think he ended up selling because I could never call him on it and he never replied to text messages.

Sitting in Tangipahoa Parish Jail, part of the time in isolation in the hole, I made well over six figures selling twenty-dollar phones and AA batteries. A single Duracell battery was valued at five dollars and a minimum of ten had to be purchased to keep the math simple and the outside monetary transactions even simpler.

In my fifth and final week of being in the hole, I was more than ready to get out and return back to the prison population.

However, with so many unauthorized cell phones in circulation, inmates were talking too much—both amongst themselves and on their cell phones. This time, it was the outside talk that got us in trouble. Upset ex-girlfriends, estranged wives, disgruntled baby mamas, and abandoned side pieces who had little leverage over their locked-up partners started calling the prison out of retaliation for quarrels, new discoveries, and disagreements. They would tell prison officials that certain inmates had cell phones and what dormitory they were located in, and the buzz began again.

For this sting—dubbed a too-lighthearted "Operation Stop-Phone" in response to our many Go-Phones—prison officials coordinated a surprise middle of the night shakedown. Operation Stop-Phone ran under the leadership of the now disgraced, former DEA Special Agent Chad Scott, who reputedly was a glorified bully with a badge, but has since been called to give accountability under federal indictment for alleged underhanded, rogue dealings of his own.[25] They even enlisted the manpower of uniformed Tangipahoa Parish Sheriff's deputies directly off the street beat so they could hit every dorm in the entire prison at the same time, including the trustee dorm and the last stop that should have been their first—my cell in the hole.

The hole was built differently from the dorms in population, and surprises were a little harder to come by there.

---

25 Mustian, Jim. "Veteran DEA Agent Chad Scott Charged with 10 Counts in Sweeping Federal Indictment." The Advocate, October 2, 2017. https://www.theadvocate.com/baton_rouge/news/courts/article_b7a3d084-a769-11e7-a164-2f4e0544948c.html.

Prison guards had to enter two separate doors before actually accessing me. Each of the two sets of latches was loud, and the click of the first door opening had long since served as my alarm for chow or mail call.

During Operation Stop-Phone, they tried to raid my cell with just as much stealth and surprise. But I happened to be awake reading and writing when I heard the first door pop. It was obvious who was coming and what they were coming for, so I immediately occupied the toilet under the pretense of defecating. Just as I flushed the phone under the façade of feces, the second door triggered.

Prison guards rushed into my cell, snatch me off the toilet in exactly that condition. They unceremoniously put my half-stripped self in handcuffs, then turned my cell upside down, searching for a phone that had departed only seconds before.

A good number of my fellow inmates were caught with cell phones in their cells that night, charged and rebooked with "Introduction of Contraband into a Penal Institution" added to their rosters. Special Agent Chad Scott knew the gravity of that looming fate and employed tactical and strategic interrogative pressures to extract details as much as phones, promising lesser consequences in return for information.

He learned that Tyrone and I moved cell phones and batteries throughout the prison. What he didn't know but so desperately desired to, was how the cell phones and batteries got into the prison in the first place. Until now, that was information that only Monte, myself, and Deputy Camillia held as top secret.

On the word of pressured inmates alone, still lacking physical evidence to corroborate, Tyrone was stripped of his trustee status and shipped to another prison for disciplinary reasons, and I was removed from the hole and placed in solitary confinement, under video surveillance and extended administrative investigation, for the next thirty-six months.

I still had to learn that no man is an island—although like the Apostle John was excommunicated to the island of Patmos (Rev. 1:9–11, NKJV), I was about to be placed on an island of terrible design. Each of our actions carries consequences, not just for us but for the people we're connected to. I wanted to believe that everyone would follow my instructions and be fine, and they could have. But I didn't want to think about the larger consequences of disrupting the environment so much.

We couldn't control everyone's actions and responses. We couldn't control the environment. As a result, who knows how many extra years were served, how Tyrone's trajectory shifted, or what was in store for me in solitary.

TWELVE

THREE-DIMENSIONAL REDEMPTION

Darkness cannot drive out darkness: only light can do that. Hate cannot drive out hate: only love can do that.
—Martin Luther King, Jr.

f prison is designed for punishment, solitary confinement is meant to force compliance through attrition. There is some institutional acknowledgment of the dangers of complete isolation. A man can be locked down for twenty-three hours a day, but for an hour he must be permitted recreation and a breath of fresh air. He should have access to some phone usage and visitation. With the psychological risks of near total isolation, he should have basic physical provisions—normal sleeping and eating and living arrangements.

These are all rights we have as Americans, even when imprisoned. Even when we pose a risk to the safety and stability of the institution.

I won't deny the chaos I introduced, though Special Agent Chad Scott never found the direct evidence that should have been required before such steep punishment. Rather than direct retribution, however, he sought revenge. And he got it, under the directive and approval of Captain Stewart Murphy—and without the oversight of the US Marshals. Those good ol' boys out of Amite kept my disciplinary status to themselves and could do whatever they wanted with me as long as they controlled my inability to communicate.

What they wanted was a broken man. They wanted me to admit wrongdoing, to beg, to plead for reconsideration. No one would have blamed me if I did. Cell A12, a five-foot-by-ten-foot room, was my new living quarters, not for 23/7 as federal regulations defined and buttressed by constitutional rights would require, but around the clock.

Without that hour in the sun, I was left alone to test my mental fortitude against unjust, unjustifiable 24/7 artificial light and cold and complete isolation, with one repeating refrain coming through the covered slat in the door or in brief moments of interaction: *Tell us how you got the phones in. Start ratting and we'll let you out.*

Constant 50-degree temperatures settled hard into the concrete floors and walls. Dingy paint peeled where prison maintenance overlooked the solitary dungeon wing year after year. One slatted window, just wide enough to indicate night and day, opened into the less than riveting views of a solid brick wall.

Furnishings included one set of raw iron bunkbeds next to a commode that served as both washbasin and toilet. With a little bleach delivered by a trustee, it could be sanitized enough to rinse the underclothes that always come back dingy from the industrial wash. Afterward, garments could be laid out around the top bunk, air drying like we used to do on a clothesline outside when I was growing up in the country.

Above the commode was a mirror made out of metal, etched with the signatures of every unfortunate inmate who passed through this room before me. On the four-inch-thick prison door there were more scratched recordings of not just names but mental states. Words of hate and anger, insanity and confusion were scrawled over every open surface.

I had joined a society of chaos without a soul in sight.

With the lights kept on their full fluorescent settings twenty-four hours each day, it became crucial to find some sense of rhythm and pace. I found consistency in the three meals a day that passed through a door slot for food trays. Then there was the shifting light outside my makeshift window, and the radio that served as my only source of human connection. The sounds of new inmates joining the ward created another sense of shifting time, though much less welcome than the other markers.

All around me, the other cells were used as temporary holding for booking or, as I all too quickly deduced, as a place to keep terribly mentally unstable people housed apart from the rest of the prison population. All night long, with your head buried under a blanket to hide from the light, moans and groans would echo through the halls. Fights between inmates and staffers would break out. Sounds of urination and thrown fecal matter were followed by thick smells, which were followed by the high-pressure hose, or zaps of a taser or the beatings of brute force sanctioned by the badges that concealed racism and bigotry.

These are the pictures of solitary confinement that we don't see on the silver screen or America's favorite prison "reality" shows. It's not so entertaining to see a man collapsing into himself as the walls close in on him. It's not fun to wonder whether some undiagnosed mental malady has been exacerbated by extreme punitive measures, or whether he'll ever be the same, or sane, again. Very realistically, orange isn't the new black. All across America, particularly at Tangipahoa Parish Jail, Black and orange have been the same color for African Americans in a system where Jim Crow laws were never meant to be colorless—scripted and enacted by racist men who need to trade in their own suits and robes for prison jumpsuits, whoever and wherever they are.[26]

That first Christmas was the hardest of them all. The holiday songs slipping through the radio, the sense of hope and cheer that I knew pervaded the rest of the prison. The kids I left at home, celebrating yet another moment of life without me. My grandma slipping away, the rest of my family by her side, knowing I'd never see her again this side of heaven.

I paced my room, collapsed on the bed, ran my hands over my face...all of the pain of loss, all the hope of the season was bottled up together inside of me with nowhere for it to go.

---

26 *The New Jim Crow,* by Michelle Alexander is a must-read.

What I wouldn't have given for a hug from one of my kids, a piece of candy and a wink slipped to me by my grandma in her prime, a real conversation with my parents, an embrace from Nellie. Instead, there was only me and that moment, in total isolation.

I moved to the sink and splashed fresh running water onto my face. The surveillance cameras wouldn't catch me crying. In the dingy metal mirror, I stared at the person I had become. The man in the mirror who first heard my Capital One conspiracy could barely recognize the man staring back at me now.

I thought, *This has got to be the first and last. I have to get out of here. I can never come back.*

I couldn't control anything about the room I was in or close the distance between where I was and where I wanted to be. I wouldn't capitulate to my captors to be freed from that room. I didn't want any part of a false sense of freedom.

But I could bring myself back before the darkness pulled me in too deep.

I could let my family know I was okay. Let them know they could celebrate without me, save memories for me like they were leftover Christmas dinner. Some of the stories, like Christmas and birthdays, I devoured as soon as I was free. Others are too painful to bring back to the surface to this very day—at the time of writing I still haven't been able to visit my grandmother's grave. Still, I determined that I would make it back out to have the choice.

In the face of twisted justice at any other point in my life, I fought back by gaining control of my environment, personal consequences be damned. I wanted the power no matter the cost. Here, I had no one to control but myself. If I could stand it, the fire could either burn me to ashes or finally purify me.

And I chose to endure.

On Mondays, Wednesdays, and Fridays I was allowed fourteen minutes total—seven to shower and seven to use the phone. Depending on the shift, sometimes supervising heads would turn long enough to give me the entire fourteen minutes in the shower. My body enjoyed and indulged in the hot water, cutting through the chill that was nearly impossible to shake.

I stacked the two bunkbed mattresses together to make one that was a little thicker and more comfortable, leaving the top bunk for the belongings that came with me now that it was clear that solitary confinement would be an indefinite stay. I also took advantage of the constant surveillance and strategically talked to myself in the hopes of catching the right ear. I rambled about the pillows and blankets and being tired of shivering myself to sleep, until Deputy Camillia had a trustee inmate quietly deliver an extra mattress and blanket to me in the middle of the night when prison operations were most inactive.

On Tuesday and Thursday evenings, the prison chaplain unceremoniously collected me for church services. Maybe it was allowed so as not to raise further alarm. Maybe no one was paying close attention on those nights. Whatever the case may be, I looked forward to warming up, body and soul, through the companionship and camaraderie I was so starved for. It fed my very human need for interpersonal connection and stoked my spiritual need to connect with Scripture.

While I had a few friends overseeing my care, or the complete lack thereof, for the most part the prison guards obeyed Stewart Murphy and Chad Scott's strict orders.

If the US Marshals found out how Tangipahoa was violating my constitutional rights while in their custody, Captain Murphy and company would face consequences of their own. However, with my case for my innocence in the phone scam too thin to hold up to the light, revealing my mistreatment would potentially call up bad behavior records that could follow me for the next five years—maybe even adding more time. We were at an impasse, playing a constitutional game of chicken. Who would crack first, and how far would we push each other before then?

Where I couldn't find allies, I found loopholes. My federal case was still in progress, and I could not be denied access to my attorneys or legal preparation. The best place for that work is the prison library, and I even managed to get someone to take me there once. Books had never looked so good in my life. I never got another trip to the library after that, but they had to allow me access to the books themselves or it would impede my ability to do legal research as part of my preparation for my legal defense. So whatever books I requested, they brought. Whatever they couldn't bring, I requested of my attorneys, who sent fresh batches as regularly as they could. We also learned that the staffers weren't transmitting non-essential mail to my cell—several times, someone tried to send me a dictionary only to have it disappear. After that, all books went to one of my attorney's offices, and he would mail it in or deliver it by hand when he knew I needed some company.

The more I learned, the hungrier I became. Little did I know at the time, but I was moving toward the three-dimensional redemption—*re*education, *re*generation, and *re*habilitation— that could finally set me free from self-consumption, free from narcissistic ideologies, and free from the diversions and distraction of my active ignorance born of miseducation.

Education for education's sake is never quite as enlightening as we might hope it will be. I graduated high school close to a 4.0, with my senior year comprised only of electives that were complete by eleven in the morning. I was in the Beta club, the Shelby M. Jackson Institute, and a model intellectual by all adolescent accounts except one: the ability to apply myself to my work. An uncanny acuity came naturally for me, but my acumen had been stifled in my distaste for school and the world it represented.

In solitary confinement, curiosity was all I had left. The intent is to break you down, to tear down your defenses, and the bunk was always calling to me, offering a place to give up. To just listen to the radio all day, letting my mental strength, morals, and mind atrophy until there was nothing left.

In other words, I could engage my mind or lose it entirely. And not just my mind, but my spirit as well.

To give up spiritually is perhaps more dangerous than to give up mentally. It is to lose hope and faith. It is to have no regard to foresight, abandon hindsight, and let go of all insight. It is to stop praying, stop consuming your daily bread of Scripture, and to stop believing. A breakdown of faith shows through in a breakdown of character, as I had seen when my Bible went on the shelf and greed and ego became my pursuits. In prison without a spiritual foundation, there are no boundaries a person won't cross, because there are no consequences to create further restraint. Life in prison without hope is careless—not to be confused with carefree. There is nothing to live for when your life is owned by your captors.

That summer, habits of study had begun to form as I had prepared for the four Bible studies that I held each week in the dormitory. At my grandma's direction before she passed, I learned of the prayer habits of men of the Bible and brought those rituals into my own life. I stopped what I was doing three times a day—morning, noon, and night—to reconnect with Yahweh.[27] This practice correlates with Daniel 6:10 and Revelation 1:4, following the Hebrew custom of three hours of prayer, giving thought to Him that (1) was, (2) is, and (3) shall always be. This became an anchor for long days alone, with only church services to look forward to outside of solitary.

I continued to study in preparation for those services, though they weren't mine to lead. The room warmed my skin, but the study and engagement were thawing my heart and mind. From what I read each week, I would challenge the theological credentials of the pastors and bishops leading lessons and test the denominational traditions that permeated their teachings. Rather than seeking the attention that came from commanding the room, I sought wisdom.

Using the Holy Scriptures as my foundation and compass, I dove into the world's eight largest religious traditions. Brother

---

27 Psalm 55:17

Sedrick Pierre, my devoted friend from my first period of federal incarceration in Texarkana, stayed connected to me in spirit and gave me recommendations for books and commentaries to read next.

I read each and every book three times over. The first time through was a literal read, to become familiar with the author and their material. The second read was inferential, to listen to what the author wasn't saying while capturing what they intended to convey. Finally, the third time through was evaluative. I wanted to take in every word, define what I didn't know, and consume every bit that the author had created for me and more.

I studied not only Christianity but also Judaism, Islam, Hinduism, Buddhism, Taoism or Daosim, Confucianism, and Chinese religious traditions. I read about the way culture informs and defines religion, and in turn how religion is used to manipulate and control the masses. I uncovered principles and practices that made us more alike than different. My growing appreciation for cultural differences led me to a newfound understanding of our Western prejudices against Eastern religions and populations, as well as a growing gratitude for our freedom of religion in this country. Naturally, I shifted my book requests from *theology* into *history*: in order to know where I was going, I first needed to know who and where I came from.

I began with the history of the Americas and the man who discovered America...*not* Christopher Columbus. When I pulled on the string of American history I had been taught, beginning with the man for whom the continents were named,

Amerigo Vespucci, the whole fabric of my understanding of history began to fall apart.

As an African American, I wanted to learn from diversified perspectives. I wanted to read things that were authentic and that went deeper than what I was taught in school. Authors like W.E.B. Dubois, J.A. Rogers, Ralph Ellison, and Frederick Douglass, to name only a few, depicted the experience of a Black man in America, from the beginning of our nation's history. *Narrative of the Life of Frederick Douglass* connected me to the author's experience from slavery and on to freedom. He had such a beautiful mind, without any way to express it but through the power of his pen, often represented by the persuasiveness of his grandiloquent oratory. No TV, no iPhone or Android, no internet—and I could relate. Not to the measure that he did, but in an all too familiar pattern nonetheless.

It was one of the first times I saw myself in the pages of history. I began to strengthen my appreciation for my own history and where I found myself in the plight of African American history, even into present day America. A psychological struggle had been passed down after four hundred years of institutional slavery. My studies naturally shifted from *history* into the present dynamics of *sociology*.

As a kid, I hated scholastic social studies. Now, I needed to understand why society functions as it does. With a better understanding of history, I could see that our sociological struggle might not subside for another four hundred years or more. I read about reconstruction and the missed opportunity for reparations, through suffrage and white women's voting rights coming before African American voting rights. The layers of societal struggle stacked one after another to shape the world we live in today.

Through the social sciences and with a broad range of historical authors, I began to see my teenage years in a new light. I could see the hoe fields again, the cotton and the cornfields, not just as the only thing going for a rural community, but as the thing keeping us down.[28] Those fields were merely generational wealth passed down from slave owner to successors. If your lineage falls within the fields rather than behind the farmhouse door, you were only owed existence money—barely minimum wage, only granted the ability to survive, if that.

My memories of hot summer days with a hoe in hand began to change. Looking out over the fields, I used to picture that credit card and dream of a life I could make for myself in spite of it all. From the five-by-ten room I was confined to, I pictured looking over those fields to see my ancestors alongside me. At some point and place in time, they were picking that cotton in the same fields I refused to work, the same fields I drove through coming home from Texarkana, the same fields I drive past today from the air conditioning of my vehicle. I'm not hoeing fields anymore. I'm not picking cotton. My kids won't, either. But we have a long way to go before that's true for everyone.

Perhaps most importantly, my deep dive into social studies solidified a sense of responsibility. Not just for my own

---

28 I hated the hoe field for all it represented—past, present, and future— socially, economically and politically. The naked and simple truth is that I still detest it for the same reasons. The climate for social and economic change is long overdue not only in Tensas Parish, but for the entire country.

actions for my own self, because accountability and consequences for my own actions were never enough to outweigh the thrill of autonomy. Instead, I saw our interconnectedness. I saw my children born into this same society I grew up in. I no longer existed as myself alone. All of my actions affected others, either directly or indirectly. Those closest to me suffered. Those who fell into substance abuse on the substances I delivered suffered, and so did the people close to them. And on it goes, because no one is an island. We are all connected to one another.

To that point in my life, I knew there were systems and controlling factors and reasons we all behaved as we did…but I was merely a zombie in the macrocosm of America. I found what I believed was my role to play and I played it without knowing why.

In that cell, with sixteen hours a day devoted to study, I consumed all of the information I could, from the deepest intergenerational struggles to the most minute details of day to day life, like taxes and offices of government and state and federal budgets. I was hungry for it, wanting to finally understand how all of the pieces of the system work together. In these moments, unbeknownst to me, I was transforming from convict to concerned citizen.

My understanding of self in the scheme of history and culture was growing by the book—now forming a sizeable stack on the top bunk. For the first time, I was interested in how people think and why they do what they do, not to exploit them, but to help them understand themselves. And it had to begin with myself. So I turned the mirror of perception inward to begin to study *psychology*. C.J. Jung and his system of analytical psychology held my attention most notably, among others.

To this day, I remain interested in psychology and the study of the way the mind works. The human brain might be limited in size, but the mind is ever evolving, limitless in both intake and output. Each and every mind holds degrees and elements of its own ingenuity and emotion. Likewise, we each have external distractions that impede us and keep us from tapping into our greater genius.

From *psychology*, I delved into *praxeology,* which is the study of human behavior. I wanted to know why people do what they do. I wanted to understand how behavioral patterns are developed and how habits are formed. With nothing but time to myself, I could serve as my own behavioral analysis case study. I held my own attitude and actions up under evaluative reasoning, attempting to bridge the gap between who I was and why I was that way. The analysis, I've found, will never stop.

At pivotal moments of growth, such as the one I was working toward in that time of study, we must admit who we are but not accept that as our final iteration. To understand yourself, reject it, and then strive for more activates change motivation. It inspires you toward the better outcome. It is the commencement of a healthier, happier, newer you.

Questions of existence and meaning melted into the study of *philosophy*, as Socrates, Plato, and Aristotle amused and took me on intellectual rollercoaster rides that I could not easily exit. Theories, reasoning, logic are never-ending and ever evolving, layered on one another as perspective is built.

In my quest, I found that philosophical inventions are discretionary, subject to the limitations of what one has experienced either directly or pretentiously through abstract reasoning. The best philosophy, in my humble opinion, is that body of work that draws directly from empirical existence of the subject matter it intends to explicate. Short of direct observation and experience, it is only empty theory and pseudo-intellectual conjecture. Perspective, representation, and experience carry greater weights than we can often afford.

In my quest to understand the philosophical and moral differences between the Red Elephant and the Blue Donkey, I plunged into *politics*. To a degree, our differences provide check-and-balance steps to powerful institutions. But when those differences give rise to derisive debate and divisive politics, they cease to be effective. The bipartisan principle and practice find their productivity in the Holy Scriptures in Amos 3:3—*How can two walk together except they are agreed?*

While studying the political landscape of our great nation, I found it impossible not to also consider its *economics*. The two are inseparable. A nation, and especially the United States of America, cannot exist without a competent governing body, balanced power, a thriving economy, and military might.

Right there in my cell, I held a group discussion with Karl Marx, Friedrich Engles, and Adam Smith, each offering opposing philosophies regarding capitalism, socialism, and communism. I learned that Marx and Engles advanced the concept of collective enterprise and redistribution in the economic beliefs of socialism and communism, while Smith willfully ignored the evil origins of his doctrine rooted in plantation capitalism, and instead tried to repackage his tainted system of economics between the covers of his book *The Wealth of Nations*.[29] Regardless of the underpinnings, it's clear that we thrive and survive as a nation because we encourage charity and philanthropic participation without enforcing it under penalty of law and in determined and deliberate defiance to capitalistic prejudices and perjuries. Perhaps Franz Oppenheimer's theory offers a right remedy and ready solution.

Epistemology followed next, to keep myself in check—the justification and the rationality of belief. In other words, it raises the question of how you know what you know, or what you think you know. The Scriptural epistemologist, the Apostle Paul, reminds us how little we know, and how deceptive it can be to think we have it all together.[30]

For sixteen hours a day, seven days a week, scheduling eight hours for sleep and mental recoupment, I maximized the years of solitude by reading fanatically, studying deeply, praying fervently, and writing prolifically. Some of my findings were facts and others outright foolishness, but they all

---

29 This is what I learned at the time, but history is written by the victors, and my education is ever ongoing. Most recently, the *1619 Project* has my attention, and Matthew Desmond's piece, "In order to understand the brutality of American capitalism, you have to start on the plantation," August 2019. Four hundred years later, we're still reaping the trauma-borne fruits of violence wrought against my ancestors, from the very "hoe fields" me and my family worked to the capitalistic-driven society that we all thought would deliver us.

30 1 Corinthians 8:2, Galatians 6:3

lead me to form my own opinions and beliefs on various topics. On these subjects, a foundation was forming that could not be shaken.

It seemed that my subject selections were being placed before me by Divine Providence, each one leading into the next. Every topic that I tackled drew me further into the practice of studying the written word. I came to a point where I had learned so much that I wanted to learn how I was learning.

Philology, as defined by Merriam-Webster, is "the study of literature and of disciplines relevant to literature, or to language as used in literature," and was my next topic of consideration. Through so many books and with a growing and diverse appreciation for varying authors, I began to notice how different writing styles could be. It is a special ability to be able to express thoughts in a form and a fashion that captivates as much as it educates and entertains. Even with my book in hand and more in mind, I only think of myself as a writer outside of the margins of the art—but writing is more than rules. Award-winning writers win because their work is effective. It's a composition of character and charisma that commands attention and compels undivided attention.

During my inferential read, words and technical terms were clear in context, but my third, evaluative read of each book called out each and every term or phrase that landed beyond my understanding. Not only did I look up the definition, but I transmitted it through pen and paper to instill it in my mind.

My study habits were laborious and exacting but rewarding, as I no longer had the distractions of a TV or a phone or even a fellow inmate's officious disturbance and interaction. I was committed to the cause of self-improvement in hopes of retiring my existence as a social parasite. On the other side of my sentence was not only freedom from incarceration but freedom from myself. I was determined to emerge from the cocoon of that prison as a social engineer rather than a societal villain. Every day, I felt more and more ready to make positive contributions to my community, in my country.

The world unlocked by a simple dictionary fostered my addiction to *lexicography*, which is none other than the process of writing, editing, or compiling a dictionary. I might have written down the definitions of as many words as are in any given dictionary, including *Strong's Exhaustive Greek and Hebrew Concordance and Lexicon* and *Black's Law Dictionary*. I wrote the definitions of words and Scriptural references in notebooks and on sticky notes and plastered them all over what little wall space I had.

Merriam-Webster Collegiate Dictionary, Eleventh Edition, remains my preferred lexicographical reference. It is poignantly persuasive and beautifully scripted in its description of the lexicography before, throughout, and behind the book. I read the introduction repeatedly and righteously every day before I wrote down a definition from each word in alphabetical order, beginning with the word "A."

Undoubtedly my grammar is far from perfect, but *grammar* was my next step anyway. I speak how I write and write how I speak, and my subjects and verbs do not always agree.

However, I quickly understood that to have knowledge of a word without understanding how to use it in dialogue or literary discourse was about as useless as knowing how to look but not see. Having at least decent grammar is paramount to having your message heard and understood. As my word studies deepened, learning the second and third meaning of a word and its usage, respectively, so did my grammar. This self-taught construction gives a reasonable explanation to my continuing grammatical aberrance, but nevertheless, I try.

Following grammar, I ventured into *linguistics* and *semantics*, both skills serving as a bridge over language barriers within and across diverse literary compositions. Understanding and grasping different writing styles afforded me the ability to interpret and translate literature, even if only to myself and in my own way.

As my scholarship developed into an insatiable appetite for words, I expanded my studies into *phonology* as well, the study of sound patterns and their meanings, both within and across languages. This helped me to hone in and better hear the tones and tenors behind various literary styles and forms.

Etymology looked to the past, in its simplest definition, to study word origins, their historical usage, and how their form and meaning have adapted and changed over time. The etymology of a word is usually situated in the introduction of the word's key in some of the more notable dictionaries. The lexicographical format of the arrangement speaks to the word's discovery or invention, marking transitional usage from origin to present. *Onomasiology*, the study of words and expressions having similar or associated concepts, and *orismology* and a referential cross-examination of the thesaurus supplemented and buttressed my developing speaking and writing abilities.

Word selection and substitution is an art form, and vital when the speaker is trying to paint an indelible message on the canvases of the minds of their audience members. Knowing when and how to use your words underscores the Scriptural message that "Life and Death are in the power of the tongue."[31] It's not what you say, but how you say what you say, as Yahshua himself reminds us, "For by thy words thou shalt be justified, and by the words thou shalt be condemned."[32]

I could not avoid the subjects of *rhetoric* and *oration*. In fact, my first lesson in public speaking came in solitary confinement, right there in cell A-12, to no visible audience but the undoubtedly listening ear of surveillance. I paced to and fro in that cell, pulling from all I learned and continued to learn into practiced sermons and speeches. The gift of gab that had taken me so far in over my head could perhaps still be salvaged for good, in hopes of influencing and persuading people toward righteousness, human decency, and common good.

I was convinced that vocabulary can be degenerative—if you don't use it, you lose it—and I was determined to use all that Yahweh had given me. Surely the cameras picked up a perceived crazy man pacing in his room amongst the books and the notes. What they really saw was a man finally pouring himself out for Yah's glory and for our collective good.[33]

---

31 Proverbs 18:21
32 Matthew 12:37
33 Psalm 68:4

Internally, I let go of my need to control my environment and exchanged it for a deeper understanding and control of my own mind and my gifts in this world. After two years of solitary confinement, my heart and mind were light, but my body was paying for the extreme living conditions. It seemed like twenty years. My skin was pale in the absence of sunlight. I hadn't had as much as a jailhouse haircut for months.

Re-education could only go so far. In the face of such deep injustice, my redemption needed to be deeper: first through regeneration, then finally rehabilitation.

In my Scriptural faith, the concept of regeneration is known as being "born again." It includes the confession with the mouth and acceptance in the heart that Yahshua died for our sins and that Yahweh raised him from the dead. In the instant of professed belief, we are spiritually reborn, resurrected, and rescued from the death and destruction that inevitably awaits the unbeliever.[34]

As I learned for myself who Yahshua was and how he purchased my eternal salvation—not just from Sunday School, and not just through the ever-faithful model of my parents—I grew to embrace Him as my Sovereign and Savior. No longer was I too cool to admit a love for the Messiah. No longer did I leave Him on a shelf. I embraced His teachings, took on His mindset, and became a disciple in the way that my grandma knew how to pray and my parents knew how to forgive.

After regeneration follows the lifelong process of spiritual and moral rehabilitation. I positioned my faith in the *Logos*,

---

34 Romans 10:9

the Living Word, before I introduced and exposed myself to the elements of darkness that lurks around and lords over various religious beliefs and practices. Therefore, my rehabilitation was only found in circling back to my first field of study—theology—through a new lens.

This time, instead of looking for broad, new concepts, I took a deep-sea dive into Covenant Theology, Systematic Theology, and an intimate acquaintance with Dispensationalism and Millennialism. I familiarized myself with the profound works of both liberal and conservative Bishops and Preachers, Masters of Divinity, Doctors of Theology, leading Rabbis, and notable scholars. To understand and follow them to other conclusions, I learned the system of *exegesis* and the science of *hermeneutics*, which when faulty and coupled together have landed a lot of intellectuals in theological eisegesis.

I was focused and determined to let the Master Potter shape and mold me into the vessel He wanted me to be so that I could be used for His purpose, for His glory.[35] I read the Holy Scriptures countless times in solitary confinement, beginning, pivoting, and ending my day with conversations in the Word.

I memorized entire passages of Scripture and over four hundred verses, having each verse taped to the wall for review and reference as I paced the floor practicing my oration. To the natural eye, it would have appeared as if I was going crazy, but I was actually finding my sanity through the mind of Yahshua.[36]

---

35 Jeremiah 18:3
36 1 Corinthians 2:16, Philippians 2:5

Though my studies were intensive and exacting, Yahshua taught me that some strongholds can only be defeated by prayer and fasting.[37] I continued the practice of praying three times a day, giving thought to Him that is, was, and shall always be. I prayed intermittently throughout the day to develop a lifestyle of praying constantly, consistently, and without ceasing.[38] I prayed and fasted every weekend of what would become three arduous years in solitary confinement, and I extended the practice well beyond, commencing my fast on Friday evening at 6 p.m. and expiring it on Sunday at 6 p.m.

While it only takes faith the size of a mustard seed in the shed Blood of Yahshua to atone for our sins and thereby be redeemed from the wrath of Yahweh, I learned that salvation is threefold in that we are saved, are being saved, and shall be saved from taking part in the second resurrection.[39] As such, I found that the fundamental doctrines of repentance and forgiveness are essential to the faith of the Holy Scriptures and are part and parcel to the practice of our salvation, the working out of our faith.[40] I learned that a penitent spirit and a contrite heart are fruits born of true repentance, even repentance that anticipates true forgiveness.

At the same time, the doctrine of forgiveness does not require or necessitate the restoration of trust. To forgive someone is to release them from condemnation, but the

---

37 Mark 9:29
38 1 Thessalonians 5:17
39 Revelations 20:6
40 James 2:26

release doesn't require one to hold the forgiven in a position to offend or betray once more.[41]

When I better understood the doctrines of repentance and forgiveness, I understood that although Yahweh forgave me for making a mockery of His name when I motivated the Scriptural symposium while smuggling unauthorized cell phones, His forgiveness did not require that I be trusted again and restored to the prison population. Though released from the penalty of eternal condemnation, I had to endure the natural consequences of my actions in order to grow and learn through them—even to the unnatural measure by which they were applied.

The more time I spent in the Holy Scriptures, the more intimate my relationship with Yahweh became. The more I settled into my identity in Him and the gifts he had given me, the less frantic I was about my restrictive environment.

Three years in, Deputy Camillia gave me one last message on a night shift, telling me the transport was coming. At four in the morning, it was time to go. Just like that, my solitary journey had come to an end.

Though I maximized the use of time, my stay at Tangipahoa Parish Jail was well overspent. Three summers, three winters, thirty-six months, one thousand and ninety-five days...[42] However you want to count it, I spent three years of

---

41 John 11:8

42 The United Nations defines any period longer than fifteen days straight in solitary confinement as "torture." I was held captive in solitary confinement for three years, *straight*! I am a living testimony, by the grace of Yahweh, to the truth and triumph of Kalief Browder's solitary...

my life in a five-by-ten holding cell at a perennial 50 degrees Fahrenheit temperature with few breaks and constant light and noise.

By the end, the wholeness I felt through one-on-one communion with the Holy Spirit and omnipresence of Yahweh made every second warm and worth it.

The strongholds in my life had begun to crumble. The pursuit of vain glory, the lure of money, even a draw toward profanity had propped up my rise to "success" and pulled me down into stark reality. But it isn't until the strongholds are broken that we are truly free.

At each moment of capture or collapse, I had been sure that my lack of marketable vices—no drugs, no addiction—meant I was free to "quit whenever I wanted to." When you're convinced the disease doesn't exist, there's no way to find healing. I couldn't simply turn away from my past—the 360-degree turn that I took over my year of freedom had made that clear. Instead, I needed that three-dimensional redemption that's built from all sides—including, most importantly, from my inside. And that gave me something firm to build upon for the rest of my days.

...experience—one that far too many don't get to tell as victims of America's systemic and conspiratorial criminal injustices.

THIRTEEN

SECOND CHANCE, LAST OPPORTUNITY

*But [Jacob] said, "I will not let You
go unless You bless me!"*
—Genesis 32:26b (NKJV)

Federal prison was a relief compared to solitary confinement at Tangipahoa Parish Jail. This prison in particular lacked the overcrowding and underfunding that our southern Louisiana parish facilities faced, especially in that post-Katrina chaos. Federal prisons have better food, more resources, and a different kind of inmate population. There, I was well received and well respected by fellow inmates and prison staff alike. Clearly, and thankfully, my disciplinary citations didn't follow me to Bastrop Federal Correctional Institution, my next step and last stop once my case was settled. If the Marshals ever heard what happened, I would have been designated to a higher security facility under the constant watchful eye of Special Investigation Services (SIS). But I wasn't.

I jumped right into the swing of things, teaching classes on parenting, relationship building, and marriage management. I took the initiative to start a Scriptural symposium from Monday thru Thursday in the evening at 7 p.m., this time with a focus on teaching the Sacred Name Doctrine, among other fundamental Scriptural truths.

My days started, pivoted, and ended with prayer. When I wasn't teaching, I could be found in the prison library, chapel, or in my cell studying—never just casually reading. I had conditioned my mind to constant cognitive development and intellectual enhancement. Without a single infraction, this is how I coasted to my release date.

On March 16, 2011, after six years of incarceration, I was released from the custody of the Federal Bureau of Prisons and entered straight into the workforce via the McGraw and Associates Accounting Firm.

Mr. Jimmy McGraw, who accepted my reference letter without question, was not the same sort of man as the others I had worked with, worked on, and had been worked over by. Fully aware of the circumstances for which I served prison time, Mr. McGraw gave me an opportunity to prove that I was trustworthy. Not only did he give me a job, but he placed me around and amidst his client's sensitive information—every credential needed to effectively steal hundreds of identities.

I did not prove him wrong.

In years past, I couldn't stop my mind from wandering toward possibility and scheming toward theft. Now, the information at my fingertips was never a second thought. I couldn't afford to go back to federal prison and didn't need the rush of the chase to avoid it. I was simply done. My values were clear: my kids needed me now more than I needed my ego stroked and adrenaline stoked.

I'll forever be grateful to Mr. McGraw and the way his acts of faith served to redeem a community in my mind and in my life. For the full five years of my probation, we shared not only in work but in life. We each fell toward our own very different opinions and life perspectives, but we cared about each other more than about each other's differences. He could talk about his political candidates and so could I, and at the end of it all we could still shake hands, share hugs, and go our separate ways as friends. He was a Republican raised in the backwoods of Woodville, MS, where conservatism was most complicit, but he wasn't contaminated by the callous politics of his generation.

Mr. McGraw rewarded my integrity and honesty with a personal loan of one hundred and seventy-five thousand dollars, the amount I asked for, to jump-start my entrepreneurial endeavors in horticulture, hair and cosmetology, and entertainment. The businesses that I only thought of as a front for underhanded dealings in 2002 had been right there all along as the window to my true calling as an entrepreneur, and now it was time to tap into that gift once more.

Later that year, in September of 2011, I took Nellie's hand in marriage, fully intending to award her patience and support with the gifts and treasures that Yahweh had given me to share with her and with others. I had a full-fledged family for the first time in my adult life, and we set out to attempt to build our future. Kaleb Kar'micah Williams (aka, Kaleb Tha Kop or simply, KK) was born into this world on October 4, 2012. We welcomed him as the youngest of my four—Emoni, Darquise, Madisen, and now Kaleb. It was for their sake that Nellie and I held on to each other for as long as we could.

For six years, I had been on a journey of brokenness and growth, spiritually, intellectually, and morally. I was not the same person who called her from a hidden hotel room the day that she lost her job. Remembering that growth and forgiveness do not absolve us of our consequences, I could see the lack of trust in Nellie's eyes. In the absence of mutual respect, understanding, and appreciation of each other, our marriage was more bitter than sweet.

Despite all of my knowledge and know-how, it appears I was too stubborn and blinded to make my marriage work. In the same way that I let invisible strongholds pull me back into identity theft and drug deals time and again, I believed the outward symbol of marriage was enough to hold us together. Instead, we each had our own relational strongholds to tear down.

Nothing is beyond the redeeming power of Yahweh. Nothing and nobody! But the fact is, He has given each of us free moral agency and with free will we do what we want— much too often to our own detriment, in direct contradiction to His will. In the area of fidelity and marriage, I was once again the seed that fell among thorns, choked out by slipping away from spiritual practice, relying on my own will, and keeping those internal strongholds reinforced.

After five trying years of marital mismanagement, Nellie and I filed for divorce. We were each too selfish to concede pride and prioritize principle. On November 2, 2016, our separation was finalized in divorce. The devil won that round. While there's no glory for Yahweh in divorce, He still can and will be magnified in spite of the circumstance.

I've struggled with this dual life at times—trusting in the plan for my life, while always craving something more. I don't have the family unit that I've always wanted, though I'm working toward it. Nothing is truly in my control, and I'm not sure that will ever be a comforting thought.

Nothing is without consequence, and I'm still reaping surprise fruits of my long-held labor. I've earned a few speeding tickets since my release from prison in 2011, but nothing marginally close to meriting incarceration. But in June 2016, a routine traffic stop in Natchez, MS, brought up an old outstanding warrant that apparently slipped through the cracks in 2001 and somehow resurfaced fifteen years later. Like *déjà vu*, I was booked in, bailed out, and went on my way, shaking my head.

The most visceral and surprising reminder of the life I once led came at me as I was leaving a venue in 2017. Some completely unrelated altercation escalated to dangerous proportions, and a .221 assault rifle fired in my direction as I drove away to take me and my friend home.

It's the internal shock that really left its mark.

When I moved guns back in the day, I rationalized it in the same way I rationalized drugs. It wasn't my business what anyone did with the product. They were going to buy it anyway, so why not from me? I never stopped to think about what end the items might be meant for. With a bullet grazing us and the heavy knowledge that a few inches, a slip of the trigger finger, could have killed me or my passenger, I could no longer hide from the scope of what I had done.

Grace alone has allowed me to survive to this present day, whole and alive and thriving in the strengths Yahweh has given me. My children are graduating high school and all share my last name. I'm not only an entrepreneur with plenty of ventures to keep my busy mind moving, but a leader and an investor in the next generation. I have ties to the elders in our communities and attach myself regularly to their wisdom.

This repentance is complete, yet never-ending. It only becomes more demanding and exacting, tempting me toward weakness and despair, reminding me that I'll never fully escape the consequences. Asking me to carry on toward a higher calling anyway.

This life is beautiful.

On March 16, 2016, I officially completed five years of supervised probation as part of my federal conviction and sentencing. Considering my many probation violations yesteryears before, it is worthy to note that *my* completion of supervised probation was without one single infraction or incident.

Some will say that I was a model prisoner and probationer, while others will deem that I've concealed incorrigibility as a conman. My testimony is that I am a work in progress that's short of perfection. I am a man with too many faults and flaws of my own to recognize and judge unrighteousness in others.

The three-dimensional process of redemption doesn't end here. It becomes more demanding and exacting as a follow-up to this published work. For continuing education is a must, regeneration is an eternal activity and progressive rehabilitation is part of the push to "press towards the mark for the prize of the high calling of Yahweh in Yahshua the Messiah."[43]

As I bookmark my story here, I constantly remind myself of my original sin in chapter 1. Jacob's legacy of complete, generational redemption is one that I hold close to my heart. As a grown man, he fought with Yahshua in pursuit of a blessing—one rightfully earned and spoken with his own name. Instead, Yahshua gave him a new name altogether—Israel.

I hold onto the vision my parents held for me, that they held in spite of all I did to scorn their patient forgiveness. I hold onto the name and identity that they instilled in me from childhood. It is through their unfailing love that I've been drawn to Yahweh and the hope and a future He promises.

When the Messiah instructed his followers to forgive seventy times seven, my parents held fast to that difficult calling. They forgave me constantly and repeatedly, out of a deep love

---

43 Phillipians 3:14

that can cover a multitude of sins. They did so believing that their child, who had been raised up in the way he should go, would one day come back to them.

And I did. I was the prodigal son who ran away and squandered his riches, lost the teachings, gave it all up for a life of crime. When I walked back to my parents, they received me with open arms and celebration.

I make these ancient connections because, as Solomon tells us, there are no new things under the sun. There will always be the son running away to squander his gifts. There will always be the scheming child, wanting what isn't his and doing whatever it takes to change his story.

Yet that means there will also be the son who wakes up in the muck and runs home to his father. There will always be the child who fears the brokenness of his relationship and fights to come into his own and restore the life he was meant to have. There will be new struggles, new blessings, and new names.

Like Jacob, I had to wrestle to get here. I fought with consequences. I fought with my own conscience. I fought with repentance and forgiveness. I fought with control and conviction. The furnace of redemption is painful, especially when it looks like cell A-12.

Through it all, I've found my name. I've found myself. I've found my identity and purpose, straight from the utterance of Yahweh himself: ObadYah!

This is my second chance and last opportunity. This is where I show all of Heaven why Jacob's name was changed to Israel. Why my name is the only name I carry in my wallet, into a room, into whatever lay ahead for me and my family.

This is where I "let my light so shine before men, that they may see my good works, and glorify my Father which is in Heaven."[44]

May it be so! May it be done!

Selah.

---

44 Matthew 5:16

Freddie Mack Williams, Sr., always has been one of Dartanyon's favorite people on the planet. Ironically, he was also his first "test case" and identity theft victim.

Freddie Mack Williams, Sr. and his bride, Linda Roach Williams. Dartanyon's parents, first identity theft victims, and true symbols of love and forgiveness.

The cotton fields (hoe fields) of Tensas Parish in bloom. The location of Dartanyon's first job, and the impetus for and motivation of his criminal pursuits.

Guildfield Baptist Church, St. Joseph, Louisiana. The home of Sister Emma Douglas's Sunday School class and Dartanyon's first introduction to Jacob in the Bible.

Pictured here with his older brother Lamont. Dartanyon always had a plan on his mind.

Home again and all smiles after "surviving" his first scary night in jail.

After an encounter with a merciless Monroe PD Officer, the K-9 Cop
Thor. Twenty-six stitches later, DAW developed a healthy disdain for law
enforcement.

818 4th Street in St. Joseph, Louisiana. The site of Dartanyon's first
individual home and "headquarters."

Duck Pond, just outside of the town limits of St. Joseph, Louisiana, served
as the site where a young Dartanyon ventured to isolate himself, using
the isolation to discover the serenity necessary to simplify intricate plans,
complex thoughts, and design-flawless strategies to successfully execute
his identity theft crimes. As an adult, Duck Pond is the site where he chose
to return to take a mind-and-memory hiatus, and develop intellectual
properties for disruptive technologies through his software company,
DuckPond Technologies, that will forever change the way we, Americans,
and the world in general, approach, appreciate, and apprehend identity
theft and the many frauds that ensue as a result.

Fatherhood. The one responsibility that tugged on the strings of his consciousness no matter how deep he had spiraled, Emoni, Darquise, and Madisen were always in his heart and on his mind. Dartanyon is pictured here with Darquise.

LEFT: One of the apples of his eyes, Emoni Janae-Marie Williams. Dartanyon's firstborn and oldest daughter. RIGHT: Dartanyon's second-born child and firstborn son, Darquise No'el Williams.

LEFT: The second apple of his eye, Madisen Marie Williams. Dartanyon's third-born and second daughter. RIGHT: The beat of his heart and his undisputed mini-me, Kaleb Kar'Michah Williams. Dartanyon's fourth child and second-born son.

Dartanyon's inmate badge during his time as a ward of the Federal Bureau of Prisons.

During Dartanyon's 360-degrees of repentance, he issued a public cry of apology and made a plea for forgiveness in the local *Tensas Gazette* newspaper, only to end up where he once was—in prison *again*!

Dartanyon, Nellie, and Madisen during a family visit to the prison.

The determination and resolve to be released were motivated by three tiny packages who did not even know that they were pulling the strings of his heart from behind the scenes—his children. Today, DAW enjoys an open, honest relationship with his girls, his Princesses.

Meet Kaleb Tha Kop! Despite the disdain that DAW had for unscrupulous police during his formative years, during his three-dimensional redemption, he resolved that matter internally and developed a renewed sense of respect and honor for the men and women in blue who serve honorably. He passed this respect on to his youngest. For his fast-and-furious-fourth birthday, he insisted on a Police Party. More kops showed up than kids. Here, Deputy Kaleb is pictured with the Ascension Parish Sheriff's Office.

Today, when DAW meets with his attorneys, he is all smiles. He is establishing companies, licensing brands, confecting contracts, and submitting patents. He is pictured here with his attorneys and legal advisors, Patrick McKenzie and Bryan D. Stewart of Atlanta-based law firm, Morris, Manning and Martin.

The serial entrepreneur. Dartanyon founded a software development company, DuckPond Technologies, Inc. (www.duckpond.tech), named after his childhood hideout and safe place. Pictured here with his development team in Bangkok.

DAW and US Senator from Louisiana, Dr. Bill Cassidy conversing about dyslexia, legislation, and technology regarding the centralization and protection of the consumer-patient financial and healthcare information (see www.medica.systems for more information).

As fate would have it, 10 years after drafting his original manuscript citing Mr. Frank W. Abagnale, DAW shows Mr. Abagnale his own name and quote at the start of volume 2 of his memoir, *The Master Identity Thief, America's Domestic War*.

Decades apart, DAW and Frank W. Abagnale both took a turn down dark paths and perpetrated heinous identity theft crimes. Fortunately and providentially, their lives have come full circle, and the two are committed to joining forces as a dynamic duo to combat the very crimes they carried out. America will be a safer place because of this powerful union.

TRUE CHRONOLOGY IN CRIME

Arrest 1: 2/26/98 (age 18), Simple Burglary, 4th Judicial District
   Court, Monroe-La...Docket No:98F0342
Arrest 2: 8/11/98 (age 18), Theft of Goods, 4th Judicial District
   Court, Monroe-La...Docket No:98F1623
Arrest 3: 10/12/98 (age 18), Theft Valued at Over $500.00, 4th
   Judicial District Court, Monroe-La...Docket No:98F1619
Arrest 4: 11/11/98 (age 19), Issuing Worthless Checks, 4th
   Judicial District Court, Monroe-La...Docket No: 98F1579
Arrest 5: 5/01/99 (age 19), Gambling in Public, 6th Judicial
   District, St. Joseph-La...Docket No: 65, 437
Arrest 6: 6/28/99 (age 19), Possession, Distribution,
   Manufacture, Cultivation of Marijuana and Possession
   of Drug Paraphernalia, Rapides Parish Sheriff's Office,
   Alexander-La...Docket No: N/A

Arrest 7: 7/06/99 (age 19), Aggravated Resisting An Officer by Flight, 6th Judicial District Court, St. Joseph-La...Docket No: 65, 683

Arrest 8: 8/26/99 (age 19), Operating a Motor Vehicle Without a License, Speeding (71/55), 6th Judicial District Court, St. Joseph-La...Docket Nos: 65,796 and 65, 797

Arrest 9: 9/10/99 (age 19), False Pretense, Madison County-Ms, Circuit Court, Docket No: 2000-0201

Arrest 10: 12/01/99 (age 20), Felonious Bad Checks, Adams County Circuit Court, Natchez-Ms...Case No: 99-KR-1433-1

Arrest 11: 2/27/00 (age 20), Aggravated Battery, Tensas Parish Sheriff's Office, St. Joseph-La...Docket No: N/A

Arrest 12: 8/06/00 (age 20), Driving Under Suspension, Speeding (75/55), 6th Judicial District Court, St. Joseph-La...Docket Nos: 67,008 and 67,009

Arrest 13: 10/12/01 (age 21), Probation Violation Warrant, 4th Judicial District, Monroe-La...Docket No: N/A

Arrest 14: 1/25/02 (age 22), Theft, Forgery, Resisting an Officer by Giving False Information, Injuring Public Records, St. Tammany Parish Sheriff's Office, Slidell-La...Docket No: N/A

Arrest 15: 2/18/02 (age 22), Possession of Stolen Property over $500, Concordia Parish Sheriff's Office, Vidalia-La...Docket No: N/A

Arrest 16: 3/5/02 (age 22), Probation Violation Warrant, 4th Judicial District, Monroe-La...Docket No: N/A

Arrest 17: 7/22/02 (age 22), Theft, 24th Judicial District, Jefferson Parish, Gretna-La...Docket No: 02-5513

Arrest 18: 10/22/02 (age 22), Felony Theft, 19th Judicial Court, Baton Rouge-La...Docket No: 4-03-16

Arrest 19: 10/29/02 (age 23), Identity Theft, Theft, Tensas Parish Sheriff's Office, St. Joseph-La...Docket No: N/A

Arrest 20: 2/07/03, (age 23), Probation Violation Warrant, 4th Judicial District Court, Monroe-La...Docket No: N/A

Arrest 21: 3/14/03, (age 23), Conspiracy To Commit Identity Theft, United States Court, Eastern District of Louisiana, New Orleans-La...Docket No: 03-058

Arrest 22: 3/08/05, (age 25), Two Counts of Distribution of Cocaine of 500 grams or more, United States Court, Western District of Louisiana, Baton Rouge-La...Docket No: 05-93-B-M1

Arrest 23: 6/15/16, Contempt of Court Charge (15yr old warrant-2001) Natchez City Police Department, Natchez-Ms...Docket No: N/A

BOOK TWO

AMERICA'S DOMESTIC WAR

A CYBER CRISIS OF IDENTITY THEFT

DARTANYON A. WILLIAMS

יהוה

FOREWORD

Just as Sam Cook of Comparitech.com has documented, "As the world continues its relentless march towards all things digital, data is increasingly exposed. Each individual consumer's personal information now resides on dozens, if not hundreds of servers across the globe. With that fact comes a somewhat obvious result: an increase in identity theft."[1]

According to Symantac.com, Americans are significantly more likely to be victims of identity theft than anyone else. From the same reference: over 791 million identities were stolen in the US in 2016. Identity theft is ubiquitous, and the very

---

1   T., Sam, Sam Cook, Dan Dascalescu, and Nojeemdeen Giwa. "50 Identity Theft Statistics and Facts for 2018 - 2019." Comparitech. https://www. comparitech.com/identity-theft-protection/identity-theft-statistics/.

institutions that are responsible for monitoring and securing the safety of our personal information have too been victimized (recalling the Equifax and Experian breaches of recent memory), our banking systems have been accessed fraudulently, and even the United States Office of Personnel Management was hacked. The Federal Trade Commission (FTC) estimates that on average as many as 9 million Americans have had their identities stolen each year.[2]

Hollywood has tackled the subject as well, producing movies about stolen identities (*The Net* 2.0) and the illegal accessing of top-secret and classified government secrets (*Breach*). When art begins to imitate life and depictions and portrayals of crime reaches to the cinematic screen, then the problem is acute and has evolved to epic proportions.

Yet cybercriminals still find it relatively easy to access consumer data. There were over ninety-six hundred reported data breaches in the US between 2008 and 2019, with over 10 billion records stolen during that time frame, the largest being Equifax, one of the three major credit reporting agencies.[3] The number of potential victims was astonishing and astronomical at 147.9 million, but the type of information exposed was more frightening: names, social security numbers, credit card information, addresses, birth dates, and driver's license numbers.

Identity theft is increasingly a 21st-century problem. As more data moves off of physical paper and onto internet-

---

2   "Identity Theft." Crime Museum. https://www.crimemuseum.org/crime-library/silent-crimes/identity-theft/.

3   Ibid.

connected servers, the chances of that data getting stolen increases as well. Data breaches show no signs of decreasing.

There are three questions we should be asking ourselves about these breaches:

1. Who is accessing our data?
2. How are they accessing our data?
3. What are they doing with the information?

This issue of data breaches and stolen identities has created an entirely new business market that's worth billions of dollars. Credit, identity, and social security number monitoring services have popped up everywhere with various subscription fees, both hidden and blatant.

Dartanyon A. Williams has a unique perspective on this entire issue of identity theft, offering us a deep dive into its nexus between cyberspace and national security, its social ramifications, and its political implications. His background as a former master identity thief and his willingness to discuss his motivations, methods, and mechanics gives us insightful and immediate access to front-line strategies in America's Domestic War against identity theft.

Further, his discovery and exposé on a new, more sophisticated genre within identity theft, *vehicular identity theft*, sounds the alarm on how subtly involved this crime has become and how far the reach is to capture unsuspecting victims, even consumers, companies, and corporations. This revelation demands a united response from legislators to law enforcement officials, from wives to workers, from car dealers to car buyers, from insurers to individuals, and from banks to businesses...Everyone is compelled to be vigilant about protecting the identity of their person and their property.

Even as a retired law enforcement official from the Federal Bureau of Investigations, I have been a victim of credit card fraud, data breaches, and identity theft, proving that no one is exempt from this crime. Identity theft can ruin your life, take years to fix, is very costly, will dampen your morale, and can kill your spirit. We are blessed to have someone become, if you will, an Educator for the uninformed and unsuspecting citizen.

The old adage states: "Give a man a fish, you feed him for a day, teach him how to fish and you feed him for a lifetime." This is so relevant, as Mr. Williams is not only teaching us how to fish, but also training us how not to become the proverbial fish on the hook of a modern-day identity thief.

I end with the Latin phrase "Caveat Emptor" which means, "Let the buyer beware." It's traditionally used in real estate transactions telling the buyer to perform all due diligence before closing the deal. I use it here to say, let the citizen be aware of what's going on with their personal information. Ask one more question: how can we stop these crimes from happening?

Answer: *America's Domestic War: A Cyber Crisis of Identity Theft* provides solutions and a roadmap to mitigate against this type of crime.

—Darryl G. Thornton, CCA, SHRM-SCP, SPHR,
Retired Police Corporal and Former Special Agent,
Federal Bureau of Investigation

HWH

יהוה

ONE

THE TESTIMONY OF
AN EXPERT WITNESS

The police can't protect consumers. People need to
be more aware and educated about identity theft.
You need to be a little bit wiser, a little bit smarter,
and there's nothing wrong with being skeptical.

—Frank Abagnale

When *Catch Me If You Can* came out in 2002 starring Leonardo DiCaprio and Tom Hanks, I was near the peak of my criminal enterprise. I watched as Frank Abagnale's expert check forgery and quick talking played out as vintage versions of my own exploits.[4] Now, years after I've

---

4   While Mr. Abagnale's story was dramatized to great extent, the real life telling
    is significant in its own right. https://www.abagnale.com/comments.htm

stepped away from the printer and closed up shop, I still see the doors that technology opens for those who remain ready to make their millions off of the credit of others. This sweeping perspective is a dark benefit of my past, from the earliest forms of modern fraud to the most advanced tools and technology, and I am blessed to now use that experience for good. By understanding where we came from, and by engaging that formerly opportunistic mind to predict where we might still go, I hope to expose the layers of identity theft that few can understand, much less prevent.

In telling my story, I labored to expose the depth of identity theft from the perspective of a former master identity thief. Now, in this volume, I hope to lay out the pieces of what I learned along the way, like a puzzle that the FBI and Secret Service never quite figured out. A puzzle that will save your family, business, and organization if you understand it well.

Editorials on identity theft tend to be anecdotal testimonies of victims—consumer or merchant—or somewhat educated assumptions by self-acclaimed experts. More often than not, I have found that those assumptions are lacking. Throughout the seven chapters of this volume, there is a repeating cadence of comparison between what is commonly known and what is actually occurring.

Flying below the radar in this way, identity theft has become big business for the criminal elite—more or less its own market and industry. Millions of Americans are affected each year, to the tune of $16.8 billion annually and counting.[5]

---

5   Al Pascual, Kyle Marchini, Sarah Miller, "2018 Identity Fraud: Fraud…

It is an art and a science for the practiced thief, ever matching and outpacing the security professional.

Where's the justice and liberty in ignoring an odious crime that is continually watched but largely passed over for activities that fit the more "traditional" criminal profile? With the subjective analysis of a former criminal mind, I offer a better understanding of the psychology, science, and sophistication of identity theft, so that we can become more proactive rather than reactive in our prevention and apprehension efforts.

CAUSE FOR NATIONAL CONCERN

From 1998 to present day, identity theft has been ranked among the fastest growing crimes in America for twenty-two consecutive years, and it's one that isn't going to solve itself. Not only is a proactive response necessary for personal protection, but for those under our care as well. We can no longer afford *not* to be our brother's keeper. And who is our neighbor but any man, woman, or child who lacks the means to protect and provide for themselves?

As parents first, our children are widely understood to be overlooked victims of identity theft. As business owners, we owe protection of information and financial holdings to the employees in our care and to the customers of our commerce. And as Americans, we are each other's national siblings, electing

---

...Enters a New Era of Complexity," Javelin Research, 2018. https://www.javelinstrategy.com/coverage-area/2018-identity-fraud-fraud-enters-new-era-complexity.

and charging our big brothers and sisters on Capitol Hill with the higher calling and responsibility of national protection.

When I began this work as an outgrowth of my three-dimensional redemption, I did not set out to sound an alarm and spark a call to emergency action. The more I wrote, the more heightened the decibels of a national emergency began to ring. In my story, I am the marginalized criminal expert, a minority in so many ways, speaking to the misinformed and misdirected majority. In this book, I aim to represent the interests of the people I once targeted, who may have seen themselves as exemptions to statistics that will almost certainly claim them without careful prevention.

I write to the consumer and to the merchant, to the voters and to the electorate, to the law enforcement community at large, as well as to Capitol Hill and the White House. To merely *talk* about legislative reform and not *be* about it is to have engaged in the dreaded "more of the same" that we all decry in an election year. What I describe as my story in volume one is, in fact, our national story.

As a convicted felon, my right to vote was reserved for a time. As a restored and concerned citizen, I hope to see our government of, for, and by the people protecting the very identities that now vote that same government into existence.

We are not strangers to redemption of this sort, at least from our highest offices. Recalling only the most recent presidential administrations, none have been without fault—yet all have spoken on the virtues of forward motion.

President Bill Clinton, who said, "I'll never forget who gave me a second chance, and I'll be there for you till the last dog dies," was given his second chance and remained beloved by urban and country communities alike in spite of his indiscretions.

Although he was not speaking of his misdirection around those now infamous weapons of mass destruction, President George W. Bush valued redemption as well, saying, "America is the land of second chance, and when the gates of prison open, the path ahead should lead to a better life…"

President Barak Obama, though indicted by his own race for allegedly not doing as much as he could have for the African American community, spoke in favor of me and my fellow ex-offenders when he said, "I believe people who have paid for their crimes should have the opportunity to contribute to society again."[6]

And in our most recent administration at the time of this writing, for all of his polarity and scandal, President Donald Trump relayed a sentiment I wholeheartedly support: "America is a nation that believes in the power of redemption. America is a nation that believes in second chances—and America is a nation that believes that the best is always yet to come!"

No individual leader will ever measure up. No individual will ever be blameless. Scripture reminds us, "For all have sinned, and come short of the glory of God."[7] There is no way to create a completely safe and victimless society, which means I cannot merely present prevention measures or to-do

---

6　I believe he meant it, too. https://www.usatoday.com/story/news/education/2019/07/11/barack-obama-prison-reform-inmate-felon-clemency-ban-box/1707154001/

7　Rom. 3:23

lists and expect the world to fall in line. Our broken world, which I admittedly contributed to, requires a constant cycle of redemption and second chances, always striving toward the better world that is yet to come—the world I want to finally contribute to in positive ways.

With that in mind, I have presented a combination of pro-active societal structures and potential reactive responses—which cannot be complete without also unraveling the psychology behind the crimes themselves. How else would an employer know that underpaying their employees makes them vulnerable to exploitation as Info Operatives? Neither could I condense my background into a single, neatly tailored introductory paragraph—how else would legislators see the web that is spun when white-collar crime is given a wink and a pass?

It takes a complete understanding of both the facts and experience surrounding identity theft to understand just how thoroughly this crime stretches from the cradle to the grave or from the womb to the tomb. I do not brag or boast when I acknowledge that I was a master identity thief, but I want to use this platform and opportunity to give testimony as an expert witness so that I will be a part of the solution and no longer part of the crisis, whether by omission or commission.

IDENTITY THEFT 101: A BRIEF EXPOSÉ

Without understanding the angles identity thieves use to come at us, from every angle of our lives, we don't realize just how vulnerable we all are today.

Identity theft is adequately, if incompletely, defined as:

the assumption of a person's identity in order, for instance, to obtain credit; to obtain credit cards from banks and retailers; to steal money from existing accounts; to rent apartments or storage units; to apply for loans; or to establish accounts using another's name.[8]

Consider this: if identity theft has remained the fastest growing crime in America for twenty-two consecutive years, and with the picture of Abagnale's checks and impersonations in the mid-century and my own at the millennium, then it's not so far-fetched to name it the crime of the century. How fitting that our era is marked by its unwillingness to simply be ourselves.

Although statisticians may beg to differ, I assure you from experience that this crime is not restricted by race, sex, religion, or age. The laws and strategies and even the software and security measures that are designed to impact this particular crime simply cannot keep pace with the creativity of its perpetrators.

When I tried to write a check to myself with my mom's checkbook or used my dad's credit card account—or when Frank Abagnale forged checks—the official crime was *instrument fraud*. When I printed identification cards and assumed someone else's identity to bolster fraudulent purchases, or

---

8 "Steal an Identity." The Free Dictionary. Farlex. https://legal-dictionary. thefreedictionary.com/Steal+an+Identity.

when Mr. Abagnale posed as an airline pilot, a lawyer, and a doctor, it was *identity theft*. However, in my estimation, the lines between the two are so blurred that they frequently blend into one and the same.

Unfortunately, most people don't take the initiative to educate themselves about these possibilities and distinctions until they become victims themselves, and even then, we are often skewed by our own experience. The danger of this crime is that we have little reason to think of it until it's too late. It targets the most commonplace aspects of our lives, which are often still vulnerable even if we have some kind of a security subscription in place.

NAMING OUR VULNERABILITIES

There are five pieces of identifying information that the identity thief finds value in: your name, your social security number, your date of birth, your driver's license number, and your primary billing address.

The single most important of the five is your social security number (SSN). This is a government-issued, computer-generated, numerical birthmark that identifies you as a free and willing participant in the digital community as an American citizen. Without a SSN, you are virtually nonexistent—to an identity thief, that's exactly what you are: a mannequin, void of life and livelihood.

From elementary school to college, from the gainfully employed schoolteacher to the hopeful retiree at the steel mill to the honorable US military personnel, the SSN is part of daily life for us all. It is how we draw unemployment and retirement benefits alike, how we secure the startup of a new company or apply for a job in tech, or sign with the New York Yankees. No established member of society is exempt.

I'm not asking you to disconnect and get off the grid. To do that would be to give free rein to the unlawful and restrict ourselves entirely. The fact of the matter is that you do have a SSN, and likely all of the rest of these key identifiers, which makes you attractive to the identity thief in many ways.

Your name and SSN complement each other just as wet is inseparable from water. Sure, your name can be changed and your SSN can be deactivated, legally replaced, or illegally substituted, but every change you make in one will ultimately tie back to the other. While there's not much you can do to protect your personal name from circulating within the public domain, the security of your SSN is also limited. It is the most important nine-digit number you will utilize, and with the right vigilance, enables you to live happily and freely, without unwanted invasion into your personal life.

A determined identity thief targets his victims based on names, listed occupations, residential addresses, and creditworthiness. Situated between these inseparable identifiers is your date of birth (DOB). Your DOB is the record of your arrival into the world. Its use determines whether you meet the age criteria for participation in respective venues, assuming an identity of its own. Even in general society, this number assigns you to the baby boomers, Generation X, Generation Y, millennials, or Gen Z classifications, along with all of the implications associated with those groupings.

It doesn't matter if it's your brand-new baby or baby boomer parents, when thieves know where to categorize you, they know how to commercialize you. Using your DOB in concert with other important personal information, the thief will capitalize on whatever your data can provide—like unapproved birthday gifts from you to them. Just as the illegal use of your DOB is essential to the commission of identity theft, your protection of it is as equally, if not more, important to the disarmament and discontinuation of an identity thief's criminal operation.

The fourth essential piece of your systemic identity is your state-issued Driver's License Number (DLN) or Identification Number (IDN). Either can and will sometimes function as a substitute for both your SSN and your DOB, but for the purposes of our discussion here, we will focus our attention on the DLN. Attached to your name, your SSN, your DOB, and your primary mailing or billing address—as well as physical identifiers such as your height, weight, gender, eye color, and even your voter registration status—the DLN is the operational equivalent of your SSN, required for everything from a passport to employment to nearly all forms of lending.

With a valid DLN, an identity thief with counterfeited documentation could perpetuate nearly any scam. Of course, a savvy identity thief can circumvent a valid DLN by using a bogus number instead. Doing business in a technologically advanced society means consumers conduct business with lifeless computers while conscious humans act as little more than monitors. An unconscious, unsuspecting computer allows bogus numbers to slip through undetected until it's too late.

As a potential or former victim, it is healthy to remember that an identity thief can only steal your identity to the extent that you allow them. Admittedly, in today's society of customer convenience, protecting your DLN is difficult, if not impossible. This forced vulnerability compromises the integrity and security of the very data that comprises your identity. Precaution is still better than a cure, and proactivity often prevents the need for a painful reaction. If you take steps to protect the personal data that your DLN represents, you can effectively limit your exposure to the danger and damage of identity theft.

The fifth and final piece of valuable information that's integral to the theft of your identity is your primary mailing or billing address—the location where prospective creditors prefer for you to have lived at least a period of two years in order to show stability. The address an identity thief seeks does not have to be a physical address—remember, I used my dad's post office box address that he had used for more than twenty years with his own creditors.

The use of any other address than what is in your credit profile will trigger the security feature during the instant credit approval process, thereby prompting the need for further verification, which is typically a process of answering various questions centered in and around your credit history. To avoid raising these red flags and security questions, experienced identity thieves will use your registered billing address to get the credit application approved, only to call the creditor back within hours or days of the transaction to provide an alternate address for billing statements. In rare and exhaustive cases, the identity thief won't even bother changing the address to prevent early detection of her scam. This usually occurs when your personal credit has been maximized and depleted and is of no further use to the identity thief.

Your primary address has an important function in the theft of your identity, but like the other pieces of your core identifiers, the effectiveness of its use by an identity thief will ultimately depend on your proactive prevention or quick reaction. These are the essential ingredients to the recipe of identity theft, and determined identity thieves will spare no effort or expense to steal them and spend your life away.

Before you read another word, take this one step to add three layers of security to your identity: call all three major credit bureau agencies at the numbers listed below and place a fraud security alert in your credit profile, even if you have not yet been a victim of identity theft. Before anyone can make a significant purchase as you or in your name—including yourself—the potential creditor will have to verify the legitimacy of the transaction by first verifying the security measures you established in your credit profile. This minor inconvenience is worth the added levels of protection and should be done for anyone in your care as well.

- Experian: 1-888-397-3742, www.experian.com
- Equifax: 1-800-525-6285, www.equifax.com
- Transunion: 1-800-680-7289, www.transunion.com

This cannot protect a business, a bank's customers, or a military or legal organization—so certainly read on to learn how to protect yourself and those in your charge in other ways. But for individuals, that single step goes far in the efforts of identity theft prevention and protection.

As a final introductory word before we dive into the ways thieves obtain and use these identifiers, I must acknowledge that the contents of this book may be used by deviant-minded persons as a means to commit the heinous crime of identity theft. This is not intended to be a map for the tempted but a countermeasure for the audacious. I intend to disarm the identity thief by equipping you with a thorough education on the subject matter.

May the moral law of the universe bend toward the justice that pleases and satisfies the will of Yahweh as expressed in the commandment, "Thou shalt not steal."[9]

---

9   Exodus 20:15

TWO

———————

IDENTITY THEFT 201

*If you adequately educate your community, you
will find that the politicians will be scrambling
to become better educated themselves.*

—Helen Caldicott, M.D.

Common security advice tells you the thief might look over
your shoulder while you access personal information,
much in the manner of my intended strategy at the age
of fifteen, before I realized just how limited my chance to
catch my mom doing the bills would be. Over the years, the
more identities I stole, the more ambition I sought. And the
more confidence I gained, the more conspicuous my informa-
tion traps became.

As this lesson develops, it's important to know and under-
stand the difference between varying types and degrees of

identity theft. First, there is the distinction between instrument fraud and identity theft. Instrument fraud will take your card information and use it as-is to make fraudulent purchases. Often, this is at the degree of petty theft—the stuff of modern-day swipers transaction by transaction, on a relatively small scale, and simple enough to undo. But while your bank was busy looking for red flags in spending patterns and purchase history, I was hiding in plain sight, ready to use as much of your identity as I could get. This is when the degree levels up to aggravated identity theft, collecting enough identifying information to assume someone else's persona and wreak financial and reputational havoc. All are at risk from the most obvious yet least considered avenues.

For example, no one is thinking about the restaurant employee who brought the check and ran your card after dinner at your favorite restaurant. No one thinks twice when picking up a quick bite to eat at a fast-food drive-thru, making a grocery run, or stopping by the bank. We trust our healthcare providers, hotel clerks, and tax preparers. We spout off personal information to retail employees and car salesmen. And as a master identity thief, I was waiting for your card, details, and verification—and I never had to step foot in the door to get them.

The identity thief believes that every commercial establishment employs someone with whom he or she can collaborate to steal valuable information. Often, they are right. The rationale is that an irresistible temptation—the financial opportunity that minimum wage employers refuse to provide—will appeal to even the most honest and hardworking people.

Employees who are living check-to-check and working endless hours can't afford to let such an easy supplemental income source pass them by. [10]

In my story, you saw me take boxes of carbon and photocopies of cards out of hotel storage rooms, fish through trash, and employ willing staffers from car dealerships, hospitals, tax preparation firms, banks, and almost anywhere else sensitive consumer data was accessible. But Info Operatives come in all occupations and professions. One of the easiest is through the use of skimmers, which are readily available data collector devices for anyone who wants to find them.

In that scenario, the identity thief will usually propose to give the compromised employee, turned Info Operative, thirty to fifty dollars for each driver's license and five to fifteen dollars for each credit/debit card they swipe through the skimmer. This is an obvious, significant increase in pay compared to the hourly wage of $7.25 to $10.00 they might otherwise make.

Surely you can remember a time or ten when you were out dining with family and friends or having a few drinks and you gave the bartender or courteous waitress your credit/debit card to settle the ticket. With their back turned or out of sight, the contracted side-hustling, underpaid employee could have easily swiped your card through this second data collection

---

10 If we're looking for solutions, we have to start with living wages for honest work. You'll notice that the same conditions that draw people into identity theft roles also lock them into the underpaid agricultural fields that my family worked and that effectively enslave children trying to help their families survive. https://psmag.com/social-justice/the-young-hands-that-feed-us

skimmer that's about two inches in length and a half-inch in width. If you're even paying attention at all, that second swipe appears to be part of the intended transaction. More likely, you never see a thing.

Australia has caught on to these creative, accessible, and all too easy identity theft and device fraud techniques. There, service personnel employ a best practice of prevention by processing card transactions in your presence, right where the services are rendered. Though we don't yet hold a similar law or policy in the US, lifeless self-checkout terminals, if anything, aid and abet credit card fraud in the absence of animated intelligence with real people. The dated security measures at point of sale and self-checkout terminals are skillfully circumvented and defrauded.

Your internal wheels might be turning right now, beginning to see where new dangers lay and what you might do to protect yourself while waiting for policy to become more proactive and practical. The answer is certainly not to stay away and never make a purchase again—after all, this is just one quick example of a near endless supply of tools that the identity thief can use. To give an example of each trap that can be and has been laid to catch your personal information would require a catalog of its own.

With that quick example, I trust your eyes are now opened a little bit wider, maybe your eyebrows are a little bit higher. It's becoming clear just how little consumers, merchants, and policymakers know about the risks we all face. Solving this problem will require a combination of simple solutions (such a table-side, real-time card-swiping policy), innovative prevention (such as thorough industry experts who think like industry expert criminals), and complex consideration (such as resolving our underpaid, overworked employment system).

In this chapter, we're going to continue to uncover the broad tactics identity thieves use in order to better understand where to direct those solutions, prevention techniques, and systemic considerations. Let's begin with what I see as the three mainstream categories of identity theft: cyber, suicidal, and social. There's yet another category that exists all by itself that I call "Vehicular Identity Theft," which I'll address specifically in a later chapter.

CYBER IDENTITY THEFT

Arguably, the form of identity theft to which we are most frequently exposed, cyber identity theft is almost exclusively carried out in cyberspace as part of designed treason and determined espionage. This is the stereotype of dark hackers using technological tools to access and steal your identity from the data systems of private enterprise and public corporations, often in partnership with or under the direction of foreign entities.

These types of thieves usually have no intentions of interacting with you personally. For them, it's a numbers game. They steal as much personal information as they can and group it together in packs (personal information package, or PIP) to sell to the highest bidder. A single PIP might contain a couple dozen or several thousand stolen identities and can cost a prospective buyer as much as ten thousand dollars, depending on the source and quality. The smaller PIPs, containing maybe twenty-five stolen identities, cost as little as three hundred dollars.

In my experience, cyber identity thieves are usually independent operatives, though frequently contracted by or connected to organized crime in some way. Some will hack into your private networks and steal personal information for sport or for some side money as they sell PIPs off to more hands-on identity thieves, while others work with the direct intention of robbing you blind. Granted, the authorities do sometimes catch a hacking cyber identity thief, but only when carelessness or greed take over and lead to sloppiness.

This is the most difficult kind of identity theft to catch, because the cyber thief often works from satellite or remote locations through a convoluted labyrinth of links, IP addresses, and milli-nomadic pings. Most of the organized crime through which PIPs are filtered and sold have strong customer relations and high fraudulent activity in Mexico, Brazil, and in the United States, while the thieves themselves are often working within the United States.[11] I knew of cyber thieves who had the ability to compromise mainframes while sitting in a public park or riding around in a residential neighborhood. This type of breach is rather simplistic. While the platform of this book does not permit me to delve into the deeper and darker mysteries of cybersecurity breaches at large, near and far, cyber identity thieves are masterminds with ransomware, malware,

---

11 While a good deal of this is from my experience in the field, you can track the stats here https://www.comparitech.com/identity-theft-protection/identity-theft-statistics/ and www.paymentcardsandmobile.com

viruses, Trojan horses, spyware, and increasingly sophisticated tricks of the cyber trade.

High-tech cyber thieves are responsible for the data breaches you see making the headlines of the evening news— from credit bureaus to banks to schools[12]—though the purchase of a PIP is not as easy as you might think. They are typically posted for sale under the guise of US-owned and operated company websites, using encryptions and purchased access codes that can only be interpreted or identified by professional identity thieves or informed law enforcement.

While most of us do business with companies that have had or will have big data breaches, the amount of times we change our passwords does not correspond with actually stolen identities. Those PIPs are challenging to access and come in sets of thousands, which means the odds of organized crime actually obtaining and using your information from one of those sets are not as high as the odds of your information landing in the PIP in the first place. I applaud the increasing awareness around cybersecurity and the attempts to keep consumers safe, but our identity

---

12 "Equifax Data Breach Settlement." Federal Trade Commission, September 9, 2019. https://www.ftc.gov/enforcement/cases-proceedings/refunds/equifax-data-breach-settlement.

   CBS/AP. "Capital One Data Breach Hits More than 100 Million People Applying for Credit." CBS News. CBS Interactive, July 30, 2019. https://www.cbsnews.com/amp/news/capital-one-data-breach-2019-more-than-100-million-people-applying-for-credit-affected-today-2019-07-29/.

   Murphy, Justin. "Not Just Capital One, Equifax: Data Breaches at School, Risking Your Family's Security." USA Today. Gannett Satellite Information Network, August 4, 2019. https://www.usatoday.com/story/news/education/2019/08/03/data-breach-back-to-school-2019-cyber-security-hacker-ransomware/1899331001/.

theft prevention measures cannot stop there. There are major atrocities in process all throughout America's political system.

SUICIDAL IDENTITY THEFT

In recent years, a new form of identity theft has emerged, heretofore uncategorized and unnamed, but that I refer to as suicidal identity theft. It is the act of fraud committed against yourself using your own personal information. I've termed it suicidal identity theft. Instead of exploiting the instant credit market, this type of fraud is typically perpetrated on existing accounts. It is self-imposed. We most readily connect it with insurance fraud, such as setting your house on fire to collect a premium, but it goes much deeper than that.

Maxed out credit accounts and tapped out bank accounts are the norm rather than the exception, but suicidal identity theft never intends to climb out of the pit. These individuals would hit their limits intentionally, then report the activity as fraudulent. Or, for example, when we talk about instrument fraud, they might float checks on an account that has no balance. These subversive strategies are rampant with college students who have no concept of budgeting or consciousness of the consequences for their actions. But there's another demographic for this type of fraud, fueled not by ignorance but by desperation: the middle-aged, mismanaged, middle America.

I venture that suicidal identity theft reached its zenith during the height of the Great Recession. From 2008 to 2010, a great majority of the American proletariat felt powerless— victims of the insatiable greed for excess that rocked Wall

Street and consumed Main Street. Wall Street wasn't the only complicit participant in those financial crimes—the borrowers were guilty of securing fraudulent loans they could not afford to repay. The world watched as Middle America blamed everything and everybody but itself for the frauds committed and still needed to commit to merely survive. We watched as big bankers executed the same fraud and deception for which average Americans would have been prosecuted if the tables were turned. While "too big to fail" corporations got bailouts, the American people got pink slips as their losses rippled into their investments, their savings, and in some cases, into a loss of regard for the rule of law. In that first year, there were 11.1 million new cases of identity theft reported. When the economy began to show signs of improvement in 2010, that number dropped by 3 million.[13] Watch the math and follow the numbers.

A sense of desperation tinged with revenge opened up a window of opportunity to defraud creditors using the information most readily available to them: their own. Of course, if Wall Street regulators would have checked their own egregious, often fraudulent business practices instead of accepting bribes and kickbacks to lay back and not blow the whistle—it is possible that fewer consumers would have hit that point of desperation.

Less dramatic but undoubtedly more common is the unscrupulous college student, a role I played for a semester. Student credit cards are maxed out and reported as lost or stolen every day, with the false impression of being victimized

---

13   Javelin Strategy and Research's 2011 Identity Fraud Survey.

by a white-collar criminal. The case is made all the more convincing when a false police report is filed and mailed or faxed to the credit card company's security department. Not only is the perpetrator initially cleared of all suspicion, but they soon receive a new card with a refreshed spending limit.

Just in case a mischievous mind reading this might be tempted to commit fraud in this way, please be admonished that it is not in your best interest to try your luck, no matter how tight your finances. Self-victimization is only realized to the extent of the need for financial relief—and one run through a credit card is rarely enough to get and stay out of a debt-riddled hole. This kind of identity theft is typically detected when someone tries to commit the scam more than once, not knowing that after the first false claim was honored, they were put on the credit card company's high-risk watch list.

SOCIAL IDENTITY THEFT

The scheme of manufacturing and counterfeiting identification documents is what I call social identity theft. Here the thief engages the community under the cover of a stolen identity to perpetrate fraudulent scams for personal gain. I cannot emphasize enough how this is by far the most damaging and devastating form of identity theft.

The dangers of social identity theft not only target the consumer and devastate the merchant, but they also breach law enforcement and military communities, largely undetected. I have seen police badges replicated to be used to impersonate police officers during traffic stops, to conduct illegal searches and seizures, to gain access to private homes, and to enter privileged communities. Military IDs can easily be duplicated to gain access to otherwise prohibited areas, and manufacturing facility IDs of any kind can be reproduced for dubious entry as well. Here in Louisiana, we house two of the largest petroleum refineries in the United States, belonging to Shell Geismar Chemical and Exxon Mobil in Baton Rouge. The ever-present threat of a terroristic identity theft scheme to gain access and explode devastation is more real and possible than we realize.

There are also college IDs, employee identification cards, and club membership identification—if it requires identifying documentation, an adept social identity thief has the means to replicate it. It's an economic concern, a security concern— even part of the undocumented immigration concerns.

A social identity thief intends to reproduce your identity using specific tools: high-quality digital camera, a laptop computer, a scanner, copier, and paper printer; plus some special but easily accessible equipment: an ID printer, laminating machine, the skimmer I explained earlier, an encoder, and an embosser. With your identity stolen, they will reproduce every piece of paper and/or plastic needed to exhaust your creditworthiness and deplete your liquid assets.

Even though there is a paper trail to be followed, catching a shrewd social identity thief is not all that simple and will usually require a slip-up or misstep on his or her part. While my early record of repeated arrests drew enough attention to build a case against me, the FBI never understood the full extent of my crimes, and after that eighteen-month sentencing, they never caught me again for those offenses.

While we're all much more heavily exposed to cyber identity thieves than any others, there's only a chance that your stolen identity will be exploited in those breaches, but if you are a victim of a data breach on any level you should take steps to protect your identity. On the other hand, if a social identity thief gets his hands on your personal information, it's only a matter of time before looming doom turns into definite disaster, especially if your credentials carry the potential to net multiple thousands of dollars within a fourteen- to twenty-one-day window of opportunity.

In both cyber and social threats, the instant credit market is the vehicle to fast fortune. The instant credit gateway to debt was born of what I identify as the econo-psychology behind instant gratification, a palatable term for the instant greed of human nature. But it is also necessary to recognize that the "instance" works both ways, for and against the consumer and merchant when a feigned need begets the real fraud of identity theft instantaneously. Without the convenience of instant credit, identity thieves would be forced to "take over" their victims' existing credit accounts, causing them to have a greater risk of detection. Instead, the poorly regulated instant credit market empowers the identity thief to open up new accounts and max out those new lines of credit within days, all before the scam is even detected. The instant credit market removes the time barriers that would otherwise delay the approval process and require further verification. Instant credit is the go-to niche for most social identity thieves—and for the master identity thieves, as documented in my story, instant approvals are instant access to transact instant wealth.

A cyber identity thief is only one source of supply for the identities that a social identity thief uses to perpetrate his scams. In fact, I rarely used the capabilities of the cyber thieves that worked under my direction. Instead, I obtained most of my victims' identities from Info Operatives within the employ of hospitals, banks, hotels, tax companies, cell phone companies, retail stores, gas stations, restaurants, phone companies, local law enforcement, and a host of other businesses who unwittingly supplied me with enough people (on paper) to populate a thriving middle class metropolis. This was the shortcut to my former riches, and as the largely misunderstood and underestimated side of identity theft, will be the focus of much of this volume.

THE SCIENCE OF IDENTITY THEFT: SOCIAL ENGINEERING

Social identity theft has many manipulations, all of which exist as part of a crime that has developed into a criminal science. They are masters of engagement. As I recounted the social tools and strategies I developed and used to enhance my craft, I identified the multifaceted structure I coined years ago called social engineering.[14] Mastering the practices of my past

---

14 Recently, I have been surprised to see an increase in use of this same term. https://www.youtube.com/watch?v=Vo1urF6S4uo and https://en.wikipedia.org/wiki/Social_engineering_(security)

and for identity thieves over the years took deep introspection. How did I do what I did? How do identity thieves consistently slip under the collective societal radar? In this section, I will unpack the multifaceted nature of the science of identity theft social engineering.

I believe there are seven components to identity theft social engineering, which is the extraordinary ability to deceive and defraud under false pretenses in the midst of ordinary circumstances. If the number seven is said to be the number of completion, then these seven characteristics combine to complete the criminality of the social identity thief.

1. STUDIED DECEPTION

A cyber identity thief, social identity thief, and a suicidal identity thief all share this common trait of studied deception, inherent in each of their mentalities and intrinsic in the nature of their crimes. These thought processes are at once proactive and premeditated—the identity thief must practice the crime in both mind and manner prior to its actual commission.

Studied deception happens in a quiet place, where one can contemplate and formulate ways to deceive the victim of the scam. I found those contemplative moments during retreats to Duck Pond Road, in the hoe fields, driving back and forth between towns, waiting to bond out of jail, and in my print studio, where every stolen identity and scam came to life.

To help you gain an idea of how studied deception works in practice, I recall a time when I needed two key pieces of information in order to deepen my access to an account, so I simply called the victim at home.

My first thought was that the victim likely had caller ID, which made it necessary for me to place the call with a prepaid calling card that would show up as a 1-800-number, "Out-of-area," or "Unavailable." Then, once I got the victim on the phone, I would pretend I was calling from a computer terminal at company headquarters, with all his account information displayed on my computer screen. With these factors in mind, I gave him a call from an untraceable number.

With the victim on the phone, I announced that the purpose of my call was promotional, then addressed him by his complete name. I also took the initiative to verify some of the personal information I already had on hand. While I recited his SSN, DOB, and home mailing address under the pretense of verifying accuracy, I typed on the computer keyboard loud enough for him to overhear. This, of course, made him comfortable enough to answer any question I would ask afterward, thereby putting him in a vulnerable position to provide the detailed personal information that I needed to complete my scam.

When it was clear that he trusted my story, I reversed the conversation and asked him to answer two more security questions to complete the identification verification process. He easily offered both his dog's name and mother's maiden name, the missing pieces I needed to take over any of his accounts on which he had added these two names as additional security information. This procedural practice is called "vishing" and is one of many ways that studied deception is manifested.

The entire scam could have been exposed if he had asked (and insisted) to call me back at a specified number to complete the call. If, in fact, the incoming call was computer generated as I had lied and said it was, then surely there's always a call back number that would route through a similarly secure automation system. This is just one of many manifestations of studied deception, obstructed only by the informed mind who can manage to think ahead.

2. MNEMONIC DISCIPLINE

An oblivious mind is of no use to an identity thief. This practice requires constant awareness and an impeccable memory. Mnemonic discipline is the trained ability to memorize and shuffle names and numbers of stolen identities to use them collectively or interchangeably as the occasion requires.

The memory of an identity thief is conditioned by the demands of the crime. At one point in my practice I developed both a photographic and eidetic memory. I could capture and commit all sixteen credit card numbers and their expiration dates to memory at a single glance. While the detailed personal information to any given victim's identity is rarely committed to permanent memory, the season of deception requires a fabricated biography that accompanies impersonation. For the suicidal identity thief, the biography is their own, but it will usually include embellished life stories that they must memorize to avoid personal exposure during a potential investigation.

I personally committed as many as twenty victim identity profiles and fabricated biographies to memory at any given time. My memory served as the back up to the memories of my Field Operatives, who were required to assume five stolen identities alternately, just in case one of the identities went bad while navigating their weekly merchant itinerary.

Wherever memory would fail me or my Field Operatives, I kept reference files and folders on a jump drive connected to a lanyard that I wore around my neck. At all times, I knew which identities were active and which could be a phone call away in the event that someone needed me to affirm any portion of the personal information from their profile.

To this very day, I still remember some of the names of my victims, and not just my parents and grandparents. If you fortify your identity, creating brick walls and dead ends for a potential thief, it will never be a second thought.

3. PRACTICED PERCEPTION

Any form of identity theft requires its perpetrators to be insightful and thorough in order to perceive and, therefore, prevent probable arrest and prosecution. Practiced perception is a heightened awareness—the sixth sense I spoke of many times in my story. It is the ability to read the room through the lens of a controlled paranoia rooted in silent suspicion. The analytical mind of a social identity thief is heavily self-aware, as well as cognizant of the ambiance, character, and conduct of the environment in which the scam is committed.

The characteristic of practiced perception is not much different from Extrasensory Perception (ESP). I do not at all intend to imply that identity thieves possess some kind of clairvoyance, but there does seem to be a subconscious, almost telepathic intuition moving between the minds of criminals, consumers, merchants, and cops. Maybe these keen and uncanny abilities are inspired by principalities and powers of darkness. I can't be sure or certain of this latter possibility, but the experienced identity thief can perceive which associates are more lenient or lackadaisical. They can gauge the environment to know when loss prevention is on alert and where plainclothes enforcers might be.

Whether it's an intrinsic skill, demonic possession, or experiential knowledge, practiced perception is vital for any identity thief. Each of my criminal arrests later became part of training for freshmen Field Operatives.

One such lesson was that, for some reason or another, I found that most plainclothes cops liked to adorn themselves with a particular pocketknife that has a stainless steel or black metal clip used to tuck the knife on the inside of their pants pockets. I wasn't sure whether the pocketknife was used as a survival tool or if it is some kind of fad in the law enforcement community, but after one particular arrest, I perceived it to be an outward sign of the undercover police badge it represented.

Whenever I would spot a supposed customer wearing that pocketknife in the vicinity where I intended to commit identity theft, I retreated the scam and instead proceeded to purchase an insignificant item with cash to erase any suspicion. In fact, that knife made such an impression on me that it became required insignia for my Field Operatives and they wore them whenever it might be beneficial to communicate any meaning and purpose attached to it.

For the social identity thief, no signal is too small or insignificant. As such, more goes unnoticed by security staff, detectives, and investigators than the practiced identity thief in action.

4. PERSONALITY PERSUASION

If you think about it, the very nature of identity theft is rooted in impersonation. When we consider iconic Hollywood roles, we can plainly see how Oscar-worthy performances persuaded us to become fans and even devotees of these respective actors, regardless of their everyday roles and real-life personalities. Although an identity thief might not write their plans out like a Hollywood production, the scam still has its script.

As the writer, director, and executive producer of countless identity theft operations, I have watched, worked, and walked within the scene of many scams to witness personality persuasion performances worthy of any accolade or award. The role of a social identity thief requires the Field Operative to be both personable and professional at the moment of the scam. This pretended propriety aims to silence the alarm of suspicion.

Personality persuasion is not so much a natural talent or gifted ability as it is a cultivated and calculated persona. One doesn't need to have inherent and emanating virtues of charisma to defraud their victims. The persuasion of their scam is predicated on intentional deceit.

5. COSTUME COMMUNICATION

The attire of a social identity thief is the voiceless but visual complement to personality persuasion. Looking the part counts for a solid half of the social identity thief's operations and subsequent success—even an amateur knows better than to adorn herself as a wolf when the scam calls for her to be dressed in sheep's clothing. Biblical Rebekah knew that young Jacob lacked the training in personality persuasion and needed some supplemental cover. So she accessed Esau's wardrobe in order for the scam to be successful.[15]

The attire that matches a chosen, stolen identity must be both selective and seductive, simultaneously detracting from suspicion and drawing the right kind of attention. If the thief can spark colloquial inquiries of unsuspecting merchant victims, they can control the conversation and steer it away from suspicion—as the next quality will convey.

Many merchant-victims all too often fall into the same trusting acceptance that Isaac did when he felt for his eldest son's furs.[16] Instead of confirming their suspicions, they second guess themselves to avoid causing offense. This is why my Field Operatives ranged in gender and age to match the Beacon score we knew would maximize profit potential. Typically, the costume must communicate a reflection of the purchase price if the scam is to be successful.

Retailers and merchants can learn to subvert the deceitful disguise of costume communication by adopting a policy and practice of objective customer analysis—properly trained rather than fueled and fooled by stereotypes and profiling—to address the social identity thief as they attempt to distract you with the surefire characteristic of calculated conversation.

6. CALCULATED CONVERSATION

This sixth characteristic is not a product to be confused with the gift of gab but is a learned art form that's specifically crafted

---

15 Genesis 27:15
16 Genesis 27:22

towards closing the deal. Calculated conversation is the live performance of previous experiences. It is the anticipation of certain responses within situational verbal exchanges. Sometimes it's casual, sometimes concise, but always controlled.

With calculated conversation, the identity thief seals the impression of legitimate business. Each talking point is controlled and directed. Small talk is useful only if the thief dominates the dialogue and moves it along toward a successful transaction.

My own calculated conversation was rooted in common courtesy. In my infancy as a wordsmith, I deliberately elevated my vocabulary to intimidate, intrigue, and impress the sales associates of my merchant-victims to distract them from the true purpose of my presence. My rhetoric was a disguise for fraud. While not all social identity thieves go to the lengths that I did to structure their conversation, most refine their language and all learn about the objectives of the people with whom they intend to transact business.

Calculated conversation can be identified by a learned set of ears. If someone appears to know more about the product or objective than its representative, for example, there's a good chance that you are transacting with some identity theft social engineering. Be mindful of the content of the transacting conversation and try not to allow your commitment to customer service silence an irrepressible cause for alarm.

7. PRESENCE OF MIND

Whenever a social identity thief perceives that you sense the insincerity of his calculated conversation, presence of mind will activate to maneuver and manage the sudden disruption. This is the seventh and last characteristic that completes the science of identity theft social engineering. A social identity thief's ability to think and act quickly in reaction to the discovery of the scam is vital to their continued liberty and to the entire operation. If practiced perception functions as an alert system, then presence of mind is the alarm mechanism that springs them into escape mode to evade capture.

Presence of mind is the characteristic that informs the details of an escape plan that advises the social thief to attend a transaction terminal that's close to an exit. A getaway car or two, usually within walking or running distance in case things get really bad, is often on hand—but presence of mind is what gets the thief there at all. Without this characteristic, the entire operation will be precariously destined for debacle. The mindset is one of "ball but don't fall," with the goal of surviving each transaction without arrest, then repeating it until the escapade suspends in voluntary recess to avert the conclusion of forced retirement due to criminal arrest.

This internal drive assisted me out of many close calls as a master identity thief, yet ironically, it is the characteristic that we most need as potential victims. Direct your presence of mind to the ever-impending threat of breach of security that surrounds your identity. The security of your identity will be decided by your ability to think ahead about the potential of identity theft and to act quickly to reduce your risk of exposure to victimization.

Of course, there's only so much you can do as a single individual. Our present fight against identity theft is disadvantaged by the lack of state and federal laws that would do much to protect us, notwithstanding the limited manpower and strained efforts within the law enforcement community that can't keep pace or track of transient and trending crimes that evolve daily.

COLLABORATIVE IDENTITY THEFT

The identity thief who operates solo will often do their work in a similar manner that I stole my parents' identities, without the knowledge and assistance of anyone else at all. With exception to the petty fraud of suicidal identity theft, the requirements for an efficient operation of any kind of expanded identity theft are exacting. For this reason, most cyber and social identity thieves seek various collaborations in order to have a supplemental system of support.

Collaborations require a network of individuals where everyone feeds and functions off their interdependent roles. The freelance cyber identity thief often collaborates with the social identity thief to supply the latter with PIPs, who in turn processes and materializes the stolen identities. When social identity thieves collaborate, it's typically within the operation of a full-scaled, structured organization.

An identity theft organization will most often be made up of four key positions: a Superintendent, a Printer, Info Operatives, and Field Operatives.

During my tenure as a master identity thief, my organizational *modus operandi* invited me to assume the respective duties of all the key positions in the operation at varying points, with the exception of the Info Operative. At different times, I acted as a Superintendent, Printer, Field Operative, and the less involved Superintendent-as-Financier.

By all accounts and authorities, the Superintendent is the ringleader of the operation. This is the person who bankrolls the entire operation—from defraying the cost of publishing counterfeited documentation to providing costume clothing, traveling expenses, and legal fees to setting and meeting the payroll for the entire organization. If a dollar is spent, the Superintendent funds it.

There is rarely a chain of command within an identity theft ring, as every decision and direction comes solely at the discretion of the Superintendent. The Superintendent usually works from behind the scenes, creating roadmaps in the form of merchant itineraries and merchandise lists. This person is a jack and master of all trades respecting his craft, highly competent and unwaveringly capable of meeting all the requirements of the three remaining positions.

In recent years, this role has changed somewhat due in part to the extended reach of identity theft conspiracy charges. Superintendents are becoming less involved in the day-to-day operations of their organizations and are eliminating their interactivity with Field Operatives in a strategic move to limit the reach of conspiratorial allegations. Most supervisory duties are delegated to the Printer, leaving the Superintendent as more Financier than direct manager.

With the role moving further away from regular operations, more and more people without a working knowledge of identity theft are turning out to be Financiers of identity theft organizations. An investment of ten thousand dollars to cover the startup costs of a three- to four-member ring can very easily bring a two to three-week return-on-investment of one hundred thousand dollars. This is altogether too attractive, irresistible, and addictive for a conscience that pretends not to know better. These "throw the brick and hide the hand" criminals might not know the ins and outs of identity theft, but they recognize opportunity and opt to engage and enlist someone who does.

The Superintendent might be the drive behind the organization, but the Printer provides the movement. This is the person responsible for reproducing and fabricating every document needed to perpetrate a single act of identity theft. The Printer works with PIPs (Personal Information Packages) and VINs (vehicle identification numbers), as well as the printing supplies and operating software and hardware for the operation. With Superintendents taking the back seat to invest cash into crime, these days Printers are doubling as Superintendents of identity theft rings in all but name, with more oversight and control than ever before. As the brain and heart of this organized deception, the Printer is the wizard behind the curtain of today's identity theft Land of Oz.

Without Info Operatives—the role responsible for stealing your personal information in the first place—an organization would be victimless. Their main job is to exploit their day-to-day position in life by stealing your personal information from supposed safe spaces—banks, hotels, retail spaces, and so much more—and positioning it for resale. Without the flow of personal information, there can be no lucrative operation. The Info Operative is only limited by the age

requirements of employment. Everyone else has great poten-
tial. You never know who, where, or when they're at work
right before your eyes.[17]

The Field Operative is just as covert, embodying the coun-
terfeited documents produced by the Printer and executing
the plans envisioned by the Superintendent. An operation
might target a certain set of stores in a specific region, dis-
trict, or entire state, and that becomes the Field Operative's
assignment. This is the person who engages and expresses the
seven characteristics of identity theft social engineering to the
greatest degree. This is the biggest money maker and risk taker
among those who receive salaries within the organization.

TRICKS OF THE TRADE

Probably the oldest way that identity thieves gain access to
your personal information is to simply *steal your wallet or
purse*. By stealing your wallet, an identity thief has immediate
access to key pieces of information that identify you. Losing or
having your purse or wallet stolen is a terrible feeling, but hav-
ing their contents fraudulently exploited is a matter of serious
consequence. While this is no longer a predominant way in
which identities are stolen, the pickpockets and purse-snatch-
ers of today know that your personal information is more
valuable than the couple of hundred dollars you may have in

---

17 Not even the sky's the limit—identity theft occurred from space in 2019:
"NASA astronaut accused of stealing identity, accessing bank account of
estranged wife while in space: report," *Fox News*, August 24, 2019.

cash. Identity thieves are opportunists, after all, and no effort should be spared to safeguard your personal property.

Another one of the classic ways identity thieves steal your identity is to submit a *change-of-address* with your local post office. The intention is to reroute your mail to a designated address that will grant unrestricted access to the sensitive information you receive via the postal system.

US Post Offices don't ask many questions when submitting a change-of-address form, which in the past meant anybody could reroute your private mail to any address without having to do so much as provide valid identification. Today, there are some minor verification steps involved that make this a more challenging step without much reward—they have to provide a credit card number that will process a one-dollar charge to "prevent fraud and make sure you're the one making the change."[18] Whether they want to provide that information depends on whether the result is worth the effort. Like stealing your wallet, the change-of-address method has become a thing of the past, used only as a last resort, but can easily be manipulated by establishing and using new trade lines in the victim's name. So much for that so-called preventative, proactive measure.

When a change of address seems to be too complicated or too time-consuming, identity thieves settle for committing the traditional method of mail theft. This occurs when identity thieves simply walk or drive up to an accessible mailbox,

18 "Change Your Address and Other U.S. Post Office Services." USAGov. https://www.usa.gov/post-office.

pretend to be delivering or collecting the mail, and steal it. This method of stealing personal information may very well be one of the oldest, but nonetheless, it remains one of the most effective ways that identity thieves steal your personal information.

If your mailbox isn't situated in the local post office or secured by a lock and key or door slot, *mailbox theft* basically guarantees the identity thief the personal information they seek. Mailboxes that are stationed by the roadside or fixed to the house are most vulnerable to mail theft. Whether you put mail out for pick up or have it delivered, either way, your personal information is readily accessible to identity thieves who might ride from neighborhood to neighborhood in search of potential mailbox victims.

In my opinion, the boldest, riskiest (and stupidest) way to steal personal information is by *shoulder surfing*. This method merely requires a desperate identity thief to look over your shoulder or position a recording near where you're making a verbal transaction. If you recall, this was my initial intended strategy with my dad's Capital One card. This is the Peeping Tom stepping out of the darkness and into the public arena to capture a glimpse of your personal information.

Shoulder surfers are not as obvious as their name suggests. They are skilled socialites armed with the intent and purpose to steal your identity. However, serious identity thieves deliberately bypass it because of the associated risks.

Another set of tools that harken back to my youngest days was that of *trashcan pillaging and dumpster diving*. This is the method I adopted to get my dad's credit card information when shoulder surfing was clearly too risky. It's how I gained access and set myself on this path in the first place.

Dumpster diving differs only in the location and scope of the trash in question. While trashcans are typically pillaged on an individual basis, dumpster diving often targets corporate America. Taking a dive into a commercial dumpster may be less suspicious than pillaging through residential garbage, but both methods are equally dangerous to the potential victims. Until recently, corporate America as a whole was quite careless with the disposal of documents containing sensitive information, giving dumpster divers privileged access to all kinds of confidential data. With the arrival of onsite shredding services and digital data storage, dumpster diving has become less attractive to identity thieves, causing them to become inventors and innovators of more advanced technological thievery.

Although industry experts love to hype up the scenarios, you are hardly likely to find an identity thief rummaging through the garbage in your backyard. Still, because prevention is better than reactionary resolutions, care should be taken to properly dispose of any documentation that contains sensitive information.

Most identity thieves prefer to take a low profile, which is where the *skimmer* comes in. This is the device we discussed at the beginning of the chapter, which collects your information right under your nose. It is difficult if not impossible to defend against a skimmer when it's not so easily identified. You will also hear reports of skimmers being affixed to self-service gas pumps and to ATMs as well, wherever you slide your card down or across for scanning as opposed to inserting it into the machine itself. It is much safer to use ATMs at reputable banks rather than the independently owned and operated machines in gas stations and on curbsides that have higher fees but less money, less security, and less monitoring.

When skimmers become too risky to install or operate, *overlays* are used to do the trick every time. An overlay is a device that gives the appearance of authenticity and is laid atop the card entrance of the ATM or gas pump card reader to collect your personal banking information as your card is inserted into the machine. The ATM transaction will continue normally, and at the same time, your account information will be transmitted to a remote computer to be exploited in the future, sometimes within hours after it has been stolen.

By the time overlays are discovered, the damage has been done and the thief is nowhere in sight. Like skimmers, overlays remain one of the most effective ways to steal your personal information. They are completely concealed from the natural eye and are often discovered by trained security professionals.

The example I shared within the art of studied deception was one of *vishing*, which is simply placing voice calls under the pretense of a legitimate company or reputable organization seeking to gather your personal information. Even in today's marketplace, it is still effective for identity thieves to prey on the elderly and youthful alike, intending to exploit both their ignorance and incognizance.

When dumpster divers and trashcan pillagers can no longer count another's trash as their treasure, social identity thieves immediately turn to either their retail spaces or to the methods and rewards of *cyber identity theft* to supply them with unlimited amounts of personal information. Some of these methods are more complicated than others and require specialized skills to engage, while others are less sophisticated and just as lethal. The remaining identity theft tools are indeed evolutionary, accelerating identity theft to a level beyond capture and control.

For years data breaches have been the stuff of breaking news. Almost every day we hear or read news reports that some major company's databank was hacked and millions of consumers' PII—personally identifiable information—was lost or stolen. Some of the companies are just plain careless with their consumers' personal information—systematically, cybersecurity software needs to be manned and monitored with automatic updates to stay ahead of hackers. But in many ways, humans are smarter than the computers they make. Data breaches will never stop occurring as long as companies continue to have computers monitor computers instead of the living people who built and installed the computer security software to begin with.

Online shopping is another vehicle identity thieves use to beguile you into handing over your personal information. They will duplicate the online storefront of a reputable retailer and offer unbeatable deals to entice you to use your PII as a customer on their website. The identity thief will then log into the back office of the fictitious website to collect your personal information and use it to complete a legitimate transaction in your name with a real retailer to avoid immediate detection, then hold on to that information and use it in future fraudulent transactions.

File sharing and P2P (peer-to-peer networking) has become another attractive way for identity thieves to gain access to your personal information. Any websites on which files are shared on the same hard drive carries with it the possibility of public disclosure of your personal or profile information whenever you connect. This usually happens by triggering a glitch in the operating software, giving identity thieves ease of access to the shared library when the window of opportunity opens.

Like vishing, *phishing* for information is the practice of asking certain questions to get specific answers, but in the cyber world. Phishing gathers and collects your personal information using bogus emails feigned as legitimate businesses. Phishing attempts are not easily identified and will usually be some type of solicitation that gradually takes you through a series of links until you've provided enough information about yourself to have your identity stolen. It's usually that email from a lottery corporation, bank, or loan company offering you money, free trips, or rewards in exchange for a little personal information about yourself, or through social media ads dressed up as credible news with a clickbait headline that entices you to engage.[19] Another recent variant might be called *SMShing,* or phishing over text messaging. Thieves will pose as a legitimate business and send text messages to your cell phone directing you to a website that's designed to collect

---

19 Or how about games? Did you play the "old me" challenge via FaceApp? https://nypost.com/2019/07/17/faceapp-security-concerns-russians-now-own-all-your-old-photos/

your personal information. Avoiding unsolicited emails and text messages is probably the best practice to avoid becoming a victim of an identity thief's -*ishing* attempt.

Another not so distant development is *keystroke logging*, perpetrated with the use of malware installed on your computer without your knowledge to record your keystroke patterns as you use your personal information to log into secure websites. The recorded patterns of your keystrokes enable identity thieves to decipher your passwords, login IDs, and other pertinent online account information that can be used to steal your identity.

Other malicious software programs usually show up in the form of a pop-up ad pretending to be some well-known software company offering free downloads of its merchandise. Once the malicious software has been downloaded, programs are run on your computer to spy on activity, then categorize, collect, and transmit all pertinent data over the internet to a remote computer where the cyber identity thieves will use the information fraudulently or package it for resale as part of a PIP. Ransomware, which is a type of malware designed to capture data, most often consumer information, and hold it hostage for a ransom, is nothing short of Cyber Identity Theft. Ransomware is in a race with Child Identity Theft to ascend to the lead as the driving force behind America's Domestic War against identity theft.

Skills, tools, and technology will continue to advance, even as security measures increase and enhance. There is little the average American can do to stop the identity thief from trying. While cybersecurity and consumer privacy are hot button issues in today's news feed, I am of the opinion that the systemic lack of understanding leads to a lack of collective action. Prayerfully and hopefully, this book will play a role in raising public awareness to get you the protection you need.

THREE

VICTIMS OF A
FRAUDULENT ATTRACTION

*I don't need to worry about identity theft
because no one wants to be me.*

—Jay London

A t the height of my experience in identity theft, I no longer
saw people as people. They were only numbers and the
profit those numbers could turn for me. Identity theft is
potentially the least personal crime, completely depen-
dent on a process of impersonal selection specific to a number
of factors appreciating qualifying credentials. From corporate
data breaches to restaurant patronization, consumer bank-
ing, or hotel registration, consumer information is available

for purchase and accessible for mass exploitation.[20] Whether you become that victim depends on chance and the protective measures you put in place.

The cyber identity thief is even more impersonal and motivated entirely by numbers. Data breaches are completely indiscriminate and cover people en masse. In a practical sense, cyber identity theft is only made relevant by social identity theft. While it's still impersonal, the instant credit market favors some profiles more than others. Victims of data breaches that end up on the digital black market are more of a gamble than a guarantee due to unverified credentials. For the identity thief, these factors become the pivotal information that points to profit.

In the last chapter, we mentioned aggravated and petty identity theft as scales of attack, and those scales will correlate to the choice of victim as well. The phrase "aggravated identity theft" was first introduced to us by the "Identity Theft Assumption and Deterrence Act of 1998":

> Statute 18 USC 1028A—Which provides that a person is guilty of aggravated identity theft where he or she commits a crime and also knowingly transfers, possesses, or uses, without lawful authority, a means of identification of another person.[21]

---

20 A full 66 percent of small businesses are at risk for a data breach. My company, DuckPond Technologies, Inc. is working on this problem as we develop our cyber security and data sharing products DataCop Solutions and Medica Systems to centralize and secure America's identity and consumer-patient information. Find out more at www.duckpond.tech
21 "Identity Theft and Assumption Deterrence Act of 1998." Identity Theft and Assumption Deterrence Act of 1998. http://www.ckfraud.org/title_18.html.

Here, I'll introduce a third scale: calculated identity theft. Contextually, by comparison, the term *calculated* is derived from my personal and professional experience as a master identity thief and connotes the processes of inclusion and exclusion when identifying and targeting victims. Master identity thieves are investigative. They identify and target their victims by what their profile can turn into profit, then employ the diabolical art of studied deception to devise the most lucrative schemes to maximize the damage. When calculated identity theft recurs to the scale of the ongoing operations that I carried out undetected, we might even escalate to *serial* identity theft.

The bottom line is that social identity theft is no respecter of persons, with no qualms about age, race, religion, or gender, yet the most devastating cases of aggravated identity theft will be drawn to specific, credit-driven regard for social profile and profession. In this chapter, I will borrow from my own experiences to uncover the characteristics that make you an attractive target for aggravated and calculated identity theft.

FROM THE CRADLE TO THE GRAVE

Most condensed sources of information on identity theft will caution that children, the elderly, and college students are the most frequently targeted victims of identity theft.[22] While this is absolutely true in some cases, there may be some

---

22 "Who Is Most at Risk for Identity Theft?" LifeLock. https://www.lifelock.org/risk-identity-theft/.

suicidal identity theft or petty scale theft skewing the numbers for college students. Seasoned identity thieves are drawn to newborn babies up to approximately fifteen years of age—young enough to establish fresh credit without being caught for many years. Identity thieves are drawn to adults, particularly, starting at thirty-five years old and older.

The marginal gap between fifteen years of adolescence and thirty-five years of adulthood is the double-decade building stage for young adults that is fraught with financial inconsistencies and social challenges. This is the developmental period of constant transition between relationships, careers, finances, lifestyle, and living arrangements. It's a precarious production that's saturated with trials, errors, and rehearsals. This instability represents a maze of mishaps, misses, hiccups, and hang-ups that more often than not result in wasted resources for the identity thief that targets this demographic.

From thirty-five years of age and older, the social security number of any qualified victim is usually established, secure, and sure in its credibility. At this stage in life they've most probably resolved their identity crisis in recognition and acceptance of who they are and have a clear compass of where they're going in life. They are established homeowners, with one or two vehicles and at least two credit cards that have positive balances that reflect utilization less than thirty-three percent of the cards' credit limits. Their debt is good, and so is their credit. This unwary but probable victim is way more valuable to the social identity thief than a twenty-year-old with newly established but precarious credibility.

When I qualified my targets, I actually went a step further and added ten years to that, going after the victims that were forty-five years of age or older. Any qualified candidate that did not meet my age criteria was of no immediate attraction to me. Correspondingly, all of my Feld Operatives were in their forties and fifties as well, except the disqualified mistake of Kenisha. I learned early on that the older and more mature you look, the less suspicious you are when committing social identity theft. Sometimes I had to flee point of sale transactions because my youthful appearance did not match up to the high credit lines I was being approved for via instant credit application inquiries.

Another reason I preferred to exploit the merits of older victims is because they were almost always rewarded with higher credit limits than younger victims. Occasionally, there was an under-forty and fruitful victim whose credentials yielded high returns on my investment, but it was rare. I needed to meet my minimum quota of twenty-five thousand dollars on all qualified identities, and that was most probable with my older victims who were more established in life.

For the social identity thief, the middle stage of life induces a different kind of crisis for the victim, the real midlife crisis of identity theft. While you're in a more established phase of life, taking care of teens and potentially aging parents, do not listen to the generic advice that markets to your fears and directs your identity concern on their protection services alone. Everything you have built to this point is at risk if a savvy, serial identity thief gains access to your personal information.

A WORD ABOUT CHILDHOOD IDENTITY THEFT

I need to pause here for a second: I raise not one but both my hands to heaven as a testimony that I've never ever applied my mastery to the trade and commerce of childhood identity theft. But for the unscrupulous cyber and social identity thieves that do, it is common practice in all too familiar territory.

As a parent with minor children and godchildren, I can only imagine the violation and injustice involved in destroying a child's identity. Yet this is a disgusting and depressing reality that we must face.

Crime experts are announcing this as the "new identity theft," but it is new in name only. For decades, parents and predators alike have used their kids and other people's children's personal information to connect the lights, cable, and water utilities, or to file false income tax claims with a promised monetary return for each child sold to the claimant. What differs between the parent using their children's personal information and the cyber or social identity thief stealing and selling that same information? Perhaps the differences can be underscored by the differences between need and greed—which can be argued both ways for any parent making hard and sometimes necessary decisions that qualify as the lessor of two evils.

The cyber and social identity thief, by contrast, has absolutely no justification or claim to use any information relevant to a child. This heinous crime has evolved into a booming business.

Here's how it works: children are issued social security numbers at birth but have no credit history for years, which makes their social security numbers ripe and ready for a credit building process known as "piggybacking." This is simply linking a dormant or less active social security number and name to an established credit profile that has a positive history of both revolving and installment trade lines. This is typically happening with people who have suffered from a credit crisis or crunch that prevents them from obtaining new credit using their own credentials. To escape their conscience and thereby evade moral accountability, they knowingly purchase the children's social security numbers under the misleading misnomers "Credit Profile Numbers, Credit Privacy Numbers, and Credit Protection Numbers," aka, CPNs, which are none other than children's social security numbers without the hyphen marks auctioned off by so-called CPN Firms.

An innumerable amount of web-based, data-scraping companies use software to scale public data and find dormant social security numbers that have no credit activity or history. These social security numbers usually belong to children and are packaged and sold by CPN firms in PIPs (Personal Information Packages) or as singles, at prices ranging from the low hundreds to thousands of dollars.

Once acquired and situated with viable credit history, the CPN holder can either sustain and manage the new creditor obligations without detection or abandon the CPN for a new one and start the process afresh using a different child's social security number. This process can be repeated over and over again without detection or until the CPN holder has repaired, restored, and regained personal credibility.

This scam is vicious to its victims and erects a barricade against their futures. When the victims of childhood identity theft become of legal age, they are often met with the nightmare of discovering that identity thieves have stolen their financial future. Childhood identity theft disrupts and delays qualification for financial aid and student loans. It derails and disqualifies the young adult from first-time buyer's programs for home and automobile purchases or credit card offers—all of which are designed by creditors to jumpstart the young adult's consumer credit profile.

Children are the closest humans to Heaven, yet they are the most vulnerable to the wiles of identity thieves. Divine sovereignty and human responsibility must link in this regard to shelter and shield America's children from both the kidnappers and hijackers of their minor identities. I willingly offer myself as a vessel through which this link between heaven and humanity can affect America's posterity and prosperity—past, present, and future.

THE GENDER FACTOR

From a physical and emotional perspective, women are more attractive to the social identity thief than men, both literally and criminally. When targeting a victim or selecting a co-conspirator alike, the recurring theme seems to be "ladies first."

By all appearances and credentials, the female identity thief disarms her victims with a perceived air of innocence and victimhood herself. Her charm is persuasive, and her charisma is poetic but poisonous and powerful, even magnetic and mesmerizing in such a way that the merchant almost never questions the perceived righteousness of the transaction, neither by phone nor in person. I methodically recruited and trained female social identity thieves for a number of reasons. They were more intelligent in the field, more attractive and disarming, more ambitious, more disciplined, more adaptive, and more receptive of instructions than male Field Operatives.

In stark contrast, the male social identity thief has natural traits of dominance as a man that constantly need to be checked and balanced in an alpha male dominant situation. Men like to assert their physical presence, thereby making their reception restricted and reserved. At the point of sale, the transaction becomes an intangible game of chess, with the victor succeeding not necessarily because he was more dominant, but because he was more discerning or more deceptive.

To cut past the potential testosterone-fueled stalemate, I trained all of my male Field Operatives to seek out transactions with female interactions at the point of sale. When I mapped out merchant itineraries, my mission reports documented detailed notes of everything, including the staff's sexual orientation and their shift changes and rotations. By design, the male/female balance extracted the possible tension and softened the line of communication. It also conducted the potential for distracting flirtation.

If the opportunity presented itself, I always flattered and flirted with female sales associates to flatline any doubt or suspicion she may have had about my representation. This same dynamic works in reverse from the female social identity thief towards male sales associates. We see the art and power of a woman's touch, her influence, and her feminine persuasion at its truest form in the Scriptural accounts of Samson and Delilah or King Ahab and Queen Jezebel, although historically these two women have not been held as virtuous.[23] So follows and flows the reputation of the female social identity thief.

MILITARY APPEAL

In this stage of my life, I have great respect for our military personnel, each and every one of them. My brother and sister are former military service members, and some of my closest relatives and friends are veterans. Much praise is owed to all the men and women of the United States Armed Forces.

However, my appreciation and respect for the men and women who embody the four branches of the US military has not always been virtuous. To the contrary, my appreciation for them was more of an evaluation and attraction to the merits and might of their occupation from the perspective of a social identity thief. Ironically, for their secure status in this country, active duty service members and veterans alike are easy targets for identity theft. They are highly exposed.

In our America, there's no better guarantor than the backing of the United States government. If you recall just how valuable instant credit is, you'll begin to see the military ID from the lens of the social identity thief. From certain discounts and special purchasing programs to privileged access and opportunities, the stolen and replicated identity of a military veteran comes with many perks and profits.

---

23 Judges 16, 1 Kings 21—all counter to the virtuous woman of Proverbs 31.

From four-star generals to boot camp trainees, I personally had access to the identities of entire companies, squadrons, battalions, platoons, regiments, wings, and fleets. When I sought out military victims—eliminating or enlisting based on age, gender, and rank—I always hit the bullseye. There's absolutely no doubt that this trend has continued long since I stopped—military personnel are assumed to be at double the risk of civilians.[24]

Clearly, no matter what amount of arsenal or defense mechanisms are at their disposal, military men and women cannot fight against what they cannot see. In this regard, identity theft has rendered them as the united unarmed forces.

CROSSING THE BLUE LINE

The men and women of the US military are not the only targets of attack because of their occupation. Their counterparts in law enforcement have long been designated as sitting "pigs"—the terminology that embodied my distrust and fueled my attacks. For the criminal, anything and anybody that poses a threat to the luxury and leisure of the criminal lifestyle presents a liability and is relegated to sentiments of disdain and disgust.

For many years, I truly hated cops, likely originating on the night of my first criminal arrest for commercial burglary. When the Monroe City police officer released his K9 partner

---

24 Duttweiler, Raleigh. "Military at Double the Risk of Identity Theft." Military.com. https://www.military.com/spouse/military-life/military-at-double-the-risk-of-identity-theft.html.

to attack me, even when I clearly had no escape and was moving in compliance with his every directive, that trauma sealed my perspective of him and his occupation.

My rage toward law enforcement soon turned creative. I paired cops against each other as unwitting perpetrators. I used the stolen identity of one cop to participate in the theft of another cop's identity. I convoluted and crisscrossed credentials, attacking and adding their true and real identifying information to the financial crimes I orchestrated for those occasions, intending to make them the subjects of departmental internal affairs investigations. I would plant and use relative information like badge and patrol unit numbers as passwords to various accounts I opened in victims' names. For me, borrowing the thought process of a thinking cop, I would have connected the dots of glaring investigative leads. But I don't think there was enough competence or concern to follow the maze of malicious mastery back to me. In more than one case, I even implicated my K9 attacker "Thor" in financial crimes he clearly was incapable of committing.

You may now question and be uncomfortably curious about my access to police officers' personal information, and rightly so. Let me just say this: the only US citizen's personal information I couldn't compromise was POTUS—President of the United States—and with the way things have changed in the last fifteen years, I'm certain that those limitations are no longer valid for today's cyber identity thief.

I spared no resources to brutalize their lives. I had folders and files on cops dedicated to social identity theft exploitation. It had become a sport for me, termed "Pig Identity Theft," that I shared with cyber and social identity theft contacts in Alabama, New York, Houston, Chicago, Washington, DC, Atlanta, and Los Angeles. From their personal information to advisable social exploitation, I was the go-to guy for profiling cops and targeting them for identity theft, undoubtedly in exchange for the attack on me that had been galvanized in my eighteen-year-old brain.

While there is no justification for my actions, there is something to be said for the adversarial relationship that police brutality, profiling, and disdain that is so often directed towards Black and Brown communities, most aggressively towards the African American community. Given that this particular platform does not afford me the luxury to explicate the dynamics of race tensions and how they inform and influence the colorful disparities within America's criminal justice system, perchance a different set of circumstances will invite me to deliver my comprehensions in full measure, but only to move the needle towards irrevocable change.[25]

If I had no regard and respect for my own parents and grandparents to not steal their identities, who outside of them qualified for an exemption from victimization? Absolutely no one who met my age criteria—and certainly not someone who had declared me an enemy worthy of attack. I detested

---

25 As I put the finishing touches on this manuscript, imagery of the brother of Botham Jean and the judge presiding over his murderer's case have conveyed forgiveness for Amber Guyger. In this instance, I find common ground with the perpetrator and the desire for a fresh start in life. I hope to unpack this more in the draft I've begun, tentatively titled *Happy New You*.

everything a cop represented. I hated the tailored uniform, the black boots, the white t-shirt under the uniform, the impression of the bulletproof vest through their shirt, the shades. I hated the weapons, how they'd rest their forearms on those weapons, how they stood and their posture at post. I hated their haircuts, their cop cars, and most of all, I despised, abhorred, and detested their handcuffs. I was an enemy of the state, and in return, police officers everywhere and at any time were my nemeses.

Today, with a stronger foundation of healing, repentance, and growth, I see the men and women of blue in a much more nuanced light. I recognize them as the most courageous, selfless, and sacrificing body of people I know. On a daily basis, they vow to protect and serve their fellow citizens, mostly complete strangers, and by doing so they faithfully uphold the honor of the badge. They are, by and large, honorable men and women who embody and enforce the laws of the land and should be consistently held in the same respect and admiration as any hero.

Ironically, my youngest son, Kaleb Kar'Micah Williams, is fascinated with police officers everywhere. Every chance we get we partner with the men and women in blue to capture a picture and secure insignia. In his mind he's a real cop with play guns, always ready to serve and protect his toys from cousins, friends, and strangers alike. In the grand scheme of it all, those who I once despised I now love in all that my son represents as "Kaleb Tha Kop."

So why is their identifying information still so accessible and unguarded?

In recent years, thirty or more Baton Rouge police officers, both active and retired, were targeted victims of aggravated social identity theft. Per WAFB news, the social identity thief purchased names, social security numbers, and birth dates of several individuals but only victimized the police officers that were identified on that list.[26] The social identity thief apparently had a gambling addiction, and reportedly lost approximately one hundred and fifty thousand dollars to local casinos. If the cash came from converted fraudulent purchases, that suggests that he used those stolen identities to make retail purchases totaling at least four hundred thousand dollars.

Now, he was a one-man show and wasn't too smart about his process, so his spending spree ended there. Reportedly, Special Agent Sean Connor of the United States Secret Service tracked his merchant itinerary by placing a GPS on his vehicle once he became a person of interest, and that was that. Yet even in his deliberate ignorance, he was able to do striking damage. Why? Because only the sitting president's personal information is sealed and monitored.

Believe me, I witnessed efforts to steal George W. Bush's identity for sport met and forever deterred by impenetrable fortresses. That notwithstanding, qualifying presidential candidates should all have their identities similarly secured and sealed from public record as a condition to entering the presidential campaign. Unless it is the incumbent president,

---

26 Jim Shannon, "BR man arrested for allegedly stealing identity of local officers and deputies," WAFB, 2009. https://www.wafb.com/story/10056686/br-man-arrested-for-allegedly-stealing-identity-of-local-officers-and-deputies/.

each of the competing candidates are fully exposed to social and cyber identity theft. If a presidential candidate turned president of the United States of America finds their identity compromised pre-election, then the Commander in Chief of the most powerful nation in the world becomes subject to the whims of foreign entities, governments, and their hired identity assassins (after all, that is what hackers really are). There is enough conversation about compromised presidents these days that we hardly need to follow that path into national emergency.

Identity theft is an astronomical problem, with military and law enforcement personnel specifically identified and targeted because of their noble occupations. They are exploited for sport, for practice, and for illicit profits and purposes. This level of deep and dark calculated social identity theft requires unprecedented, exigent and extreme, concentrated, concerted, collaborative, and calculated measures to protect those who protect us and to prosecute the criminals who persecute the badges and boots of our protection agencies without conscience or deep consequence.

THE SOCIAL GOLD STANDARD

The last factor for victim selection tells the most about a credit profile, and that is social status. I used to gauge my victims' social status by the neighborhoods they lived in, the vehicles they drove, the restaurants they patronized, whether they parked with valet services, their careers, etc. Attorneys, local, state, and federal politicians, police officers, military veterans, preachers, doctors, nurses, college professors, engineers, farmers, teachers, entrepreneurs—all of them carried a social status that was attractive for fraud.

I had a class and caste system, identifying and targeting the driver of an S-Class Mercedes Benz in preference to the driver of a Toyota Camry. I discriminated among potential victims, selecting only those who appeared to be more affluent. A few of those victims were drowning in debt and ready to die in bankruptcy, but most of my potentials were on target and perfectly situated for aggravated social identity theft.

In case you think social status might rule you out, this is not the same as targeting for celebrity or notoriety. Those targets are much too heavily in the spotlight. Whatever happens to them becomes the center of attention as well. The social identity thieves who dare challenge the consequences of notoriety usually find themselves the notorious subject of the evening news stories.

Case in point, we can think of a handful of celebrity personalities and professional athletes who have been victims of aggravated social identity theft. When you read the reports, the social identity thieves who tried it were opportunists and not learned professionals or experts—with one exception of cyber identity theft involving the queen of talk shows.

Ms. Oprah Winfrey, the crown jewel of talk TV turned media mogul, was the victim of an elaborate identity theft scheme years ago. Reportedly, a restaurant worker living in New York devised and developed, by way of engaging studied deception, complex methods and means to obtain sensitive information. He had social security numbers, birth dates, home addresses, and financial records belonging to some of the world's richest, most powerful and influential people. The perpetrator employed cyber technology and used computers at public libraries to piece together the identities of his victims and to pick apart their finances.[27]

Instead of establishing new credit accounts as is routine for social identity thieves, he engaged account takeovers to access and expend the abundant riches and resources that were already in place. This was smart, because he would have brought immediate scrutiny to himself if he would have applied for new credit using Ms. Winfrey's personal information. His criminal enterprise came to an abrupt end only after six months when he tried to cross over from cyber identity theft to social identity theft. He was arrested when trying to take the delivery of twenty-five thousand dollars' worth of equipment that's used to replicate credit cards and other forms of identification. That's what happens when the cyber identity thief gets comfortable and cocky about his operation: he gets caught.

Steven Spielberg, the Oscar-winning filmmaker, in company with his counterpart Mr. George Lucas, the genius behind the Star Wars saga, were targeted and attacked by the same cyber identity thief that victimized Ms. Winfrey. What he did not appear to know was that the bigger, more recognizable the target, the bigger and louder the beep is on the radar.

---

27 Staff, CBSNews.com staff CBSNews.com. "Cybertheft Case Skewers Celebs." CBS News. CBS Interactive, March 21, 2001. https://www.cbsnews.com/news/cybertheft-case-skewers-celebs/.

Targets with celebrity social status live on a platform for all to see, scrutinize, judge, celebrate, demonize, mischaracterize, and victimize.

Celebrity status should not be held against its achiever, but far too often success is envied and coveted when it cannot be emulated. Thus, the hater and stalker are born at once, sometimes in the same person, and the attacks ensue in some form or another.

A social identity thief who had been previously caught, charged, and convicted for stealing former Atlanta Hawks star Steven Smith's identity came back on a different occasion to tackle *The Fresh Prince of Bel-Air* himself, the one and only Mr. Will Smith.[28] The social identity thief's crimes were both calculated and aggravated, presumably motivated by a physical resemblance shared between the victims and the thief. How else could someone socially present themselves as Steven Smith or Will Smith if not tall and of a caramel complexion? You'd have to look like them or actually be them to forge ahead with that kind of temerity and determination.

Maybe he just has an affinity to the last name "Smith," it's hard to say. What's certain is that he had a fraudulent attraction to the fruits of their celebrity and targeted them because of it.

In his first incident regarding the theft of Mr. Steven Smith's identity, the social identity thief acquired and used a

---

28 AP. "Jail For Will Smith Identity Thief." CBS News. CBS Interactive, December 29, 2005. https://www.cbsnews.com/news/jail-for-will-smith-identity-thief/.

single credit card to charge up purchases in excess of eighty thousand dollars. This was bold and daring, undoubtedly two of the main ingredients for his arrest and capture. For lack of thorough tracking measures, in most cases, greed is the predominant reason that most cyber and social identity thieves get caught.

For Mr. Will Smith, the same social identity thief used his personal information to acquire not one, two, or three credit cards but a mind-blowing fourteen fraudulent credit cards. This is not just greed but a clear example of one who suffers from my self-determined Excessive Compulsive Disorder.

I never directed more than six new fraudulent accounts to be opened in a single victim's name over a two- to three-week period, and unless it was connected to vehicular identity theft, I've never kept a stolen identity active for more than thirty days. If and when I did, I either got caught or had to flee the scene because my scam had been detected. Consequently, the social identity thief that stole both Will Smith and Steven Smith's identities was eventually convicted in both cases and was sentenced to thirty months in prison for aggravated identity theft charges.

Similarly, why any professional identity thief, no matter how learned or brilliant he or she might be, would want to touch "The Tiger" when he was exerting his loudest roar on the golf course is far beyond me. Nevertheless, Tiger Woods was targeted at the zenith of his career.[29] The social identity thief,

29 Rovell, Darren. "The Other Tiger That Lurks in the Woods." ESPN. ESPN Internet Ventures, November 1, 2002. https://www.espn.com/sportsbusiness/s/2002/1031/1454033.html.

again, used Mr. Woods's information to apply for a fraudulent twelve or more lines of credit in this one name. Before he got caught, the social identity thief was able to charge approximately fifty thousand dollars' worth of purchases in Mr. Woods' name. He already had two prior felony convictions and for his crimes against Mr. Woods, he received a staggering but sobering sentence of two hundred years to life.[30]

Then there is the case of social identity theft focused on account takeovers, for the thief who made himself an authorized user on Mrs. Kim Kardashian-West's existing accounts. He actually changed the address on the accounts and requested that replacement cards be mailed to him directly, at his real home address where he lived with his mom—evidently his partner in crime. The social identity thief was only nineteen years old, clearly an amateur in his criminal craft. He was ultimately sentenced to forty-two months in prison. However, his novelty did not prevent him from gaining the social security numbers, bank account information, and credit reports belonging to Mr. Bill Gates, Mrs. Michelle Obama, and Mrs. Beyoncé Knowles-Carter.[31]

Whether you have celebrity status and invite the attention of reckless envy and admiration, or simply have an established career and attract the studious professional identity thief,

---

30 *Wow!* This guy either was sentenced under some type of habitual offender statute or the judge was a fan of Tiger Woods. I believe it's the former.

31 "U.S. Probes Hack of Credit Data on Mrs Obama, Beyonce, Others." Reuters. Thomson Reuters, March 13, 2013. https://www.reuters.com/article/us-usa-cybersecurity-hacking/u-s-probes-hack-of-credit-data-on-mrs-obama-beyonce-others-idUSBRE92B12520130313.

social status is a welcome mat for identity thieves. Of course, we've now seen that no one is exempt from becoming a victim of cyber or social identity theft—no one!

YHWH

FOUR

THE PSYCHOLOGY OF IDENTITY THEFT

For as he thinketh in his heart, so is he...
King Solomon, Proverbs 23:7 (NKJV)

Throughout this volume, you might have noticed an interchangeable usage of pronouns when referring to the identity thief. I deliberately constructed the material to be gender inclusive to conversely document the equality of men and women across an ever-widening spectrum in our collective fight against the social injustices that we face on both sides of the law. Identity thieves are not confined to any particular demographic—they aren't just one gender, race, or ethnicity group. No one type of person dominates that dark industry over any other. So what makes an identity thief? It is this development of a criminal life that motivated me to tell my full story and not simply allow for assumptions to be made. As I thought back over my years in identity theft, I needed to understand not only how I committed the crimes but why. Not to come to an excuse or justification—I had done plenty of that while I was active in that world—but to know more about myself. As a society, we need to do the same. Simply expecting criminals to stop without understanding what it is we expect them to stop will only create that 360 degrees of repentance that led and landed me right back into the folly from which I had been delivered.[32]

As much as we need to understand the methodologies of identity theft, we should also appreciate the motivation. From the various branches of psychology—notably, the landmark research of psychologists Samuel Yochelson and Stanton Samenow in their published work, *The Criminal Personality*—to the disciplines of sociology and criminology, experts have sought to understand the rationality of crime.

Notable psychologist T.W. White wrote three volumes on this subject, and in the federal system there is a program called RDAP (Residential Drug Abuse Program) based on it to help prisoners identify the errors of their criminal thoughts and actions. Those thinking errors that are hypothesized to lead to higher rates of recidivism include: 1) Mollification, 2) Cutoff, 3) Entitlement, 4) Power Orientation, 5) Sentimentality, 6) Superoptimism, 7) Cognitive Indolence, and

---

32 Proverbs 26:11

8) Discontinuity.[33] In this chapter, I will lean marginally on components of T.W. White and Glen D. Walters' "Psychological Inventory of Criminal Thinking Styles (PICTS)" as a framework for exploration.

During my second term of federal imprisonment (2005–2011), RDAP was one of the only diversionary programs that could lead to an early release, earning the successful participant a reduction of one year off of their sentence. It's intended to help prisoners identify the thought and speech patterns that motivated their criminal behavior and to choose wise alternatives if they were ever inclined or tempted to reengage criminalities.

However, RDAP is limited to prisoners who admit to substance abuse. Though I didn't take the program, I drew from it thanks to fellow prisoners who had taken it, and I researched T.W. White's findings on my own. The more I learned, the more I saw myself in the criminal thought patterns he identified.

The one exception I take to these measurements for the identity thief specifically is T.W. White's concept of "cognitive indolence." If there is any category for the effort that it takes to execute a successful identity theft operation, "lazy" would not be it. Sure, petty identity thieves might steal a wallet, use a credit card, try to pass for someone else with a quick flash of their driver's license, then move on to something else. But that's not the same for social identity theft on a calculated,

---

33 "Publications." NCJRS Abstract - National Criminal Justice Reference Service. https://www.ncjrs.gov/App/Publications/abstract. aspx?ID=118464.

aggravated scale. Preparation for a successful aggravated identity theft campaign is anything but lazy. A great deal of work is required behind the scenes for anyone reaching beyond the scale of petty theft.

Instead, I believe the identity thief's emotions are relative to their actions and thereby provide a foundation for understanding the cognition and condition that make up their lifestyle choices. With this in mind, I have overlayed the seven remaining thinking errors from White and Walters with what I believe inspired my thoughts, fed my emotions, motivated my actions and, to some extent, formed my criminal character. Thus, what follows is intensely personal and should not be misconstrued as a pre-treatment plan for complicit or contemptible behavior.

I am not a licensed clinical psychologist and have no goals of diagnosis or prognosis here. I wrote this chapter with profound and purposed empathy, with the hope of understanding myself better at its conclusion than I did when commencing it. Moreover, my observation has been that most criminals develop their crime as a habit without choosing to understand the rationale behind their actions. Others can only be shown their folly and fallacy through fact. This is my labor here. If I am able to lead at least one recidivist or identity thief out of a life of crime in this effort of exploration and discovery, then this chapter will have accomplished far more than I initially intended. But by prayer I trust that we'd be grateful for their praiseworthy rescue and return from the deep and dark depths of incorrigibility.

It's a discussion worth starting. In that spirit of understanding, let's explore the identity thief's psychology.

MOLLIFICATION AND SENTIMENTALITY

By whatever means and at all costs, the criminal mind *mollifies* their work, making self-serving excuses to justify their behavior and erase their own anxieties about right, wrong, and damage. During my tenure as a master identity thief, the more I stole, the more I gave, erroneously thinking that my generosities justified, and in some ways pardoned, my criminal behavior and permitted it in others. In the midst of even my most elaborate crimes, I was sure I had done no wrong.

Dating back to the days of my adolescence, I saw the limited opportunities in my environment and used them as motivation and incentive to pursue ambitious goals built on the fatal premises of faulty promises spoken to me as a self-serving false prophet. Instead of criminality, I could have followed my peers into college or the military, but I chose this path and felt justified in doing so. This is the way I found a convincing and compelling argument every step of the way—for stealing identities, for selling drugs, for targeting cops, and for anything else I did.

A close cousin to mollification is *sentimentality*—as I shaped my own reality, I needed and wanted to be perceived and received as heaven's gift to the hood. Now having ears to hear and a heart to understand, I must confess that my former perspective blurred my vision and led to the eventual blindness that narcissism creates in the life of its occupant. I couldn't see past myself and thus became twice deceived. All roads led to me, and this self-centered design caused me to be self-deceived. Self-deception is the worst kind and the only way out of such dark delusion is by the self-discovery of your real identity in your true reality. To offset the negative reputation that invariably rises in the community as a cool criminal, even when no one has seen your misdeeds, you shape your own public image, like Denzel Washington did as Frank Lucas in the movie *American Gangster*. My reputation as a nice guy needed to overshadow my record and report as a criminal.

I would take kids on random shopping sprees. I would loan money throughout the hood knowing people weren't going to pay me back. Despite my disdain and disgust, I even donated money to police departments—which of course was more self-serving and gratifying than anything else, but it still felt like a good deed in the moment.

On one Mother's Day, I went through the whole community and gave out a card and ten bucks to every single mother I saw. I felt like I was on top of the world, doing something politicians and community leaders don't and wouldn't do. The good deeds kept piling up until I was certain they would overshadow the misdeeds.

Unfortunately, my story is not that of Robin Hood, who stole from the selfish and gave to the poor. I'm sure I stole from both good and bad people and gave to both bad and good people. But I placed more value on the deed of giving than on the need to whom I was gifting. Good deeds cannot overshadow a thing as long as the motives and intent are impure.

The more good I did in the community, through empty sentimentality, the more I felt justified and mollified in my actions. Thus the circle was complete, and that circle became a ring around me that kept me more and more secluded from any real sense of connection.

CUT OFF, ENTITLEMENT, AND POWER ORIENTATION

The mindset of *cutting something off* can manifest in many kinds of practice. It's seeing people as numbers and weighing the potential they could earn you rather than weighing the worth of their character and humanity. It's suspending your emotions and abandoning your conscience in favor of your crime.

When I targeted police officers, I deliberately chose their dehumanized street name of "pig" to further distance myself from what I was doing. I "cut off" fear of consequence and incarceration so that no one could slow me down.

Ironically, prison itself is the act of cutting people off from society and relationships. It's the literal embodiment of the figurative isolation that has already grown in the criminal's mind.

Especially for the serial offender, there comes a time when you feel like you're on an island. It is abnormal to view your fellow citizen as both a budget and a bottom line, but the identity thief knows no other system of evaluation. When fully engaged, I cut off all normal feelings and suspended my emotions. I became robotic in my pursuits and removed my conscience from the transaction.

A criminal of this mindset and magnitude doesn't care about anyone or anything. Every waking moment is about exploitation. It spills over into relationships and spreads like a cancer. You don't care about race, religion, color, creed, gender, or age. You only want what's coming to you next—and thanks to the thought process around entitlement, you're sure you deserve only the best of what's to come.

Drawing from the justification that was fostered through mollification, and then reinforced the longer you are cut off from reasonable society, entitlement becomes the fuel on that fire. *Entitlement* tells you that you deserve that extra cash, the nice car, the expensive clothing. It destroys contentment and ensures that no amount of success will ever be enough. You will always need more.

For me, the thing I felt most entitled to led into the next thought process: *power orientation*. I wanted to keep playing cat and mouse until the roles could somehow reverse. When that sense of power is threatened, the criminal seeks to alleviate the feeling by manipulation or even assault. My standard was to manipulate the merchant, but occasionally—as with the baseball bat—I would step into other means in order to secure my sense of pseudo power.

The most depressing and disappointing moments, thinking back over my story, were when I lost control entirely. I truly believed that I needed it. I needed to be the wizard behind the curtain, pulling the chains and pushing the buttons. Even within prison walls, I needed something that I could control, so I manipulated guards and fellow inmates alike until I felt like my fate was back in my own hands again.

The surprise came in solitary confinement, in my most isolated and cut off moment, when I had absolutely no power or influence at all. It was not by design of the system, which was meant to aggravate each of these thought processes and break me into submission, but by heavenly intervention. People lose themselves in isolation, only to never rediscover who they are and why they exist. Instead, against all odds and in spite of the circumstances, I was able to redefine myself and begin to break the strongholds that held my thoughts captive and enslaved to erroneous thinking.

We must always remember to "cast down imaginations, and every high thing that exalteth itself against the knowledge of God, and bring into captivity every thought to the obedience of Christ" lest we lend our minds to satanic influence.[34] Once our psychology becomes the domain for demonic criminal thinking, those thought patterns lead to obsessive criminal behavior. I write from my experience as an expert witness, and yet I also testify that Scripture is true when Yahshua says that "This kind (demon) can come out by nothing but prayer and fasting." (Mark 9:29, NKJV)

SUPEROPTIMISM

Superoptimism is a double-edged sword that both drives criminal innovation but weakens criminal enterprise. The identity thief relishes in success as a criminal, and the longer he evades capture, the stronger his spirit of arrogance becomes. What follows his arrogance is the false confidence that plans a future in fraud with no preparation for the consequences of capture. A sense of superiority develops and thus the identity thief puts himself above the law and it is within this augmented

---

34 2 Corinthians 10:5 (KJV)

reality that the identity thief's sense of invincibility inevitably realizes definite incarceration. [35]

I was emboldened by the mechanics of the scheme, enamored with the dynamics of the scam, and infatuated and intrigued by the sophistication and science of its perpetration. I felt indispensable and invincible. I truly believed I was too good to get caught, eventually realizing that superoptimism often exceeds capabilities, which in turn fails and falls captive to the pride that precedes criminal convictions.

By believing I was smarter than the next identity thief, I not only thought outside the box but brought others in with me. I designed and developed a new method for vehicular identity theft, then charged fifty thousand dollars in cash to teach others how to do it. People flew in from all over the country to learn this lesson in evil, to practice the method, and perfect its outcome.

These are the interactions that confirm a sense of superoptimism and further embed it into the criminal's brain—not unlike the near complete oversight of identity theft charges. It's not enough to assume that the criminal's ego will take them down. By depriving them of consequences, we feed the beast and allow their ingenuity to run unchecked far too long. There's no doubt that I've gotten away with far more crimes of identity theft than I've been accused and suspected of, prosecuted for, and that inspired me to continue on.

---

35 The self-described "GOAT" of credit card fraud met a humbling end to his optimistic streak: "Rapper Selfmade Kash bragged he was the 'GOAT swiper' of credit card fraud. 'In fact, he is not,' feds say," Washington Post, March 2019.

YHWH

This is not kleptomania by any measure. I believe, with deductions from C.G. Jung's process of analytical psychology and Sigmund Freud's system of psychoanalysis, that practiced identity theft is a pathological personality disorder with an inherent uncanny ability to adopt and adapt to multiple profiles and presumed personalities. I further theorize that the greater challenge is steeped in what I would classify as "excessive-compulsive disorder" (ECD). Unlike obsessive-compulsive disorder, excessive-compulsive disorder is driven by an inextinguishable desire and insatiable appetite for more. There is no sense of enough. This drives the mind of the identity thief to rehash, rehearse, and repeat his crimes incessantly.

DISCONTINUITY: THE LAST STRAW

When I ponder the sophistication with which I approached a full-fledged identity theft operation there's absolutely nothing "cognitively indolent" or lazy about it, which is where T.W. White and I stand in opposition on this one notion. Cookie-cutter crimes like robbing the local convenience store at gunpoint under video surveillance or committing burglaries or car jackings might be driven by this thought process. Those kinds of crimes require little to no thought given to planning, preparation, and execution, though they require a certain amount of audacity (and a lot of stupidity) to carry out.

In no way do I intend to boast or recreate a class and caste system among criminals—my point is that different criminals think differently.

When I wasn't supervising my identity theft operation during the day, I was devising, orchestrating, and manufacturing the next mission at night. Truly, there is nothing cognitively indolent about a lifestyle identity thief, in thought or behavior.

In that frantic desperation that is so far from lazy, the last of the thought processes becomes evident. *Discontinuity* eventually takes its toll.

When I was a master identity thief, I suffered from insomnia before I knew what the sleep disorder was. My brain was a 20/7 machine, always in motion except for a sporadic four-hour nap out of every twenty-four-hour day, seven days a week. If I slept longer than anticipated, I felt like I had missed out on life's biggest opportunities.

The mind of an identity thief is tantamount to a fragmented puzzle—disconnected and disjointed from the parts and pieces that make it complete. There are multiple realities to contend with: the reality of their environment, the reality of what's needed to change the conditions of that environment, the reality of the benefits of those changed conditions, and the all too real consequences that await.

From a sociological perspective, much of what a person is or becomes is in part based on his roots and reality—the conditions of existence within their environment. There are hereditary factors such as intellectual abilities, disposition, and demeanor. Then there are external conditions such as community, education, family members, and friends. There are some exceptions to these social norms, on both good and bad sides of the equation, but the general rule applies:

we are all limited in some way by what we are given in this life. We don't begin to go and grow beyond those conditioned limitations until we dare to challenge and change the status quo.

The identity thief defies the conditions of their environment by acquiring someone else's reality. The self-talk required to enable this behavior is intense and difficult to sustain. There is a rotation of thoughts that randomly shift in three different directions: digressing, regressing, and progressing. The identity thief lives in two different worlds: a world imagined and a world realized.

The distinction between these two worlds creates a dichotomy of distraction—a discontinuity that breeds the internal confusion that eventually manifests itself in external chaos. A gradual loss of purpose will land the social identity thief in an ironic but inevitable identity crisis, losing sight of true self amidst the assumption of multiple identities—often tipping toward a kind of personality disorder itself and dramatic reruns of psychotic episodes.

At this stage, the identity thief goes from assuming the identities of his victims to being consumed by the crime itself. There are no worthy goals to reach—nothing optimistic, justifiable, or admirable—if the means you take to reach them are impure and unsustainable. But the identity thief doesn't weigh results. He only affixes a value to "good intentions" and endless effort. He can try to fill the void with a sense of sentimentality, but in the end it's not the law that determines a criminal's fate. It's his own aspirations.

BREAKING THE PATTERNS

Criminal thought patterns don't necessarily go away, but they can mature. This is why we reduce puppy love to adolescence or new relationships. As you grow, the way you think about people and things and your true self begins to change. You discover a new measure of identity and set new definitions about yourself and alter your perspectives on life as you adjust and redefine yourself throughout the growth process.

For identity thieves to abandon these criminal thought patterns, they have to first discover their own identity. They have to step into the true values and virtues that define them, rather than being defined by their criminal exploits.

I still chase life to excess. I have multiple businesses. I have an extensive jewelry and watch collection that I enjoy gifting to some and giving to others—as my need for more abates over time. I want more children (I would love to adopt paternal twins). I have struggled with infidelity. The excessive compulsive tendencies didn't stop because I exited crime, I just do a better job of managing them; but not all of the redirected energy has been productive. Some of it created a lot of hurt and damage. I've learned a lot about me *from* me, but I don't know nor do I expect to know myself completely on this side of eternity. Admittedly, I'm a "working process," but I'm also a model for many things—especially imperfection. It's part of who I am, and my imperfections are accepted realities that I have to work with and through, not against but as part of my lifelong process of refinement, reprioritization, and ongoing rehabilitation.

YHWH

This is why identity theft is growing at the rate that it is: Not only do we need to protect ourselves better as individuals. Not only do our merchants need to abandon tired stereotypes and gain better training. Not only do our law enforcement officers and legislators have a mighty long way to go. There's also this societal element that asks us as friends, parents, and peers to help our young people grow up into stronger, more stable versions of themselves. There's a personal element that asks current identity thieves to break long-held thought patterns. We can only break these patterns by truly seeing, valuing, and fighting for and alongside each other. What that fight actually consists of is the subject of a different discussion surrounding criminal justice and prison reform, but I hereby present my testimony as a spark to ignite a greater collective and more united effort over time.

FIVE

THE EVERYDAY THREAT OF FRAUD

The type of scheme is as endless as the human
imagination...And often as frustrating as a whack-a-
ball game...You shoot one scam down and dozens more
arise. That's why informed consumers are one of the most
powerful tools we have. Because the best prevention
is consumer education, and care and self-protection!
                                    —US Senator Richard Blumenthal[36]

C yber identity theft is certainly a risk, but it has its place
front and center in the minds of consumers. Whether we
comply or not, we know that our passwords should be
secure and our online habits airtight. The niche that my

---

36 March 21, 2017: Staying a step ahead: Fighting back against scams used
to defraud Americans

story conveys is that identity theft doesn't need the internet to be alive and well, as our age moves beyond a user ID and password protected society. We're headed towards biometric authentication of everything, everywhere. While this will be enough of a challenge enough for cybersecurity professionals, we will always have the human factor to contend with.

I accessed identities from people doing everyday business with trusted merchants and service providers. It wasn't through suspicious emails or texts—it was through your tax preparer, your doctor's visit, and your dinner date night.

Fifteen years ago, my victims didn't know that the counter clerk at the gas station at the corner of Highland Road and Seigen Lane was working for me. They didn't know that the new administrator behind the desk at the family doctor's office needed some extra cash so they agreed to funnel files my way. They didn't know how many times the waitress ran their card just around the corner, so they couldn't know that their information had been uploaded to me for use at a later time.

Now that you have a better understanding of the tools and techniques identity thieves use, and even some motivation behind their action, it's time to look at how it affects you directly. I might have been unique in my age and the scope of my enterprise, but I'm certainly not the only master identity thief to walk the Earth. In spite of the massive damage that identity theft causes each year, we're still only given outdated advice about our risks, like suggesting your risks lay in eavesdropping or social media profiling.[37]

---

37 Long, Emily. "6 Common Habits That Put You at Risk for Identity...

Keep in mind that this is a chapter that focuses on fraud, which strictly speaking is separate from identity theft. However, in terms of practice and effect, the lines tend to cross. Most identity theft statistics include fraud in their totals, and the consumer is affected just the same. I would be remiss not to cover it, so in this chapter, we're going to look at some of the major risk areas for the everyday consumer or business owner: card and check fraud, and vehicular and insurance fraud.

YOUR CARD, YOUR CREDIT, MY ACCESS

From corporate America to organized criminal enterprises, the selling and reselling of identifying consumer data is big business. Legally referred to as "access device fraud," credit card fraud has become more prevalent in practice and perpetration in recent years. Access to consumers' private and personal identifying information, whether by methods of deliberate deceit or massive data breaches, is more readily available now, within arm's reach of the fraudster who can turn your personal information into dollar signs and wonders.

Separate and apart from some of the sophisticated data breaches accomplished by card skimming-malware—most notably at Target for forty million credit and debit card numbers, followed by another 56 million credit and debit cards at

---

...Theft." NBCNews.com. NBCUniversal News Group, August 20, 2018. https://www.nbcnews.com/better/business/6-common-habits-put-you-risk-identity-theft-ncna899251.

Home Depot—I want to draw your attention to some of the more deceitful ways that studied deception leads thieves right to your financial door.[38]

Before a package of digitized information (PIPs, from chapter 2 of this book) is parsed out for use, it is typically grouped based on number sequences. Then, it's sifted into the dark market within the public domain for open bidding. As a master identity thief, I never really cared for the breach pipeline to gain access to personal information. I always assumed that the feds were on the other end of the online transaction as part of some sting operation to catch identity thieves in the act, and I never trusted purchasing any information over the internet.

The illicit practice of data gathering I perpetrated upon my victims was a bit more intimate and practical, based in part on locality and in part on demographics divided among and across all races, both genders, every profession, and most religions. Data collection for my criminal enterprise relied heavily on carefully and strategically placed Info Operatives who worked for various entities, businesses, and corporations by day while simultaneously working on my covert mission to collect and gather personal information.

My fraudulent credit card exploits were part and parcel to the larger scheme of my identity theft operations, and I often committed both crimes in connection with each other. The Info Operatives I employed were paid a salary based on weekly

---

38 Sidel, Robin. "Home Depot's 56 Million Card Breach Bigger Than Target's." The Wall Street Journal. Dow Jones & Company, September 18, 2014. https://www.wsj.com/articles/home-depot-breach-bigger-than-targets-1411073571.

quotas. Armed with handheld devices that can be concealed in pants pockets or disguised in plain sight, they were equipped with skimmers with the directive to collect a minimum of one hundred credit card numbers a week in exchange for one thousand dollars in pay, each and every Sunday. Some of the credit card numbers collected were repetitive if she worked in a fine-dining experience, specialty clothing store, or salon/spa where customers patronized frequently, but I had computer software that would flag the numbers that were already active in a scheme, about to be used, or had already been used as part of a previous scam.

Once the stolen credit card numbers were delivered, I categorized them by card type based on the first four numbers on the card, a process that enabled me to easily group the four major credit card issuers. Once categorized and grouped, numbers from each group were strategically selected based on the issuing bank and card expiration date(s). I always targeted the credit card numbers that were hosted by the household names such as American Express, Citi Bank, Capital One, Chase Bank, and Discover Card, just to name a few. My reasoning was that the bigger the bank, the higher the credit limit; the longer the expiration date, the newer the card. Chance and transaction would occasionally remind me that neither of my theories were proven, though they were probable. Some credit card expiration dates are renewed annually, and the larger credit card issuers make their money off issuing credit cards with lower limits, higher interest rates, and longer expiration dates.

Because credit card numbers don't have faces attached to them—the industry tried pictorial credit cards for a while but it failed miserably—they numerically represent consumer profiles, domicile addresses, and spending patterns. So the place where you chose to use your credit or debit card determined whether you were exposed to my credit card fraud. Now stolen, chosen, and subject to my discretionary exploitation, your credit card numbers underwent the meticulous process of credit card replication.

THE CARD REPLICATION PROCESS

Credit and debit card replication is an awful art and a mad science that attends to the aesthetic attractions as well as to the electronic and security measures of both authentic and counterfeit credit and debit cards.

The obvious and physical aesthetics of a credit card is what first captures the merchant's attention. A flawed or poorly replicated credit card will certainly alert and alarm the least suspecting. The Printers within my organization knew I was a painstaking perfectionist, and I taught them how to replicate credit cards in a way that rivaled the actual cards issued by the banks. The embossing had to be perfectly measured, spaced, and glossed properly just in case the credit card had to be physically handled at the point of sale for manual entry of its numbers.

Type-ins, or numeric manual entries, are always a last resort for the merchant because it's treated as a "Card Not Present" transaction, thereby causing the merchant to be more liable for any potentially fraudulent transactions. Before the EMV chip technology was introduced into the US market—in October 2014 by Executive Order: 13681 for added security as a third factor of authentication—a credit card carried, and still does carry, its electronic identity on the black magnetic-sensitive strip that runs across on back of the card. All of the credit card's information was encoded on this strip, and by one swipe through a skimmer device, that information could be collected and transferred to a card with its own blank magnetic strip. Once produced, the replicated credit card functions at the same level of proficiency as does the authentic card originally issued to the primary cardholder.[39]

Uploading and encoding your applicable personal information from a skimmer onto a counterfeit credit card requires special and specific abilities. But the most daring and demanding task about credit card replication is a Printer's ability to replicate the artwork and science of the "unseen" security features known only to the bank that issues the card and to the merchant that accepts it as a method of payment. This includes everything from multi-color, translucent holograms to staggered and layered company logos to inverted and encrypted card identification numbers. A special black light and decoding software enables the Printer to see and replicate all security features on any credit card. Furthermore, what retail associate has the time or interest to verify all the security features on a credit card at the point of sale, despite what they are trained and instructed to do in orientation?

39 "Executive Order—Improving the Security of Consumer Financial Transactions." National Archives and Records Administration. National Archives and Records Administration. https://obamawhitehouse. archives.gov/the-press-office/2014/10/17/executive-order-improving-security-consumer-financial-transactions.

USING FRAUDULENT CARDS

My personal, practical, and professional approach to credit card fraud was a combination of credit card counterfeit and replication as well as through "account take over," beginning twenty-five years ago before this scam was ever given a name. That is, when I was fifteen years old I "took over" my dad's Capital One credit card account and exhausted his existing line of credit.

As an identity thief, I had access to all my victim's credit profiles, which contained their full credit reports. I earned this unprecedented and privileged access to existing credit card accounts by assuming the identity of the cardholder. Too much was involved in account takeovers, however, and I quickly pursued and perfected "new account" fraud by applying for new credit using stolen identities.

These new, fraudulent accounts were guaranteed to be approved when I confirmed credit score criteria as a prerequisite to victimization. I carried those credit reports as "cheat sheets," either on my person or in my memory as I applied for new credit online or in-store. As my identity theft schemes evolved by way of trial and error, so did my credit card scams.

Instead of undergoing the laborious task of "account take-overs," and risk premature discovery of a freshly stolen identity, I discovered the shortcut to credit and debit card replication. In 2002, I developed an elaborate system of "hybrid identity theft," these days referred to by its misnomer "synthetic identity theft."[40] Though misidentified as synthetic identity theft,

---

40 Kagan, Julia. "Synthetic Identity Theft." Investopedia. Investopedia, August 11, 2019. https://www.investopedia.com/terms/s/synthetic-identity-theft.asp.

there's absolutely nothing synthetic about the crime or its victim impact. Whichever term you choose, the stolen identity is used in combination or conjunction with a stolen credit card number belonging to a completely different person that had been replicated to match the name of the stolen identity.

For example, I might steal the identity of an African American woman and replicate a credit or debit card belonging to a Caucasian male, but replace the original cardholder's name with that of the stolen identity. Retail associates almost always like to match names between any acceptable form of identification during the credit or debit cards transaction authentication process, but rarely if ever do they match the name on the printed transaction receipt to the primary form of identification. That simple step would spot the fraud, but it's never checked, and so the crime continues.

Some forms of credit card fraud are more detectable than others, but for the most part, there are far more successful credit card fraud transactions than there are defeated ones. In today's industry, credit and debit cards have adopted and adapted new security features to combat against the rampant and random credit card fraud of today's marketplace. For a good while, the three-digit CVV code (Card Verification Value) on the back of a card served as an authentication measure. It was introduced by credit card companies to reduce fraudulent transactions over the internet or by phone. For a small span the CVV code provided a level of security against the "Card Not Present" transactions. Those days are long gone.

To circumvent the CVV security feature, I encouraged my Field Operatives to rely on their mnemonic discipline and engage "Match Memorization" to collate the last four digits of the account number with the CVV code. My Info Operatives that worked at hotels simply photocopied the credit cards—this was before debit cards could be used to check into a hotel—front and back, along with the driver's license at check-in. The CVV code never fully nor effectively served its purpose in my network of scams, which gave necessity and invention to its cousin the "EMV Chip." However, the EMV chip is already obsolete and its security measures are easily circumvented.

By the time the EMV (Europay Master/Visa) Chip was mandated by Executive Order into the US economy in October 2014, my career in credit card fraud had been over by more than a decade. However, I've considered the technology with all of its fancy features, encryption technology, and additional factors of authentication. In summary here, if you compare and contrast two of your credit or debit cards issued by different banks, you'd notice that the EMV chips may slightly vary in size as you compare your credit card to your debit card. This is a security measure aimed against the card replication and "device access fraud," but the raw and real truth is that a perpetrator can order thousands of EMV skimmers and chips, holograms, and blank gift cards straight from China, in all shapes and sizes *right here, right now, in real time.*[41]

As a former master counterfeiter of credit and debit cards, I've recaptured the zeitgeist of Duck Pond Road back in St. Joseph and cell A-12 in Tangipahoa Parish Jail to develop what

---

41 It's true. https://m.alibaba.com/amp/showroom/emv-card-skimmer.html

I believe to be the technological panacea that will disrupt and stop credit and debit card fraud once and for all, thus declaring it the "be all end all" to the problem of device access fraud. My heartfelt desire is to introduce and implement my disruptive technology here at home in America and then throughout the world wherever credit and debit cards are an acceptable form of payment to once and for all stop the fraud that infiltrates and contaminates the card processing transaction.[42]

CHECK IN AND CASH OUT

According to some experts, the Romans devised the concept of check writing around 325 BC, but widespread acceptance and usage weren't realized until eighteen hundred years later in Holland. In the sixteenth century, Amsterdam was a major international trading depot. As a more secure option to storing up mattress-money at home, people started depositing their cash with Dutch "cashiers." Eventually, the notion of writing and depositing checks as a payment arrangement soon found its way to England.

The first printed checks are traced to 1762 and a British banker named Lawrence Childs. The word "check" also may have originated in England in the 1700s when serial numbers were placed on these pieces of paper as a way to keep track of, or to "check" on them. In the United States, the first checks are said to have been introduced in 1681 when cash strapped

---

42 I've developed technology for this need via DuckPond Technologies, Inc. See www.duckpond.tech for more info.

businessmen in Boston mortgaged their land to a "fund," against which they would write checks.[43]

As the checking system evolved, so did the check fraud schemes and scams. According to the Federal Trade Commission, over the last three years, the number of complaints has steadily increased, and so have the dollars lost.[44] A report written by the Better Business Bureau reminds us that check fraud is a "huge problem" with "millions of fake checks worth billions of dollars circulating every year."[45] Most check fraud is committed by use of a monetary instrument—a paper check.

The most common type of check fraud known to us and practiced every day in our society is *check kiting*. This process hinges on the "float" system, which is when money in the banking system is counted twice, for a brief time, because of delays in processing checks or any transfer of cash. There is a float time between check issuance and checking accounting deduction. So check kiting is a matter of calculated manipulation that takes advantage of the float system to access and make use of non-sufficient funds in a checking or bank account. When this happens, checks become a form of unauthorized credit instead of being a date and time stamped negotiated instrument.

Another commonly practiced form of check fraud is plain, old fashioned, writing *bad checks*. Bad check writing is simply

---

43 Infoplease. https://www.infoplease.com/.
44 "Consumer Information." Consumer Information. https://www.consumer.ftc.gov/.
45 "BBB Study Shows How Fake Check Scams Bait Consumers." BBB. https://www.bbb.org/en/us/article/investigations/18409-bbb-study-shows-how-fake-check-scams-bait-consumers?bbbid=0000.

knowingly and deliberately writing a check and presenting it as sufficient payment for goods and services without the intent of making the check good for payment by the hosting banking institution. I learned how to float checks only after writing enough bad checks, for which I was judicially held accountable. I wrote them with absolutely no money in my accounts, not realizing at the time that jail would be the ultimate consequence for this type of check fraud.

Another type of check fraud is called *abandonment*, and it's often perpetrated by individuals known as "paper hangers," which is another name for the check kiter that fully intends to abandon the account with no intention of balancing the float. Abandonment occurs when the paper hanger deposits a bad or fictitious check into his or her account. Once the funds clear or are made available for withdrawal, which usually is the next business day, but before the bank is notified, the fraudster makes an immediate cash withdrawal. I often orchestrated and engaged abandonment as part of my social identity theft operation. Using stolen identities, I instructed my Field Operatives to open bank accounts to run check scams and schemes through as we were nearing exhaustion of the stolen identity in use.

The art and science of replication is not restricted to counterfeit credit cards and IDs, but is rather applied to any and all aspects of a person's paper and plastic reality, checkbook included. I stayed away from taking over my victims' pre-existing personal checking accounts because the monetary contents therein were monitored with a heightened level of scrutiny. Any sign or symptom of impropriety associated with such an intimate account triggers an alarm that has the potential to discover my silent, sinister, more lucrative schemes of identity theft much sooner than I had projected. So instead, I reproduced counterfeit checks on real entities in the name of the stolen identity—four or five different checks—and made a group deposit on Friday just before close of business in preparation for a Monday morning cash withdrawal of 80 to 90 percent of the available funds.

This complex scam worked each and every time, though it could never be used at the victimized bank twice. To avoid suspicion and possible detection when having large sums of money withdrawn, sometimes I directed my Field Operatives to simply get a cashier's check made payable to the counterpart of yet another stolen identity that would be assumed by a different Field Operative. They would take the cashier's check and cash it at a different bank branch.

My check fraud and counterfeiting experiences didn't just start and stop with counterfeiting commercial checks. Two of my most promising counterfeited checks were top-rated insurance companies and federal government-issued income tax checks. Banks and local check cashing stores don't hesitate to cash either of these two checks, as long as the amounts aren't astronomical.

When closing out a stolen identity with "abandonment" being my last stop, two of the three to five counterfeit checks that I would have deposited were always insurance and/or income tax checks. Funds for these checks were made available the next business day, but I would always monitor check clearance and availability online, then never return back to the initiating or hosting bank for withdrawal. In today's check industry, check security and verification technology have advanced to combat and curb this fraudulent practice, but so have the mastermind criminals who thrive and survive off this industry.

When counterfeiting checks, a host of other crimes are committed in the process. For example, identity theft and forgery were a necessary part of my check fraud operation. Yet there are those rare occasions, as in the case of master check forger Frank Abagnale, who employed at least two methods of check fraud in conjunction with identity theft: forgery and counterfeiting. Mr. Abagnale defrauded the banking system by putting incorrect MICR numbers at the bottom of the checks he wrote so that they could be routed to the wrong Federal Reserve bank for clearing. The technology of digital banking has virtually made this scheme impossible in our present-day era. Thanks to such depictions, forgery is widely known. But because of technological developments, it is less practiced and perhaps the simplest way to get caught committing check fraud.

The newest type of check fraud is called *advance fee* check system, popularized and primarily perpetrated by criminal elements based in Nigeria, Romania, Jamaica, Russia, and India. Have you ever received one of those emails requesting you to send a small amount of money via Western Union or Money Gram in order to receive a large sum in the form of a check? As the scam unfolds, the process is reversed and the issuer overnights you a fake check but cautions that before you can deposit the check or attempt to cash it you must first send, usually wire, the "advance fee" associated with cashing the check. The advance fee check scam manifests in various forms, but there's no doubt that this scam specifically targets you as its victim.

Check fraud in the United States is a persistent and pervasive annoyance. Law enforcement can't track nor keep up with the constant technological advancements of criminality. They are just outnumbered, and necessarily, this domestic war with foreign invasions must be fought from a technological platform. America's economy is in need of check security technology that no longer meets the criminal at the fraudulent transaction but beats him there and awaits her arrival.[46]

THE REAL GRAND THEFT AUTO

In America, auto theft has always been problematic in the automobile industry, making it a black-market business that cost automobile owners, various insurers, and taxpayers billions of dollars annually. With the advent and use of today's technology, the traditional method of stealing an automobile is a thing of the past and auto thieves, and thieves in general, are rapidly adapting to meet the demands of their criminal trades of choice. The 2002 flick *Gone in Sixty Seconds* suggested that an automobile is stolen every sixty seconds or less here in America. While I do not contend with the notion of how often or how much time it takes to manually steal an automobile,

---

46 My company, DuckPond Technologies, Inc. is currently developing disruptive technology that will introduce and expose the fraudster long before their scam meets success. More information on my disruptive technologies can be found at www.duckpond.tech.

I provide a different perspective and reality—that more and more automobiles are being stolen over a span of less than sixty *days*, in a complex and sophisticated process I've termed vehicular identity theft.

Absolutely no one—not any of the experts in the identity theft security industry, the automobile industry, law enforcement, or the American populace—identifies with the modernized, materialized, and monetized crime that I have designated as vehicular identity theft.

In his article "Protecting Against Car Identity Theft," Pat Goss of *Motorweek Magazine*, referenced one concept of this method.[47] According to him and to other warnings about vehicular-related identity theft, the threat is that someone will walk by your car, copy your VIN, and use it somehow and somewhere else, preventable by placing a piece of aluminum foil between the windshield and VIN.

Now, I applaud the effort to bring awareness in this regard, but what follows describes an entirely different process and is on a completely different planet all by itself. For the remainder of this chapter, I will rely solely on my experience as the expert witness to differentiate idealistic assumptions from everyday realities.

THEN AND NOW

Throughout the '80s and '90s, auto theft required stealing the entire vehicle, whether by hot-wiring or carjacking. Once

---

47 "Protecting Against Car Identity Theft." MotorWeek. http://www.motorweek.org/features/goss_garage/protecting_against_car_identity_theft.

stolen, the vehicle was taken to a local chop-shop for dismantling and redistribution of its parts. By the late '90s and early 2000s, cyber and social identity theft started to become prevalent, and auto thieves and identity thieves began to collaborate their initiatives to defraud their victims. Instead of having to carjack or use a shammy to hot-wire a vehicle, auto thieves were now consulting me on how to use the personal information of an automobile owner to steal their vehicles without having to resort to any means of force by way of entry or possession.

My first resolution was to assume the registered automobile owner's identities and, with a replicated driver's license and automobile registration in hand, attend the local dealership to request or simply order a duplicate key for the vehicle identification number to the automobile targeted for theft. However, when automobile dealerships across the nation became aware of this scam, it proved too much of a risk to take.

I had been using stolen identities to purchase new vehicles from dealerships since my teens when I purchased a Lincoln Mark VIII off-site, using my dad's stolen identity. As my identity theft organization and its operations evolved, I used stolen identities on the regular to purchase and re-sell new automobiles to aspiring black market buyers, but it became too much of a headache when I found myself having to manage the maintenance of the vehicles regarding monthly payments and insurance premiums to avoid detection and the eventual compromise. By 2004, the auto theft black market needed a less risky and more sure way to capitalize on the auto theft market.

I needed to adapt and meet the demands of the black market. This branch of identity theft as I designed and developed it, is the crossmatching of selective automobile vehicle identification numbers to automobiles of like characteristics to create a multi-level transaction that is difficult or impossible to track. It is a high-level crime, given its complexity and unusual sophistication, that I detailed in part as I came to understand it in my story.

My dark technology was originally inspired by auto thieves from Modesto and Arizona that began flying in to consult with me to discover a remedy to rectify the developing problem of security measures that were being introduced in the scheme and scam of things.

THE AUTO THEFT PROCESS

From the approach of social identity theft, I first identified a victim with a credit beacon score of 721 or more to ensure the auto loan approval process wouldn't require proof of income, although that too was doctored and readily available if requested. I then identified automobiles of choice by going on a lot-hopping mission to determine which dealerships were ready to sell a vehicle almost at any cost. Once my dealership of choice was targeted, I armed Field Operatives with the qualified identities and orchestrated the "purchase" of a vehicle of my selection. After the loan agreements were finalized and full coverage insurance verified, my people took possession and delivered the newly purchased vehicles to me.

On the surface, these stolen automobiles look like legitimate purchases, but they were nothing more than the poisonous fruit of fraud and profitability in process. No matter how perfect the paperwork was, the lender always required proof of full coverage insurance before the buyer could take possession of the vehicle, which I always prearranged via the insurance quote process once I targeted a vehicle for acquisition.

Under the normal process, the original VIN on the fraudulent vehicle would be initially registered with its resident state, in keeping with the high probability that the identity thief used an in-state address. To significantly reduce the risk of detection during any stage of my process, I eliminated potential conflicts by never again using the true credentials of the vehicle once it left the dealership. The stolen vehicles needed to assume a new identity by assignment of a new vehicle identification number.

To assign a new VIN to the fraudulent vehicle, I dove into the treasure trove of the internet to find unregistered and uninsured automobiles that matched the year, make, and model of the fraudulent vehicle that needed a new identity to advance. Neutral VIN numbers were readily available on sites like autotrader.com, cars.com, and carmax.com. In some instances, when local insurance agents required or requested to photograph the actual car but the exterior paint didn't match the VIN that was provided to get the quote, my simple solution was that the vehicle had recently undergone a custom paint job. Needless to say, this lie worked every single time some scrupulous insurance agent wanted to physically examine the vehicle before issuing coverage. With the fraudulent vehicle now quoted at retail value for full coverage insurance under the description of the stolen VIN from the internet, the next phase of this scam was in order.

Using the neutral VIN from the internet, I replicated the bill of sale and title documents to reflect a cash purchase for insurance and state registration purposes—now using a completely different stolen identity, completely disconnected from the one that was used to originate the scam.

I preferred to replicate and submit an out-of-state title of ownership that would have to undergo the conversion process of the resident state. The intent of an out-of-state title of ownership is to impede any possible detection of the scam before the real benefits can emerge. Alternatively, my Field Operatives would attend the local satellite tax/title/license outlets that charge higher convenience fees for their services but were less stringent than the Office of Motor Vehicles. I juggled the tax, title, and license locations to push paperwork, to be easily accessible and escapable if the scam was ever discovered, like the OMV on Independence St. in Baton Rouge that had state police working the parking lot conducting vehicle inspections and a host of other things.

The conversion process of an out-of-state title of ownership took approximately thirty days to mature, sometimes sooner, as does the first month of a stolen vehicle insurance premium. Once the fraudulent vehicle was fully insured and registered with the hosting state under the description of the VIN swiped from the internet, in time I would make sure the vehicle was staged at some major event or parked at a hotel in the locality where crime was high. Once the fraudulent vehicle was situated on the scene and relocated back to safekeeping, a false police report was filed with the local police alleging grand theft auto.

The insurance companies typically investigated auto theft claims up to thirty days before they honored the claim or extended its investigation. The insurance companies already had counterfeit bill-of-sales on file reflecting ownership by the insured, so the claim handlers automatically knew that the claim would be a cash settlement based on present day market value or the appraised retail value of the fraudulent vehicles.

In approximately thirty days, sometimes a little longer, the insurance companies all issued full settlement checks over the full retail or appraised value of the automobiles—naturally, I always added increased coverage for custom upgrades that were never actually added to the fraudulent vehicles.

Once the insurance settlement checks came in the mail to the registrant's address on file, they were deposited into the checking accounts that were opened, always using the credentials of the substitute stolen identities. They typically clear in one or two days, but my Field Operatives got them cleared on the same day of deposit by simply requesting the bank manager to verify the authenticity of the settlement check and authorize its immediate availability for withdrawal.

After the funds were authorized and made available for immediate withdrawal, I instructed my Field Operatives to deplete the checking accounts of all funds between two to three branch locations if a single branch could not accommodate such a large cash withdrawal. Once the process of vehicular identity theft was perfected, it was light work and worked like clockwork, every time.

The turnaround for a perfectly orchestrated vehicular identity theft scam takes approximately thirty-five to forty-five days on average but can take up to sixty days as part of admin-istrative bureaucratic protocol when settlement checks are over a certain threshold. Each and every time after I cashed out on this scam, I either repeated it with the same fraudulent vehicles but different used identities, insurers, and vehicle identification numbers obtained from the internet, or I sim-ply sold the original stolen vehicles to chop shops.

For an investment ranging from twenty-five hundred to five thousand dollars and over not more than a two-month period, my return on investment was a minimum of fifty thousand dollars and graduated to an excess of one hundred thousand as I scaled industry loopholes, human ignorance, and systematic deficiencies.

AN ADVANCING SCAM

Unfortunately, today's auto theft black market industry has become very lucrative and liberating thanks in part to the sci-ence of identity theft and its ever-evolving schemes and scams. Vehicular identity theft is a lucrative crime that's just now getting exposed and never gets classed or caught because the cyber identity thief, the social identity thief, and the auto thief have metamorphosed into the singular *vehicular identity thief.*

And to prevent a massive perpetration of multifaceted fraud it is necessary that I pivot here and not delve into the virtual aspects of vehicular identity theft, the dark dynamics and deep dangers of which does not permit me to partially explicate or even hint at the details of its operation via this medium. It is enough here to put America on notice that there are untold risks that exist in the cyberspace of virtual vehicular identity theft.

HWH

Technological advancements have enabled vehicular identity thieves to steal your vehicle while it remains in your possession, much in the same way a cyber or social identity thief steals your identity while it remains in your wallet or purse, subject to your discretion. Traditional chop-shops have been upgraded and are less visible, with a virtual inventory that operates off of an on-demand order policy over the internet. The risk of running a "live-wire" chop shop full of hot merchandise has been reduced to the convenience of a laptop computer.

In the old days, greed led to capture. Nowadays, contentment and calculated thefts translate into continued capitalization. The more intelligent vehicular identity thieves aren't burglarizing and hot-wiring automobiles as they did before. Though it is the predominant motivator, insurance and bank fraud aren't the only aspects that vehicular identity thieves find to be lucrative, as many a stolen automobile can be auctioned off on the street to unscrupulous buyers seeking a good deal.

NOT JUST SPORTS CARS

My experience with vehicular identity theft was not restricted to the theft of automobiles alone. Just about any mobile device with a vehicle identification number is subject to the realization of vehicular identity theft. I have used stolen identities to purchase all kinds—the most popular items were ATVs and zero turn radius lawn tractors, which were some of the easiest vehicles to steal. They guaranteed a minimum of four thousand dollars for each item upon delivery—and not the cheap ones you can purchase just off the side of the road from a pop-up supplier. They were industry recognized brand name items that had exorbitant retail prices attached to them.

These items were in such high demand that I had begun to purchase and store them (using stolen identities, of course) in an effort at proactivity to supply the increasing demand. But I could never keep up, sometimes selling three and four ATVs or lawn tractors to a single customer, who often were the "straw customers" for anonymous buyers.

Second to automobiles, motorcycles were also in high demand. Vehicular identity theft works the same way with a motorcycle as it does with an automobile. Compact water-craft, such as fancy jet skis and a full array of boats, are also some of the main attractions to a social identity thief that engages vehicular identity theft. Just like ATVs, jets skis, lawn tractors, small heavy-duty equipment, etc., motorcycles are purchased in groups of twos and threes from respective dealerships using the creditworthiness of stolen identities to secure instant credit financing.

While I have not personally stolen nor crossmatched the vehicular identification numbers of any watercraft to commit vehicular identity theft, I do know that it can be done following the same schematic that I used to explore and exploit the automobile, insurance, and banking industries.

Most of my experience in stealing and reselling stolen watercraft using a stolen identity has been with various fishing boats that came with specific motors, per customer requests. My watercraft customers were not necessarily interested in purchasing the body of a boat, but they always requested boat motors that retailed from fifteen to twenty thousand dollars. Instead of the headache of purchasing, pulling, and disposing of an entire boat, I often settled my scam in the purchase of just the motor, which circumvented the boat registration paperwork and did away with all the extra cargo to make the commission of the scam more convenient and easier to perpetrate, selling them at a 40 percent discount from the retail cost.

However, had I been given an order for a cigarette boat or even a yacht, I could have delivered both items with relative ease using one of many stolen identities I had on file that reflected credit profiles with high loan amounts in both revolving and installment credit accounts.

ADDRESSING THE THREAT

In my research, I cannot determine where state or federal law enforcement agencies, legislators, identity theft protection providers, insurance companies, state or federal departments of transportation, nor any of the findings of the leading research institutions on the subject of identity theft that either acknowledge or confront the real and direct threats of vehicular identity theft.

The purpose of exposing each of these scams is to spark policy for prevention, methods for detection and prosecution, and disruptive technology for protection, as well as the legislative jump-starters I propose among the bonus material that closes this book. As part of a concerted and ongoing effort to reverse some of the diabolical trends to which I have made impactful contributions, my company DuckPond Technologies, Inc. is also developing *new* technology that will disrupt and eradicate vehicular identity theft before it ulti-mately rewrites national vehicular crime statistics.[48]

To be entangled in a social identity theft scam as an inno-cent victim is a very messy ordeal. The scams of social and vehicular identity theft almost always send its victims into a stage of mild depression, creating a sense of unconscious para-noia even after the victim's life has been regained and restored.

The adverse psychological effects of victimization are real. In my legislative bills, I also propose that a treatment plan and counseling services should be legislatively mandated as part of any identity theft protection service for which a con-sumer pays.

Each of the crimes I have detailed come with cousin crimes and extremist approaches that I feel warrants special, closed-session elaborations on both a state and federal level, where everyone can contribute to the proposed solutions. In the meantime, an understanding of the methods, motivation, and means of identity theft can help you better prevent or detect it.

---

48 Watch www.duckpond.tech for the latest updates.

SIX

INSTITUTIONAL TRUST BETRAYED

Betrayal is the worst...and the key to moving past
it is to identify what led up to it in the first place.
—Charles J. Orlando

What do we do when the service providers that we assume we can trust turn out to be in partnership with identity thieves? To this point, we've hardly had to think about it. The general assumption is that the thief will make himself known through some clearly suspicious interaction. Once institutional trust is in place, we stop thinking about everyone else.

The same underpaid, overworked employees who would be willing to swipe your card through a skimmer at the convenience store would be willing to move information from their profession to the active social identity thief or ring. There is no class, level of employment, or certain type of person to watch out for. It is simply a question of becoming more aware, then sealing protection for ourselves, our families, and anyone else in our care.

ADMITTED FLAWS IN COLLEGE ADMISSIONS

Recently, the most unsuspecting perpetrators of fraud have come to light, earning prison time and shaming a national institution: parents trying to get their kids into college. Sixteen parents were given fraud charges based on their attempts to buy their kids' way into school, with some of the bribe and fraudulent records amounts reaching into the millions for a single student.[49]

In the greater scheme of it all, they are not only the tip of the fraudulent iceberg, but they also went the longer, more expensive way around. In my former life, I replicated countless high school transcripts to get kids into colleges and universities.

When someone wanted to get into college but didn't quite possess the qualifying or preferred level of records, I would pay for an original high school transcript of an honor student, then swap the names for the student aspiring to enter college. Today,

---

49 Fieldstadt, Elisha, and Tom Winter. "Lori Loughlin among 16 Parents Indicted on New Charges in College Admissions Scheme." NBCNews. com. NBCUniversal News Group, April 10, 2019.

with everything digitized, replication looks a little bit different but is still possible. As long as you don't get greedy and also apply for federal assistance to pay for school, this is a simple way into college that happens from semester to semester.

None of these fraudulent attempts are a huge leap from the unethical essay-for-hire admissions services that so many people use to get into and pay for failing grades throughout school. The desperate parent or student is assisted in their mollification then, sure that they're only doing what any parent would, given the chance.

THE SCARE IN HEALTHCARE

Medical identity theft occurs any time an identity thief uses a victim's personal identifiable medical information, including but not limited to insurance information, social security numbers, Medicare and Medicaid numbers, or medical records to obtain medical goods and services, or to submit fraudulent claims for medical services rendered.

Out of all the known and developing forms of identity theft, I assert that medical identity theft is the most dangerous among them. It can adversely and egregiously impact its victims psychologically, financially, even physically and fatally. The application of medical identity theft can manifest for the victim in many ways, from being billed for services you didn't receive to chasing a misdiagnosis.

Medical identity thieves show up on both sides of the spectrum—as a healthcare provider and healthcare recipient alike—stealing and using personally identifiable medical information. Not a few healthcare professionals have been charged and convicted for using their patients' medical identity, costing the patient, the system, or both.

Healthcare professionals such as office personnel, nurses, secretaries, administrators, and other staff members with convenient access to medical files are equally qualified, capable, and motivated to engage medical identity theft for their own varied reasons. At the age of twenty-three, I was as healthy as they come, with no need to forge my way into healthcare, and I didn't work in the medical field, so I had nothing to gain from its exploitation. But I was interested in the identifying credentials of the hospital's patients—specifically the private hospitals in the more well-to-do side of town. I teamed up with an Info Operative who held an administrative position at premier hospitals from Monroe, LA, to Hammond to Baton Rouge and on back to New Orleans.

In those days, if the patient didn't have Medicare or private insurance, you simply could not be a customer of those hospitals. This observation suggested that most, if not every patient, was premium and a prime candidate for social identity theft, in the economic standing to be able to have your own private insurance policy. Through my Info Operatives, I had access to the medical information of every patient who ever walked in and out of those hospitals.

In that way, my practice and participation in medical identity theft were marginal at best—which is not to minimize the intrusion of having your personal information taken from supposedly secure hands. But when medically identifying information is used within the medical field, the consequences are far greater than any financial damage I might have done.

Besides the health benefits, there's little motivation to practice and perfect this form of identity theft unless you're on the receiving end from a medical billing perspective or are receiving monetary kickbacks as a healthcare professional facilitating fraudulent billing. As recently as 2019, a billion dollars' worth of fraudulent purchases through Medicare were caught as part of an identity theft and a fraud ring within the medical industry.[50]

When someone in administration is involved in medical identity theft, it's typically as we saw in my experience. They are gathering personal information and passing it along to the actual thief on a cash basis. Or they might be instructed by the doctor, who could be involved in a much larger scam.

One all too common way they profit off of patients is to use Medicaid, Medicare, and private insurance numbers to conduct fraudulent billing.[51] Across a network of hundreds of patients, small amounts that might not otherwise be noticed can add up quickly. The administrator would likely be the one to execute this scam, but only the doctor or clinic has the monetary motivation to initiate it. Not only is this unfair to the owner of the information, but it wreaks havoc on our national

---

50 "Billion-Dollar Bust." FBI. FBI, April 9, 2019. https://www.fbi.gov/news/stories/billion-dollar-medicare-fraud-bust-040919.
51 Outreach, Education &. "Health Care Billing Errors and Fraud—Reporting Health Care Fraud." AARP. https://www.aarp.org/health/health-insurance/info-05-2012/health-care-billing-errors-and-fraud.html.
   Piper, Charles. "Fraud Magazine." Fraud Magazine. https://www.fraud-magazine.com/article.aspx?id=4294976280.

systems. The money we allocate for Medicaid and Medicare should go to the patients who need it. Instead, our taxpayer dollars are lost to the tune of a billion dollars every year.[52]

Medical identity theft is likely committed by healthcare providers and professionals at much greater levels than by a cyber or social identity thief in need of medical goods and services themselves. There are those instances, however, and enough of them are reported and accounted for. This kind of medical identity theft wreaks havoc on the lives of unwary and unsuspecting healthcare recipients, sometimes fatally.

In the US, we also have a significant problem with "patient mix-ups."[53] While the official story is one of gross incompetence, I cannot help but wonder how much of it is actually tied to intentional deception. If someone gathers up your identifying information and beats you to the hospital with it, or to a facility you haven't been to before, those new records enter the system with their unique health information tied to it.

The reports we have begun to see about the mix up of patients' information is gaining in frequency and consequently, fatalities will follow. It is no small matter when a patient's medical identifying information is compromised to the extent that otherwise accurate medical records have been

---

52 "Fifth Annual Study on Medical Identity Theft." Medical Identity Fraud Alliance. Ponemon Institute, February 20, 2015. http://www.medidfraud.org/wp-content/uploads/2015/02/2014_Medical_ID_Theft_Study1.pdf.

53 May, Patrick. "How Big Is the Patient Mix-up Problem in the U.S.?" RightPatient. Patrick May, January 11, 2018. http://www.rightpatient.com/blog/how-big-is-the-patient-mixup-problem-in-the-us/.

contaminated and confused with misinformation. Far beyond billing questions, now there is the potential for misdiagnosis and mistreatment.

Medical identity theft is a subtle epidemic that's weaving socio-disease into the very fabric of our healthcare system and community as a nation. Having diagnosed this unwanted disease, we must align our efforts toward a cure. We need more secure records, more accountability, more centralization of medical data access and analysis, and more careful consideration of the patient in front of providers.[54] Otherwise, our healthcare system will eventually be bankrupted and stolen via medical identity theft.

INCOME TAX IDENTITY THEFT

Within the last five to seven years, this form of identity theft has gained enough momentum to make headlines and spark warnings.[55] I write with limited personal experience in this arena, owing to its rise within the last decade. Income tax identity theft is an evolutional hybrid of cyber identity theft and social identity theft that enables the unauthorized use of your personal information—particularly and primarily, your social security number—to file a fraudulent tax return or claim tax benefits.

---

54 DuckPond Technologies, Inc. is working on a solution to medical fraud via our MedicaSystems technology. Watch for updates at www. duckpond.tech
55 "Taxpayer Guide to Identity Theft." Internal Revenue Service. https:// www.irs.gov/newsroom/taxpayer-guide-to-identity-theft.

Most income tax identity thieves engage with the criminal intent of receiving a tax return, yet there's the minority among them who will combine income tax theft with child identity theft to claim specific benefits belonging to legitimate taxpayers with dependents.

For the first two months of the year 2017, more than fourteen thousand fraudulent income tax returns were filed, netting a loss to taxpayers of approximately four billion dollars.[56] By comparison, in the previous year of 2016, an estimated fifteen and a half million identities were compromised with losses weighing in at more than sixteen billion dollars, among which more than fourteen thousand fraudulent income tax returns were filed.

While those criminals will impersonate you to the IRS, another subset will impersonate the IRS to you. Few of us have been spared the call from a "202" Washington, DC number, threatening arrest and demanding payments with robocalls originating out of India. There's a market for that sort of vishing, typically directed at senior citizens. They are more likely to be established financially and less likely to be shrewd in who they trust.

As a matter of impatience, income tax identity theft for me was much too risky for my operation. The risk factors for the thief include the time appreciating tax returns and turnaround before a benefit is realized, as well as the attempt to

---

56 Al Pascual, Kyle Marchini, Sarah Miller, "2018 Identity Fraud: Fraud Enters a New Era of Complexity," Javelin Research, 2018. https://www.javelinstrategy.com/coverage-area/2018-identity-fraud-fraud-enters-new-era-complexity.)

defraud the Internal Revenue Service, who has resources to get their man, but are grossly outnumbered in futile efforts to take down a digital army of cyber identity thieves. For me, that was not simply a no, but a *hell nah*. I convinced myself that there was enough of America's money at ground level and within reach—particularly when household name tax preparation employees could siphon information directly to me and my established system of theft.

Endless streams of taxpayers' information were readily available to me. I retained an entire company's files on a single jump-drive for the current tax season and preceding year, ready to send to qualify through my process. I venture that most dare-devils who engage in income tax identity theft beyond the mere use of personal information are either organized criminal entities that have the patience and resources to score big over time, or are petty thieves and one-hit wonders who need some fast cash.[57] In equal measure, the reward was not worth the risk of having electronic fingerprints and footprints attached to a measly three to ten thousand dollars.

Unfortunately, crime data shows that the proverbial "early bird gets the worm." Those income tax identity thieves typically advance their fraud by filing fraudulent tax returns as early in tax season as is permissible by current tax laws, exploiting the delayed filing of the victimized taxpayers who would otherwise wait late into the tax season to file. They use

---

57 In Bulgaria, their prize was the data for the entire nation. https://www.cnn.com/2019/07/21/europe/bulgaria-hack-tax-intl/index.html

falsified W-2s that guarantee a large return, and once you find out it's too late. It takes months to resolve with the IRS so that you can get your real return.[58]

Under present conditions, I would recommend filing your income tax return as soon as you become eligible to do so. Otherwise, you remain exposed to this form of identity theft that's widening its reach and victimization each and every tax season.

Unlike cyber and social identity theft, the risk of income tax identity theft can be greatly reduced by a simple assignment that already exists. For those who have been victimized by income tax identity theft, the IRS issues an IP-PIN (Identity Protection Personal Identification Number) designed to verify the true identity of the taxpayer. Research shows that IP-PINs are effective against repeat income tax identity theft victimization, yet they are neither issued regularly nor used proactively.[59]

It seems counterproductive to have this measure of security as a reactionary remedy instead of positioning it as proactive crime prevention. As an advocate for the victims of identity theft in all of its facets and forms, at the end of this volume I have drafted an appeal to State and US lawmakers, along with legislative measures they can adopt to meet identity theft where it currently is and to beat its arrival to the

---

58 Weisman, Steve. "What the IRS Isn't Telling You about Identity Theft." USA Today. Gannett Satellite Information Network, January 30, 2016. https://www.usatoday.com/story/money/columnist/2016/01/30/what-irs-isnt-telling-you-identity-theft/79306984/.

59 "Identity Protection PIN Program Expands." Journal of Accountancy, February 8, 2019. https://www.journalofaccountancy.com/news/2019/feb/irs-identity-protection-pins-201920605.html.

future. One of my legislative bills speaks to the assignment of IP-PINs to every taxpayer in hopes of eliminating this pernicious form of identity theft and the emotionally draining process of resolution.

I may not have all the answers to combating the ever-widening spectrum of identity theft, but I have proposed the methods I would use in a fight against the old me and any of my previous social and cyber expert colleagues in crime.

SEVEN

A NATIONAL CRISIS
OF IDENTITY THEFT

*Identity theft, financial laundering...as well as
ransomware...all involving extortion of a hacked
institution are becoming increasingly common.*

*To truly make America safe, we must make
cyber security a major priority...for both
government and the private sector.*
— President Donald Trump

The gaps in security for our nation's security forces are
clear—the way I was able to exploit the police force and
military members years ago has no doubt continued over
the years, and will continue as long as it is unaddressed

by concerned, experience-educated minds. But this is not the only threat that identity theft poses to our national security. In fact, it is the hidden terror that we've yet to go to war against.

The threat of foreign attacks on this nation's cybersecurity merits constant vigilance from our top security agencies, yet we're still surprised when information leaks or systems are compromised. The unseen hands of visible and viable threats here at home pose a potentially greater threat, undermining our economy, healthcare systems, immigration policies, gun security, political process, and next up, America's voting democracy.

Let's face and deal with it: from both a practical and spiritual perspective, the enemy has a way of using our weaknesses against us to defeat us. Identity theft is a domestic problem that has evolved into a matter of international security.

While the world watches and continues casually, there are forces working tirelessly to damage and even take control of America. This plan of attack is being developed as part of a covert mission to infiltrate and influence, feeling more like *The Manchurian Candidate* every year. Hollywood gives us more clues than we readily accept or believe, and while I'm not saying to believe everything you see on TV, when a government cannot be overthrown by the planting of spies, treasonous tricks, and espionage, foreign agencies must resort to a cyber "sleight of hand" to perpetrate and perfect their attacks digitally.

I've mentioned data breaches and how consumer information is compartmentalized and sold in PIPs. Contextually, PIPs, are the "side hustle" to data breaches. The real money and greater catastrophe is brewing right in front of our faces, gradually but perceptively, as foreign governments bet big and buy into the massive data breaches rooted in and inextricably tied to America's economy. So why do the largest data breaches involve American consumers specifically, and where are these massive amounts of information being stored—more importantly, who is storing this data and for what purpose?

We live in the age of information gathering and redistribution. At every turn, American consumers' data is being gathered, collated, categorized, and qualified. More and more, it appears to be preparatory to a calculated redistributive infusion to manipulate the outcome of general elections. The most important goal is not to overthrow, but to infiltrate and influence the American government by way of covert control.

At this level of subtle, silent, and surreptitious foreign influence, politicians will be bought without knowing, elections paid for, policy shaped, and plans implemented to divulge and destabilize every fiber and fabric of our democracy.

It's ingenious: foreign governments can use the stolen, data-breached, compromised identities and voter registrations of Americans to take control of America by infiltrating the political process and voting system.[60] The war against America's democracy is already engaged, and by the time we realize the political casualties of this clandestine attack, the

---

60 When was the last time you looked back at what happened to your vote after you walked out of the booth? The fact that we can't is a gap in accountability that needs to be resolved. We should be able to track and measure our voting records as one step toward keeping our systems in check.

US Constitution as we live and breathe it will merely be a dead obituary of what America used to be. This, no doubt, will be the greatest, most irrevocably damaging and devastating fraud ever recorded in America's history.

Respectfully, I propose that our nation's leaders host a meeting of the minds consisting of the heads of every major institution within the federal government. We need to revamp or develop a new interagency task force to build upon and champion the spirit and intent of "The President's Identity Theft Task Force of 2007." The strategies of 2008 following this most recent task force report were indeed informative and full of ideas for its time and season, but today its application is rather obsolete.

From a legislative perspective, we need new laws aimed right at the heart of the domestic threats we face. Not superficial attempts at control, but direct responses to the methodology that drives identity theft here at home. From the executive branch, none of this will be carried out effectively unless we have the backing of our nation's commander in chief. Then, when new laws and measures are implemented, our Supreme Court justices and lower court judges must be prepared and empowered to govern a specific set of redacted and revised laws that have no allowable recourse or retreat through the appellate process for those caught and irreversibly convicted of a qualifying crime of identity theft.

To cut the identity thief off at the wrists, figuratively speaking, we must continually refresh our perspective, refine our strategies, and renew our attempts at curbing this national crisis.

QUESTIONS OF NATIONAL SECURITY

In the "9/11 Commission Report," identity theft was given a small segment of about ten pages, starting on page 393, wherein a few overly simplistic solutions are offered to address a very complex problem. The topic was given attention due to the hijackers' fraudulent paperwork during their time in the US. The report does highlight the gravity of identity theft and its attraction and connection to terrorism, noting that:

> ...impersonation, i.e., identity theft, is a key tool for terrorists. Travel documents are as important as weapons. Fraud is no longer just a problem of theft. At many entry points to vulnerable facilities, including gates for boarding aircraft, sources of identification are the last opportunity to ensure that people are who they say they are.[61]

What's noteworthy is that the 9/11 hijackers used their actual identities when boarding their flights the morning of September 11, 2001. The document fraud they committed was to enter the United States, live unsuspectingly once here, and obtain the driver's license they needed to board the planes. Just as with every piece of identity theft that I've unmasked in this work, the most obvious steps were overlooked.

---

61 Sullivan, Bob. "9/11 Report Light on ID Theft Issues." NBCNews.com. NBCUniversal News Group, August 4, 2004. http://www.nbcnews.com/id/5594385/ns/us_news-security/t/report-light-id-theft-issues/.

In an earlier report, just as the country was getting back on its feet, an identity theft expert named Judy Collins said, "What it's going to take is somebody who's really going to be married to this issue in terms of some knowledge and ability and skills and devotion and strict focus on this one single issue. And I don't know who's going to do it."[62]

Fifteen years after she spoke, the question is *when* are we going to do it?

I fully believe that the next major terror attack to be attempted on US soil will inevitably involve identity theft in some of its most deceptive and discreet forms, via some domestic entity. Among other security measures, it's time that we reconsider introducing biometrics into our nation's identification systems across the board and for all borders.

I'm speaking from expert testimony that signals the sound of the warning bell. If we ever become complacent in our attempts at regulating and controlling the problem of identity theft, I offer my story as a cautionary tale to return us to vigilance. If you're still not sure that identity theft needs a closer look, I posit the following questions of national security:

1. How many identity theft cases, mine excluded, have the FBI, Secret Service, Postal Inspector Service, and other government and state agencies with investigative authority and jurisdiction, investigated and closed since 1998—in comparison to the annual increase of identity theft victims to date?

---

62 ibid

2. How many identity theft cases have the Department of Justice prosecuted since the enhancement of the 2004 Identity Theft Penalty Enhancement Act?

3. How many tax dollars have been spent fighting identity theft in comparison to the billions lost to taxpayers over any given span of time? If the fight doesn't match the fraud, we're fighting in vain.

4. How many legislative initiatives aimed at identity theft have been introduced and passed into law over the past five years in response to the massive data breaches at eBay, Home Depot, JP Morgan Chase, Target, Equifax, Experian, T-Mobile, Marriot Hotels, Yahoo, etc., totaling well into the billions of compromised identities?

5. How many vehicular identity theft cases have been investigated and closed by both state and federal law enforcement agencies since the year 2004? In light of those investigations, how many vehicular identity theft cases have been successfully prosecuted by the Department of Justice or under the authority of each state's Attorney General's Office? In what way have those prosecutions shaped and impacted state and federal policy and legislation designed to identify, categorize, and restrict vehicular identity theft?

6. How many Executive Orders have been signed in the interest of combating identity theft and credit card

fraud since President Barak Obama's EMV requirement on October 17, 2014?

Truth be told, identity theft in its various forms has reached critical levels, and as a matter of national security, Executive Orders need to be implemented annually based on reporting and statistical data, and legislation should be revisited regularly to keep pace with changing times, trends, and technology.

Without decisive action, it's only a matter of time before our election process will be fully hacked and hijacked to steal and overthrow general elections, a new domestic attack arises, or our ongoing immigration, economic, and gun violence problems reach a fever pitch.

IDENTITY THEFT AND THE GUN VIOLENCE EPIDEMIC

As Americans, we love our guns, and we have every right to do so per constitutional provisions. As a convicted felon, my right to purchase and bear firearms remains perpetually denied, not even up for debate. However, as a former identity thief, I helped facilitate that love of guns for all willing to pay, including fellow convicts and anyone restricted by existing laws or financial restraint.

Using stolen identities, my Field Operatives would traverse the gun show circuit to illegally purchase all kinds and varieties of guns for resale purposes on the black market, neither knowing nor caring for what purpose the guns would be used. The guns I purchased and directed others to purchase were both big and small, semi-automatic and automatic, high power hunting rifles and assault rifles alike. If the clean and clear background check of a stolen identity passed—which I always confirmed pre-purchase via one of my law enforcement Info Operatives—I could purchase practically any firearm on my order sheet.

We went to gun shows, gun stores, and on some occasions, less restrictive pawn shops. Each time, our purchases were completed without question or conflict. It was then and remains now simply too easy to possess a gun in America, via systemic flaws. And each of these flaws are specifically targeted and exploited via the technical manipulation of social identity theft.

Yet for all of my repentance and regret, it wasn't until I was a victim of that crossfire shooting between rival gangs in Natchez, MS, that I truly felt the significance of that piece of my past. While leaving an afterparty in October 2017, my vehicle was hit several times. A couple of the rounds entered through the rear windshield, striking me and my female passenger in our right and left arms that rested on the center console armrest. Our injuries were minor. We were treated by the local hospital and released after our bullet fragment wounds were determined not to be life threatening.

The ultimate result notwithstanding, the bullets were life threatening as they left the barrel. Later that morning, on my drive back to Baton Rouge, I realized I was blessed to be alive and that the targeted victim had not been so fortunate. As I approached the four-way intersection in Woodville, MS— reminded of where my beloved and belated friend Jimmy

McGraw is from—my thoughts shifted and I began to cor-relate that night's experience with the many other random and senseless acts of violence, psychotic episodes, and out-right hate crimes that are so frequently perpetrated by people who never should have accessed those guns in the first place.[63]

We know the places—from Columbine High School to Pulse Night Club to Marjory Stoneman Douglas High School—but do we know the names of the people behind the weapon? To name a few, do we recognize Stephan Paddock, Omar Saddiqu, Scung-Hui Cho, Adam Lanza, Devin Patrick Kelly, George Hennard, James Huberty, Dylann Roof, Nich-olas Cruz, Eric Harris, Dylan Klebold, Robert Bowers, Dimi-trios Pagourtzis, James E. Holmes, Ian David Long, Howard Unruh, or John Earnest? These seventeen men are respon-sible for deadly shootings that prematurely and selfishly claimed the lives of three hundred and thirty-nine innocent American victims. They identified soft targets, defenseless places of worship and academia, where people should have been the safest. Seventeen men. About as many weapons. Hundreds of lives lost.

As this book moved through drafting and editing stages, Connor Betts, Patrick Crusius, and Santino William Legan joined these unholy ranks, wreaking havoc in Ohio, Texas, and California, respectively.

---

63 Nor should they be accessible to the extent that they are. In July, a man in Bel Air, CA, was found to have over 1,000 guns in his possession. This has gotten out of hand. https://www.latimes.com/california/story/2019-07-16/1000-guns-girard-saenz-felony-charges-getty-mansion

I fear that there will be more violence before production is complete, and that we will not be able to keep the text updated to publication time. The frequency at which these mass acts of violence occur is appalling and demands action. When I think back to the lives that were lost and my own that was spared by grace, I can't help but wonder why. Only by experiencing the trauma of gun violence can you really know how terrifying and humbling it is. I consistently remind myself of just how unworthy I am of life and liberty. I remind myself of how deeply our countless domestic victims deserved to be and were supposed to be safe during their hour of praise and prayer, in their classrooms of learning and development, and being together in venues where community and bonds are strengthened and life, in that moment, is joy. Instead, they were forever robbed of their lives or permanently scarred as victims in a country that can't seem to get a handle on its hate.

Only once my own life was threatened did I begin to contemplate the potential hand that I had in similar violence. I have no way of knowing where the guns I purchased went or how they were used. I can only look forward to what can be done out of experience as both victim and villain to devise a future that my children can be both safe and prosperous in.

When our loved ones are slaughtered as soft targets in places they should feel the safest, their blood is on our hands for our acceptance and dismissal of the status quo. When our loved ones are massacred in places of worship, where they should be most peaceful, their blood is on our souls for our refusal to repent of "the way we've always done things" and for settling for "just more of the same."

Who amongst us can give account for the shed blood of innocent lives in the face of conscious, cognizant, and consistent inactivity?

I have to echo Mrs. Michelle Obama's unrelated but applicable rallying cry: Let's move, America!

BONUS MATERIAL

FIFTY LEGISLATIVE PROPOSALS

The best ideas don't come from politicians, they come from citizens, people who work and live in the real world.
—Former US Rep. Bill Cassidy,
The Advocate, August 24, 2010

Clearly, the United States of America is under attack by an identity theft epidemic, both foreign and domestic. With the ability to cripple our economic system and wreak havoc on our structure and systems of national security, Homeland- and security-based initiatives should be adopted to systemically, strategically, and proactively protect the identities of American citizens.

I don't have all the answers or the definitive strategy to secure victory in this war against identity theft, but I am more than ready to enlist my services. After years embedded on the other side, I can now do my part by sharing and supporting our collective and national fight against identity theft.

In view of my former life as a cancer to society that was spreading without treatment or cure, I've purposed not to squander my second chance at life by improving upon this final opportunity to make amends. I have committed myself to a life of advocacy, giving permanent meaning and perpetual memory to my fellow Americans who have lost their finances, reputations, innocence, and lives due to indiscriminate criminality and unregulated hate in this country.

To start the conversation, I have offered here fifty legislative proposals directed toward identity theft, then ten more addressing gun safety and control reform. I consider this in the sequence of advancing against identity theft, even a part of my "Give Back to America" campaign, which includes the technological reservoir of DuckPond Technologies, Inc. as well as recurring pledges and donations from the proceeds of this book that will be used to support causes and initiatives that were once impacted by my crimes.

I wrote these proposals with the understanding that this subject matter is much bigger than me. The measures that follow are by no means intended to cause greater division, especially within a polarized community of lawful gun owners and gun rights advocates and activists. Rather, my ideas are intended to ignite healthy bipartisan debate based on indelible and undeniable evidence.

Finally, it has been argued that guns don't kill people, but people kill people. That's true—a gun can never be charged in a criminal case. However, it is almost always used as a material witness in trial proceedings. To promote domestic, recreational, and civil gun safety and control, my neuro-biometric design and ideas aim to take a proverbial shot at stopping gun violence once and for all. Our children and our children's children deserve the opportunity to pursue the life of liberty and happiness that's afforded to all Americans.

We need to engage not a whiteboard session, but something comprehensive and exhaustive—using up the walls, ceiling, and floor if needed to document means and measures that will eradicate this disease of fraud. It is likely time to rewrite policy entirely, scrapping the laws that evidently have not deterred identity theft despite enhanced penalties. This is a humble beginning, but it's a start nonetheless.

To start, the 1998 Identity Theft and Assumption Deterrence Act, Title 18, US Code, section 1028; and the 2004 Identity Theft Penalty Enhancement Act should both be revisited and amended. These measures should establish more categorized and severe penalties in this age of domestic terrorism, regional and national voter-fraud, and domestic and foreign threats to our nation's cybersecurity, as well as more calculated prevention measures.

The remaining sixty proposals should get the conversation moving further.

LEGISLATIVE PROPOSALS FOR IDENTITY THEFT

LEGISLATIVE BILL 1

Congress and/or state legislators should act to adopt, amend, or write and pass new legislation that mandates all credit reporting agencies to update consumer credit files twice a week, Sunday and Wednesday of every week; Holidays included. The US Senate and/or State Senate should sponsor or cosponsor this legislative bill.

> *Rationale:* This legislative idea aims to let potential creditors see the most recent activity in a given consumer's credit file, including real-time, newly opened accounts, when making an inquiry to award new credit. In a review of the credit file's most recent activity, potential creditors will be more able to determine whether the multiple previous requests for new credit are the result of fraudulent activity or pyramiding debt.

LEGISLATIVE BILL 2

Congress and/or state legislators should act to adopt, amend, or write and pass new legislation mandating the increase of Social Security benefits by at least ten dollars to help and enable financially insolvent but eligible senior citizens to pay the monthly minimum cost of having their identities monitored and protected by an industry recognized identity theft protection service provider. The US Senate and/or State Senate should sponsor or cosponsor this legislative bill.

Rationale: This legislative idea should be seriously considered, even if the enactment of it requires a special tax on one of the gross domestic products. Each of the fifty states should also enact similar legislation and attach it to its Medicaid program for our impoverish and uninsured senior citizens.

LEGISLATIVE BILL 3

Congress and/or state legislators should act to adopt, amend, or write and pass new legislation that mandates the credit market to verify valid state-issued identification numbers, numeric dates of birth, and social security numbers as part of the credit approval process in the same way that the automobile insurance industry uses the records of driver's license numbers as a determining factor for its verification, rating, and approval prior to issuing coverage for the insured. The US Senate and/or State Senate should sponsor or cosponsor this legislative bill.

Rationale: This legislative idea aims to heighten the security measures of the instant credit approval process with the intent of making it more difficult and less likely for the potential victim's identity to be stolen by phone, online, or in person.

LEGISLATIVE BILL 4

Congress and/or state legislators should act to adopt, amend, or write and pass new legislation mandating the creation of an independent budget that allocates funding to federal, state, and local law enforcement agencies for fighting America's domestic war on identity theft. The US Senate and/or State Senate should sponsor or cosponsor this legislative bill.

> *Rationale:* The fiscal budget for this legislative idea can be drafted from the budgets of Reagan's never-ending War on Drugs and from Bush's War on Terrorism, and perhaps should be embodied by a special interagency identity theft task force headed up by a new government agency with its own name, organizational structure, and agency chain of command that serves at the pleasure of the president of the United States of America.

LEGISLATIVE BILL 5

Congress and/or state legislators should act to adopt, amend, or write and pass new legislation mandating that all credit bureau agencies require and record up to date, valid, and accurate contact numbers in the credit profiles of consumers to reverse engineer the information reporting process, akin to the measure taken to record previous and current primary billing addresses. The US Senate and/or State Senate should sponsor or cosponsor this legislative bill.

> *Rationale:* Before approval for instant credit is awarded, new creditors will be able to verify the identity of the applicant by calling the recorded contact number(s) in the credit profile as a security measure pursuant to approval, via text reply or verbal verification. This proactive initiative is the alternative to fraud alerts that consumers can add to their credit profiles for free.

LEGISLATIVE BILL 6

Congress and/or state legislators should act to adopt, amend, or write and pass new legislation that mandates a reduction in the length of time that negative credit history stays within a consumers credit profile; respectively, late payments, charge-offs, and collection accounts reduce from seven to five years; repossessions, foreclosures, bankruptcies, and judgments from ten years to seven years; liens of any kind should come off a consumers credit report in eight years, if paid or not, after the date of origination in the credit profile. The US Senate and/or State Senate should sponsor or cosponsor this legislative bill.

> *Rationale:* This legislative idea aims to "Give A Break!" to millions of Americans and small business owners who are still suffering from the housing market crash of 2008 and its consequent recession as they stood on main street and watched their tax dollars bail out the very Wall Street bankers that bankrupted their household economies.

LEGISLATIVE BILL 7

Congress and/or state legislators should act to adopt, amend, or write and pass new regulatory legislation that mandates and limits new credit approvals to three accounts if more than three credit inquiries are made within a seven day period, reduced to a five day period beginning on "Black Friday" of every year and ending on January 2nd of the succeeding year. The US Senate and/or State Senate should sponsor or cosponsor this legislative bill.

Rationale: This legislative idea is aimed at preventing multiple instant credit accounts from being opened and depleted as is often the intended goal of a social identity thief's verification of merit.

LEGISLATIVE BILL 8

Congress and/or state legislators should act to adopt, amend, or write and pass new legislation that mandates more severe penalties for identity thieves who steal and sabotage the identity of any student (part/fulltime) that's actively enrolled in any trade school, vocational school, college, or university; undergraduate or graduate students. The US Senate and/or State Senate should sponsor or cosponsor this legislative bill.

Rationale: Any American who aspires to acquire a trade skill or to further their education to better their lot in life should not be impeded by the setbacks of identity theft. Moreover, college students are a primary target for some identity thieves and this legislative idea intends to make them less attractive as prospective victims of identity theft.[64]

LEGISLATIVE BILL 9

Congress and/or state legislators should act to adopt, amend, or write and pass new legislation that mandates more severe and specific penalties for identity theft crimes perpetrated against law enforcement, men and women of the armed forces, and

---

64 "Learn." LifeLock Official Site. https://www.lifelock.com/education/id-theft-schemes-target-college-students-kids/.

any local municipal, state, or federal official serving his/her community and country in the interest of public service. This idea should be considered in accordance with an amendment to the outdated "2004 Identity Theft Penalty Enhancement Act." Congress should further consider subsidizing state and federal programs that would allocate funding to all fields of law enforcement, public offices on a local, state, and federal level, and all four branches of the military to better protect the identities of American servicemen/women who risk and sacrifice their lives protecting and serving ours. A mandatory five-year term of imprisonment should be imposed for anyone who is convicted of identity theft against men and women of public service. An appropriate title for this act may very well be, "The Identity Theft Protection and Service Act: Honoring Law Enforcement, Military, and Public Office Personnel." The US Senate and/or State Senate should sponsor or cosponsor this legislative bill.

> *Rationale:* Identity thieves who deliberately target law enforcement, military, and public officials show a total disregard for the law and discover to themselves a greater degree of moral depravity. If there's no proactive protection for those who protect us, and no sense of security for those who serve us, then identity thieves sniper those public servants who they attack as enemies.

LEGISLATIVE BILL 10

Congress and/or state legislators should act to adopt, amend, or write and pass new legislation that mandates more severe penalties for both identity thieves and end users who exploit children's social security numbers under the guise of CPNs, better known as "Credit Protection Numbers" or "Credit Profiles Numbers." A mandatory three years of imprisonment should be imposed for the heartless criminals who knowingly exploit the identities of helpless children. Moreover, it should also be mandated that the Social Security Administration, Office of Vital Statistics, and certified credit bureau agencies establish an interagency data system that recognizes and registers children's social security numbers without the hyphens, beginning at birth. The US Senate and/or State Senate should sponsor or cosponsor this legislative bill.

> *Rationale:* This legislative bill is designed to attach a measure of security to children's innocent and fragile identities and thus position credit bureau agencies to flag a child's social security number the instant it has a financial reference in the tri-agency database. The punitive aspect of this legislative idea is proposed not as a deterrent, but as a dire and definite consequence for the virtual kidnappers and human traffickers that dare to exploit the children born of the American Dream for selfish means and financial gain.

LEGISLATIVE BILL 11

Congress and/or state Legislators should act to adopt, amend, or write and pass new legislation mandating the violation of heretofore identity theft interstate trafficking laws aimed at prosecuting identity thieves who steal, sell, trade, assume, and use stolen identities across state lines via the internet, within and beyond the borders of the US mailing system. The US Senate and/or State Senate should sponsor or cosponsor this legislative bill.

> *Rationale:* This legislative idea will give state and federal authorities more leverage and collective jurisdiction over investigations and prosecution of identity theft crimes across state lines to stymie and stop the trafficking and trade of stolen identities.

LEGISLATIVE BILL 12

Congress and/or state legislators should act to adopt, amend, or write and pass new legislation mandating that all state and federally convicted identity thieves have their conviction displayed on state ID cards, driver's licenses, US passports, and all identifying documents, as the state of Louisiana does for the "Sex Offender" that has been convicted of a qualifying sex offense as follows: "Convicted Identity Thief." Moreover, a national registry should also be established to pinpoint the locality of convicted identity thieves and used as a reference for regional identity theft crimes. This bill should not retroactively apply to the convicted identity thieves who have already completed their prison and probationary sentences and are no longer under state or federal supervised probation. The US Senate and/or State Senate should sponsor or cosponsor this legislative bill.

> *Rationale:* While designed to act as a deterrent, this legislative idea will alert law enforcement and merchants of the

persons and convicted identity thieves they may or may not be interacting with and it will also put the community on notice of the potential threat that lives among them.

LEGISLATIVE BILL 13

Congress and/or state legislators should act to adopt, amend, or write and pass new legislation mandating that the felony convictions of identity thieves be logged into their credit profiles for creditors, insurance companies, employers, merchants, and healthcare providers to engage in discretionary, not discriminatory, business practices in revelation of an identity theft conviction, thereby mandating an honest, undeniable answer to the "Have you ever been convicted of a felony?" question on job applications. The record of an identity theft conviction should remain in the credit profile for ten years; a line item and payment history of restitution, if imposed, should follow the same payment history format already established by the credit industry. The US Senate and/or State Senate should sponsor or cosponsor this legislative bill.

> *Rationale:* This legislative idea intends to make it lawful to share specific public information more deliberately and directly for discretionary decision-making purposes regarding identity theft related crimes.

LEGISLATIVE BILL 14

Congress and/or state legislators should act to adopt, amend, or write and pass new legislation mandating more severe penalties for identity thieves who target and exploit less vigilant senior citizens. The penalty for this crime should be enhanced if the victim is a former or retired military veteran, law enforcement member, or public official, thereby mandating a four-year term of imprisonment for victimizing senior citizens and mandating a six-term of imprisonment for victimizing and violating the earned and deserved senior citizenship status of the men and women of retired public service. The US Senate and/or State Senate should sponsor or cosponsor this legislative bill.

> *Rationale:* This legislative idea targets the merciless identity thieves who profile and prey upon the cyber and social weaknesses of their elderly victims.

LEGISLATIVE BILL 15

Congress and/or state legislators should act to adopt, amend, or write and pass new legislation mandating that all point-of-sale transactions involving a credit card be transacted at the register, tableside, and in the "real-time" presence of the cardholder. The US Senate and/or State Senate should sponsor or cosponsor this legislative bill.

> *Rationale:* This legislative idea is designed to eliminate unauthorized data collection by use of skimmers and other data collecting devices in the absence of the consumer.

LEGISLATIVE BILL 16

Congress and/or state legislators should act to adopt, amend, or write and pass new legislation mandating that manufacturers, merchants, and suppliers of embossers, skimmers,

HWH

specific printers, gift cards, decoders and encoders, etc., register the purchaser's information such as payment method, name, shipping address, purchaser description, and intended use, much in the same way that consumers have to disclose their identities when purchasing certain over-the-counter medications to help track and curb the methamphetamine epidemic. The US Senate and/or State Senate should sponsor or cosponsor this legislative bill.

Rationale: This legislative idea is designed to create a paper trail that leads directly to the suspecting identity thief.

LEGISLATIVE BILL 17

Congress and/or state legislators should act to adopt, amend, or write and pass new legislation mandating more severe penalties for credit card fraud based on various measures and methods used to commit the crime. Theft and resale of credit card numbers via data collection and redistribution should carry a mandatory two-year term of imprisonment, while the crime of credit card replication and counterfeiting should mandate a three-year term of imprisonment for first-time offenders and increased prison sentences for repeat offenders. The US Senate and/or State Senate should sponsor or cosponsor this legislative bill.

Rationale: This legislative idea is designed to help balance the justice system and thereby start giving white-collar crimes penalties that are commensurate to the harm they cause in victims' lives.

LEGISLATIVE BILL 18

Congress and/or state legislators should act to adopt, amend, or write and pass new legislation mandating that the credit card industry give an annual report of how many fraudulent transactions were successful and what means and methods were used to advance "Device Access Fraud." This annual report should be made available to all state and federal law enforcement agencies and legislators. The US Senate and/or State Senate should sponsor or cosponsor this legislative bill.

Rationale: This legislative idea aims to chart and track down means and methods of credit and debit card fraud to develop innovative ways to stop it once and for all.

LEGISLATIVE BILL 19

Congress and/or state legislators should act to adopt, amend, or write and pass new legislation mandating that merchants be held liable for loss due to careless business practices in acceptance of the credit cards transactions that are mediated in the absence of a single security measure that would otherwise be part of the typical or standard credit card transaction. The US Senate and/or State Senate should sponsor or cosponsor this legislative bill.

Rationale: This legislative idea intends to encourage merchants not to become complacent or lackadaisical about secured credit card transactions and not to rely on insurance reimbursement in the face of fraud.

LEGISLATIVE BILL 20

Congress and/or state legislators should act to adopt, amend, or write and pass new legislation mandating that credit card companies do more to educate both the consumer and merchant business sectors about credit card fraud, how to spot, stop, prevent, and report it in the form of a monthly newsletter to its respective cardholders as an accompaniment to the monthly online or mailed paper billing statements. Credit card issuers should be encouraged to give various "cash back" incentives to cardholder participation in the educational process via online company owned and operated portals and forums. The US Senate and/or State Senate should sponsor or cosponsor this legislative bill.

> *Rationale:* This legislative idea intends to accomplish credit card fraud elimination by constant, consistent, and continuing education.

LEGISLATIVE BILL 21

Congress and/or state legislators should act to adopt, amend, or write and pass new legislation that mandates more severe penalties for cybercriminals that make sport of hacking security systems and stealing consumers' personal information. For every identity that's compromised during a data breach, the criminal should serve four seconds in prison. For example, if 100 million consumers' identities are compromised as a result of malicious malware, the hacker(s) should serve 12.78 years in prison. The term of imprisonment should double for repeat offenders. The US Senate and/or State Senate should sponsor or cosponsor this legislative bill.

YHWH

Rationale: This legislative idea is designed to adequately and sufficiently deal justice in response to the injustice of malicious data breaches that create social panic and chaos, and in doing so, creates a matter of national security!

LEGISLATIVE BILL 22

Congress and/or state legislators should act to adopt, amend, or write and pass new legislation that mandates tougher regulation and bigger fines for the companies and corporations that are victims of data breaches due to outdated security measures, negligence, and incompetence. The fines and penalties should be doubled in severity when corporations do not report and publicize the data breach within seventy-two hours of occurrence. The same fine and penalties should be tripled when it's discovered that false or misleading information was given to the public as part of a damage control public relations plot or ploy. The US Senate and/or State Senate should sponsor or cosponsor this legislative bill.

Rationale: This legislative idea intends to hold companies and corporations accountable for negligence, dissemination of misinformation, delayed diversionary tactics, and incompetence.

LEGISLATIVE BILL 23

Congress and/or state legislators should act to adopt, amend, or write and pass new legislation that mandates corporations to inform each of its consumers directly as a follow up to the local and national broadcast. It should also be mandated that corporations and companies equip themselves and offer lifetime service of identity theft prevention, protection, and counseling services to each of their data breached victims at no cost to the consumer. The US Senate and/or State Senate should sponsor or cosponsor this legislative bill.

> *Rationale:* This legislative idea is designed to make corporations and companies accountable and more careful about consumer privacy laws and protection, and more responsible for any carelessness regarding upholding those same laws that otherwise contribute to data breaches.

LEGISLATIVE BILL 24

Congress and/or state legislators should act to adopt, amend, and write or pass new legislation that mandates consumers to hold corporations directly liable for damages incurred as a result of a data breach due to outdated security measures, negligence, misinformation, or incompetence. This mandate should stipulate that corporations establish a legal fund or escrow account designated for fair and equitable settlement as a measure not to inundate the legal system with an overload or onslaught of civil suits. The US Senate and/or State Senate should sponsor or cosponsor this legislative bill.

> *Rationale:* This legislative idea is designed to compensate the consumer for being an unwitting and involuntary victim of corporate data breaches.

LEGISLATIVE BILL 25

Congress and/or state legislators should act to adopt, amend, and write or pass new legislation that mandates more severe penalties, civil and criminal, and bigger fines for corporations that secretly and illegally purchase consumer information anonymously from anonymous or shell and shielded entities via convoluted and complex dark web and parking lot transactions as a result of a data breach. The US Senate and/or State Senate should sponsor or cosponsor this legislative bill.

> *Rationale:* This legislative idea is aimed at the unfair, under-regulated, and illegal business practices that are largely ignored and unchecked on a daily basis in corporate America.

LEGISLATIVE BILL 26

Congress and/or state legislators should act to adopt, amend, or write and pass new legislation mandating domestic terrorism laws aimed at prosecuting illegal immigrants who purchase, steal, and trade American identities to impersonate and benefit from citizenship status. Once convicted in a court of law, it should also be mandated that illegal alien criminals be immediately deported back to their native country. There, they can be made to serve out a US court imposed prison sentence as part of an extradition treaty with allied nations or part of a United Nations law, relieving the American taxpayer from the burden of incarceration of non-US citizens under "illegal immigrant" violations. The US Senate and/or State Senate should sponsor or cosponsor this legislative bill.

Rationale: This legislative idea intends to safeguard the identity of American citizens. It is also designed to expose and expel the terrorist who assumes American citizenship to keep his diabolical agenda concealed.[65]

LEGISLATIVE BILL 27

Congress and/or state legislators should act to adopt, amend, or write and pass new legislation that mandates severe penalties under domestic terrorism statutes for the identity thieves who bid and bargain American identities to illegal immigrants. A mandatory minimum sentence of five years should be imposed on the identity thief per count for knowingly or unknowingly aiding and abetting the next terror attack on our nation. The US Senate and/or State Senate should sponsor or cosponsor this legislative bill.

Rationale: This legislative idea is designed to capture and hold captive the criminals who exist to make commerce of illegal immigration and foster terroristic agendas in the process.

LEGISLATIVE BILL 28

Congress and/or state legislators should act to adopt, amend, or write and pass new legislation that encourage legal immigrant status through measures and means of a virtual vetting process based on a merit-based system of checks and balances

---

65 See US immigration and customs enforcement release on 5-8-17 entitled "Document and Benefit Fraud."

collated and compared to the model middle class American citizen, solely initiated by temporary work visas until all criteria has been met and legal immigrant status awarded. The US Senate and/or State Senate should sponsor or cosponsor this legislative bill.

> *Rationale:* This legislative idea is designed to discourage identity theft as a shortcut to American citizenship.

LEGISLATIVE BILL 29

Congress and/or state legislators should act to adopt, amend, or write and pass new legislation that mandates "tax credits" to individuals, families, and employers who pay or offer pay incentives to the annual cost of identity theft protection services. The US Senate and/or State Senate should sponsor or cosponsor this legislative bill.

> *Rationale:* This legislative idea of an "Identity Theft Protection Tax Credit" is designed to encourage families and businesses to seek and secure identity theft protection services. This legislative idea will also create thousands of jobs in the economy as the identity protection industry expands and recruits personnel to accommodate the rapid increase of supply and demand.

LEGISLATIVE BILL 30

Congress and/or state legislators should act to adopt, amend, or write and pass new legislation that mandates immediate relief to victims of "income tax identity theft" and set aside the bureaucracy of a nine to twelve month resolution period before victims can legitimately receive their tax refund. It should also be mandated that the Internal Revenue Service issues every taxpayer an IP-PIN (Identity Protection Number) as a proven security method and measure in the reduction of income tax identity theft. The US Senate and/or State Senate should sponsor or cosponsor this legislative bill.

Rationale: This legislative idea is designed to prevent taxpayers from being a victim twice to both the identity thief and to the system.

LEGISLATIVE BILL 31

Congress and/or state legislators should act to adopt, amend, or write and pass new legislation that mandates W-2 forms to be sent to the IRS much sooner than the current deadline. The US Senate and/or State Senate should sponsor or cosponsor this legislative bill.

Rationale: This legislative idea is designed to close the window of opportunity and timeframe during which income tax identity thieves steal taxpayers' income tax refunds. The longer employees have to send in W-2 forms, the greater the chance and likelihood of income tax identity theft being committed.

LEGISLATIVE BILL 32

Congress and/or state legislators should act to adopt, amend, or write and pass new legislation that mandates the creation of an independent patient medical profile system to which consumer and patient medical data are reported to certified bureaus from which information can be verified using an optional two-factor authentication portal that only allows review of the patients medical profile and restricts access to consumers credit profiles. The US Senate and/or State Senate should sponsor or cosponsor this legislative bill.

Rationale: This legislative idea is designed to merge both the medical and financial data systems into one system and make the data accessible and verifiable using different credentials assigned to financial creditors and healthcare providers.

LEGISLATIVE BILL 33

Congress and/or state legislator should act to adopt, amend, or write and pass new legislation that gives the DEA (Drug Enforcement Administration) the legal authority to investigate and pursue crimes under the previously proposed "Domestic Terrorism Identity Theft Act" for prescription fraud, insurance fraud, Medicare fraud, and related document fraud that almost always involves prescribed narcotics. The US Senate and/or State Senate should sponsor or cosponsor this legislative bill.

Rationale: This legislative idea intends to recruit another federal agency to engage America's Domestic War on Identity Theft and add to the arsenal that's needed to defeat medical identity theft.

LEGISLATIVE BILL 34

Congress and/or state legislators should act to adopt, amend, or write and pass new legislation that mandates more severe penalties and bigger fines for the identity thieves who perpetrate medical identity theft. Healthcare providers and professionals should face stiffer penalties with mandatory jail time for engaging medical identity theft because they are held to higher standards than are common and highly sophisticated criminals. For the identity thief who engages medical identity theft, a mandatory sentence of three years should be imposed for a first-time offense. The healthcare provider or professional that betrays the patient and violates the Hippocratic Oath should face double the penalties and fines respecting prison, restitution, and cost of prosecution in addition to the fine the court chooses to impose. The US Senate and/or State Senate should sponsor or cosponsor this legislative bill.

> *Rationale:* This legislative idea intends to deal deserved retribution to the deliberate and determined violations of medical privacy laws and patients' medical rights. The ramification and consequences of medical identity theft are cause for serious health concerns at least and life-threatening at most.

LEGISLATIVE BILL 35

Congress and/or state legislators should act to adopt, amend, or write new legislation that mandates strict and specific penalties to be written as an addendum to the HIPAA Laws that speak to the compromising of patients medical records.

YHWH

Healthcare institutions and their employees should be held to the highest standards of accountability and the language of amended or new HIPAA laws should speak not only to our expectations as healthcare recipients in a medically induced, over-medicated society, but also spell out the consequence when trust turns toxic in some form of medical identity theft by omission or commission. The US Senate and/or State Senate should sponsor or cosponsor this legislative bill.

Rationale: This legislative idea is aimed at prosecuting the providers and professionals that prey upon the illness and ailments of their trusting patients.

LEGISLATIVE BILL 36

Congress and/or state legislators should act to adopt, amend, or write new legislation that mandates all vehicles and automobiles of every kind manufactured in the United States of America be required to have digital vehicle identification technology installed within the vehicles and automobiles computer system by 2025, beginning with the new line of production for 2024. The US Senate and/or State Senate should sponsor or cosponsor this legislative bill.

Rationale: This legislative idea aims to protect American consumers, US automobile and vehicle manufacturers and the US automobile and insurance industry from continued victimization of the subtle and surreptitious scam of vehicular identity theft; a crime whose reported loss of billions has no statistical data that can be referenced because it's not on any of the law enforcement agencies' radar nor registered in any of their crime indexes, according to my research.

LEGISLATIVE BILL 37

Congress and/or state legislators should act to adopt, amend, or write and pass new legislation that mandates all vehicle and automobile identification numbers manufactured in and imported into the United States of America be registered with local and national vehicular identification registration agencies and privately owned vehicular registration companies. A fee-based system should be established and integrated between the private sector and government/state agencies to help defray the operational cost of transacting vehicular information. The US Senate and/or State Senate should sponsor or cosponsor this legislative bill.

> *Rationale:* This legislative idea is designed to establish a database for each and every vehicle and automobile on US soil and to establish a database to keep record of active and inactive vehicles.

LEGISLATIVE BILL 38

Congress and/or state legislators should act to adopt, amend, or write and pass new legislation that mandates all automobile and vehicle insurers be required to share vehicle identification numbers with a central portal or platform to cross-check the insurance status of automobiles and vehicles, if insurance is required by state law per automobile or vehicle, without compromising or violating consumer privacy laws. This legislative bill should parallel its counterpart and be effectuated by August 2024. The US Senate and/or State Senate should sponsor or cosponsor this legislative bill.

> *Rationale:* This legislative idea intends to foster a network among insurers wherein they can exchange identifying vehicular information openly to instantly detect potential vehicular insurance fraud.

LEGISLATIVE BILL 39

Congress and/or state legislators should act to adopt, amend, or write and pass new legislation that mandates automobile and vehicle insurance companies to share identifying vehicle information directly with law enforcement and highway patrol agencies. Presently, the state's Office of Motor Vehicles mediates the insurance verification process between law enforcement and insurance companies. The US Senate and/or State Senate should sponsor or cosponsor this legislative bill.

> *Rationale:* This legislative idea aims to keep record of both active-registered and inactive-nonregistered Vehicle Identification Numbers to curb and detect vehicular identity theft.

LEGISLATIVE BILL 40

Congress and/or state legislators should act to adopt, amend, or write and pass a body of policy and new legislation aimed at "Boxing In" vehicular identity theft. In the legislation world there is virtually and absolutely no documented laws addressing, implying, or inferring vehicular identity theft. Under "The Vehicular Identity Theft Act" it should be mandated that stiff penalties, mandatory prison sentences for first-time offenders, and steep fines be proliferated throughout the new body of legislation. The US Senate and/or State Senate should sponsor or cosponsor this legislative bill.

> *Rationale:* This legislative idea for an entire body of sound policy and sane legislation is designed to motivate the people and politicians that are charged with the collective responsibility of making informed, sagacious decisions on behalf and for the betterment of the American people.

The real grand theft auto, i.e., vehicular identity theft, both virtual and social, has been a sapient criminal's secret for years that has gone largely unnoticed and undetected but marginally mentioned in theory until now. The question before us, "How will America respond and react to this attack of the enemy?"

The next ten legislative bills, from 41–50, are short of full measure and intend to serve as starting points for topical discussion and bipartisan collaboratives approaching and apprehending the demanding subject of Vehicular Identity Theft. The rationale for each is simple: because there are no laws in Congress or on any state level that address and restrict the subject of vehicular identity theft.

LEGISLATIVE BILL 41

The politicians and powers that be should act to hold a special session and write new legislation to establish a bipartisan advisory committee consisting of automobile and vehicle manufacturers in conjunction with officials from the US Department of Transportation and other federal and state agencies to take up the subject of vehicular identity theft. The US Senate and/or State Senate should sponsor or cosponsor this legislative bill.

LEGISLATIVE BILL 42

The politicians and powers that be should act and write new legislation that establishes a fiscal budget around the subject of vehicular identity theft. The US Senate and/or State Senate should sponsor or cosponsor this legislative bill.

LEGISLATIVE BILL 43

The politicians and powers that be should act and write new legislation that gives the US Department of Transportation the means and authority to work with each of the fifty states and their counterparts to develop methods and strategies targeting vehicular identity theft. The US Senate and/or State Senate should sponsor or cosponsor this legislative bill.

LEGISLATIVE BILL 44

The politicians and powers that be should act and write new legislation that confirms vehicle and automobile titles of ownership to a centralized federal document hosted by the respective state to stop title replication and counterfeiting as the single most important document when committing vehicular identity theft. The US Senate and/or State Senate should sponsor or cosponsor this legislative bill.

LEGISLATIVE BILL 45

If Legislative Bill 44 is not mandated into law, then the politicians and powers that be should act and write new legislation that allows insurers to electronically verify the registrant's state-issued title with the Office of Motor Vehicles before an insurance claim is paid to title holders with no liens to prevent a payout to vehicular identity thieves. The US Senate and/or State Senate should sponsor or cosponsor this legislative bill.

LEGISLATIVE BILL 46

The politicians and powers that be should act and write new legislation prohibiting the public display of vehicle identification numbers in full measure by online auto dealers and certified automobile verifiers, to discourage and thereby make it much difficult to find a "twin VIN" to commit vehicular identity theft. The US Senate and/or State Senate should sponsor or cosponsor this legislative bill.

LEGISLATIVE BILL 47

The politicians and powers that be should act and write new legislation that exacerbates and enhances penalties and fines for domestic terrorism violations if an illegal immigrant or a foreign agent or entity is convicted of committing vehicular identity theft. The US Senate and/or State Senate should sponsor or cosponsor this legislative bill.

LEGISLATIVE BILL 48

The politicians and powers that be should act and write new legislation mandating automobile manufacturers share all-new vehicle identification numbers with all certified insurers to catch up to and get ahead of vehicular identity theft. The US Senate and/or State Senate should sponsor or cosponsor this legislative bill.

LEGISLATIVE BILL 49

The politicians and powers that be should act and write new legislation that gives the US Department of Transportation regulatory authority over the transaction of VINs to monitor how they are transacted in the automobile and insurance industry through the lens of vehicular identity theft. The US Senate and/or State Senate should sponsor or cosponsor this legislative bill.

LEGISLATIVE BILL 50

The politicians and powers that be should act and write new legislation mandating a specific coded vehicle identification number be assigned to the geographical location of manufacturing, thereby allowing manufacturer, insurer, and enforcer to regionalize automobiles and vehicles under the authority of the US Department of Transportation to segment an anticipatory tactical reconnaissance after vehicular identity theft. The US Senate and/or State Senate should sponsor or cosponsor this legislative bill.

TEN GUN SAFETY AND CONTROL LEGISLATIVE BILLS

*We need to stand up, go out and vote, talk
to our legislators, and get educated.*

*Can we please not debate this as Democrats and
Republicans but discuss this as Americans?*

This isn't about left or right, it's about saving lives.
—David Hogg, activist and founder
of March for Our Lives

LEGISLATIVE BILL 1

Congress and/or state legislators should act to adopt, amend, or write and pass new legislation that mandates, effective January 1, 2025, all new registered gun owners be required to undergo a virtual Q/A psychiatric certified psyche-evaluation in addition to existing state and federal requirements pursuant to gun purchases. The psyche-evaluations should be performed and results renewed bi-annually and prior to the purchase of a new firearm. The US Senate and/or State Senate should sponsor or cosponsor this legislative bill.

Rationale: To determine the mental and emotional health and establish the qualifying determining factors as a prerequisite to gun ownership. The annual or biannual evaluations should be required due to the varying changes in life that affect mental health and emotional disorders from one life event to another, often fatally resulting in psychotic episodes.

LEGISLATIVE BILL 2

Congress and/or state legislators should act to adopt, amend, or write and pass new legislation that mandates a minimum mandatory term of imprisonment of ten years be imposed for any crime of identity theft associated with the illegal purchase of a gun under newly revised or implemented domestic terrorism statutes, both seller and buyer. The US Senate and/or State Senate should sponsor or cosponsor this legislative bill.

> *Rationale:* To discourage and punish the audacity of the perpetrator that dares to undertake illegal gun purchases via identity theft.

LEGISLATIVE BILL 3

Congress and/or state legislators should act to adopt, amend, or write and pass new legislation mandating that all "Open Carry" laws be repealed and replaced on both a state and federal level. The US Senate and/or State Senate should sponsor or cosponsor this legislative bill.

> *Rationale:* The open and, most times, willful and boastful intimidation of openly demonstrated weaponry in a democratic society is unnecessary. While some will argue that the open show of guns acts as a possible deterrent to crime, I venture that the impure and purposeless demonstration of guns under "Open Carry" laws emboldens the carrier and simultaneously activates and alarms public fright and fear. People in general do not feel as safe in society when they witness fellow Americans openly carrying a

gun as they do when they see an authoritative figure, such as police officers or military personnel, wearing a gun as part of their duty to protect and serve his/her community.

LEGISLATIVE BILL 4

Congress and/or state legislators should act to adopt, amend, or write and pass new legislation mandating that neuro-bio-metric gun safety and control technology be implemented in a measure into the US gun industry by 2025 and that by 2030 all guns manufactured in or imported into the US have neuro-biometric technology as a primary component to gun design and engineering. The US Senate and/or State Senate should sponsor or cosponsor this legislative bill.

Rationale: See Neuro-Biometric Trigger Happy Technology at www.duckpond.tech for conceptual analyses relative to gun safety and control.

LEGISLATIVE BILL 5

With exception of antique and collectible guns, Congress and/or state legislators should act to adopt, amend, or write and pass new legislation mandating a "Trade-In/Buy Back" program be established and funded by the US government. Participation in this program should be voluntary and without penalty. Gun owners who participate will receive the appraised medium market value for their gun(s) that can be used towards the purchase of its counterpart equipped with neuro-biomet-ric gun safety and control technology. The US Senate and/or State Senate should sponsor or cosponsor this legislative bill.

Rationale: To position the US government to take the lead in championing new legislation and developing new programs so that America can once again claim center stage among all nations as the hallmark and model for gun safety and control as a superpower. The "Trade In/Buy Back" program will show wise investment of taxpayer dollars to make America safe and secure by adopting a technology that better enables verified gun owners to take total control over the usage of their firearms.

LEGISLATIVE BILL 6

Congress and/or state legislators should act to adopt, amend, or write and pass new legislation mandating that a submission of fingerprint biometrics and facial pixelation (headshots) be recorded as part of the gun buying process in addition to traditional background checks. The US Senate and/or State Senate should sponsor or cosponsor this legislative bill.

Rationale: Background checks alone, for gun purchaser and merchant, are not enough collective information to legalize gun ownership. Background checks can be manipulated and circumvented via identity theft. Existing fingerprint biometrics verification and facial recognition software can be used for authentication purposes and to assist in investigative matters in the commission of a crime.

LEGISLATIVE BILL 7

Congress and/or state legislators should act to adopt, amend, or write and pass new legislation mandating that a restriction to the number of guns domestically owned be implemented, per legal identity and per household, and that specific allowances be considered for guns used for gaming. The US Senate and/or State Senate should sponsor or cosponsor this legislative bill.

> *Rationale:* For example, rhetorically asking from a domestic perspective, what can be done with, say, thirty-five guns that can't be accomplished with legally owning three to five guns, per identity and per household? The Second Amendment speaks to Americans' inherent right "...to keep and bear arms," and we should. However, The Second Amendment doesn't qualify the plurality and numeric implication of what's intended by "bear arms." This abandonment to eisegesis (self-interpretation) begs the question: "How many guns does each lawful American have a constitutional right to own, qualified by civilian and servicemen/women status?"

LEGISLATIVE BILL 8

Congress and/or state legislators should act to adopt, amend, or write and pass new legislation mandating "qualifying" convicted felons be given a second chance to exercise their Second Amendment right along with the restoration of their right to vote and obligation to pay taxes. The restoration of "qualified" convicted felons' right to gun ownership should in part be based on offense and restricted to specific gun types and categories for personal and protective reasons. Certain offenses such as robbery, rape, murder, assault with a deadly weapon, etc., should permanently disqualify a convicted felon from gun ownership, while non-violent felony convictions such as perjury, misprision of a felon, etc., should qualify for restoration of gun ownership rights. The US Senate and/or State Senate should sponsor or cosponsor this legislative bill.

> *Rationale:* It would seem rather contradictory for a "qualified" convicted felon to have a restored right to vote on gun laws that exclude him/her from the benefit, provisions, and protection of those selfsame laws. Surely the right to vote is voluntary, but the law must be consistent in its application, even when lawmakers are inconsistent in their ideologies and various political persuasions. I get it; people change, nobody is perfect, and we all make regrettable decisions and mistakes in various ways and for various reasons, some less forgiving than others. I'm acutely aware that criminal justice reform and gun safety and control are two different conversations, but since both topics are social burdens that have been shelved for far too long, let's address these social pathogens legislatively, treat them judicially, and cure them executively.

LEGISLATIVE BILL 9

Congress and/or state legislators should act to adopt, amend, or write and pass new legislation "earmarking" that a National Landmark be constructed on Capitol Hill to memorialize the victims who lost their lives in mass shootings as casualties of America's domestic division of gun safety and control legislative regulation, or the lack and absence thereof. The Messiah

Himself teaches us in Matthew 12:25, "...every kingdom divided against itself is brought to desolation; and every city or "HOUSE" divided against itself shall not stand." The US Senate and/or State Senate should sponsor or cosponsor this legislative bill.

> *Rationale:* To constantly let the precious lives we've lost to gun violence remind us in their death of all we could have and should have done to keep them alive.

LEGISLATIVE BILL 10

Congress and/or state legislators should act to adopt, amend, or write and pass new legislation mandating that all gun manufacturers and distributors provide quarterly reports of gun sales to designated federal and state law enforcement agencies. Moreover, ammunition type and quantity should be mandated to follow the same reporting system and the same identifying and authenticating metrics proposed in Gun Safety and Control Legislative Bill 6 as part of the ammunition purchases when excessive quantities creates probable cause for suspicion and alarm. Legislation designed to limit ammunition quantities over a specific time span should also be considered. The US Senate and/or State Senate should sponsor or cosponsor this legislative bill.

> *Rationale:* To track and keep record of gun and ammunition distribution throughout the United States of America. It is preferable to follow bullet purchases back to the gun than it is to follow bullet shell casings back to the victims.

𐤉𐤄𐤅𐤄

𐤉𐤄𐤅𐤄

YHWH

יהוה

SACRED NAME DECLARATION

YHWH יהוה ᴣᴎᴣᴪ ஓㅓஓㄴ

Hear O Yisrael, Yahweh is our Sovereign, Yahweh is One!

In reverential harmony and sanctified unity with all of cre-
ation, transcending the terrestrial, we prostrate our very exis-
tence before Him declaring relentlessly: Holy, Holy, Holy is
Yahweh Almighty, which was, and is, and is to come (Rev. 4:8).
We further declare, "Our Father which art in Heaven, Hallowed
be Thy name..." as Yahshua the Messiah has taught us, bring-
ing restoration and veneration to Yahweh's name when he fur-
ther prayed, "...I have declared unto them Thy name and will
declare it; that the love wherewith thou hast loved me may be
in them, and I in them." (Mt. 6:9, Jn. 17:26 KJV)

We the Messianic Believers of today (Yahudims) impera-
tively proclaim the Yahwistic Kingdom message, that true and
Scriptural salvation is only in the Hebraic name of Yahshua

the Messiah (Mt. 1:21, Acts 4:12) who bore the Memorial (Ex. 3:15), Prophetic (Ex. 23:20,21), and Covenantal (Acts 2:21, Joel 2:32) name of Yahweh His Father (Ps. 118:25, 26, Jn. 5:43 et al.). It is never our purpose in this declaration to denigrate anyone's belief, but through the Spirit of meekness to enlighten and liberate by the means of a dialectical symposium to bring into fulfillment the prophetic voices: "My people will know My name (Isa. 52:6), "...That My name will be declared throughout ALL the earth (Ex. 9:16), "...in every place where I cause My name to be remembered, there I will come and bless them" (Ex. 20:24). Selah!

We remonstrate historically and spiritually that the vital legality and absolute celestial jurisdiction of the sacred name to salvation has been the primary point of attack by Ha-Satan and his seed, to impede spiritual birth, power and consciousness; subsequently distorting, altering, and suppressing the only name under Heaven whereby mankind can be saved (Acts 4:12), substituting it contrary to the commands of Yahweh (Dt. 4:2, 12:32, Pro. 30:5, 6, Rev. 22:18, 19) and placing under the curse (Gal. 1:8, 9, Ex. 32:35, Dt. 27:9–26, 28:1–68) *all* those who proclaim and worship by Another Message (2 Thes 1:7–12), and Another Messiah (2 Cor. 11:4, Mt. 24:23–26, 2 Thes. 2:3–12), and Another Spirit (2 Corr. 11:4, 1 Jn. 4:1–6).

Through historical revisionism and semantics, Ha-Satan has used the religious scribes and/or prophets of all cultures and continents to interpolate titles as names for both Yahweh the Father and His only begotten Son, Yahshua the Messiah (Jer. 8:8, 9). The Holy Writ reminds us that "In the latter days ye shall consider it perfectly, I have not sent these prophets...which think to cause my people to forget my Name" (Jer. 23: 20–27).

Essentially, a name is the reputation, the authority, the power, and the character by which one acts; more so, it is the sum total of one's internal and external pattern of behavior. Since the name is both prophetic and descriptive of the personality of the one to whom it belongs, Yahshua set forth Divine doctrine, truth, and revelation when he stated unequivocally, "Father, glorify Thy name (Jn. 12:38); and again, "We must worship in Him spirit and truth (Jn. 4:24)," promulgating that Yahweh's name is included in that truth.

Because Yahweh is immutable, so is His name. As in every case, to change one's name, there is a change of position expressed (e.g. from Kunta Kinte to Toby)—either a dignified exaltation or relegation to dependency. History deduces that to cut off one's name was tantamount to removing that person and all his contributions from existence, thus dealing him a death blow. This was Ha-Satan's surreptitious plot at being Yahicidal (killing of Yahweh), creating myriads of religions and deities, represented by visual images and idols designed to eclipse humanity's perspective of worshipping Yahweh in spirit and truth. Consequently, Ha-Satan is redirecting all worship towards himself, who is the active force behind every idol (1Cor. 10: 20, Ps. 106:36–42, Dt. 32:16,17, Rev. 9:20), as Scripture holds, behind every idol there is a devil.

Man was gifted with delegated authority from Yahweh to name Earthly creations, thereby establishing a relation of dominion or possession of them (Ps. 8, Gen. 2:19). But man's alienation from the commonwealth of Yahweh, and his alliance with Ha-Satan, filled him with false ambition, elevating him to a pedestal of pernicious pride; whereby mimicking the Fallen One (Ha-Satan), that old dragon who vaunted himself (Isa 14:14) not only to be like the Most High Yahweh, but even to replace Him and every vestige of Him, even His holy name.

If committing the act of libel here on Earth is grounds for judicial review and compensation, how much more so for *all* who conspire with darkness to blaspheme and make vain (Ex.20:7) the sacred name Yahweh be found guilty before His eternal bar of judgment?!

As the sole author of this two-volume book, vested with Messianic authority to declare the sacred name of Yahweh, I've purposed to do so verbally and grammatically, in accordance as the Ruach Ha-Kodesh (Holy Spirit) directs and instructs me. By Yahweh's divine afflatus I humbly write, merely understanding in part (1 Cor. 13:9) what he conveys through his finite vessel obedient by faith to His every command whereby He has called me by a new name, ObadYah (Servant of Yahweh).

In honoring the vow I made to Yahweh thirteen years ago regarding the declaration of His sacred name, you will find on the four corners of each page throughout this book a different four-letter depiction of the Tetragrammaton (the ancient four letter Yisraelitish name of Yahweh, occurring 6,823 times throughout the Hebrew Scriptures and validated via archeological findings throughout the known world). The four letters, like the four Gospels, connote North, South, East, and West, which confers the omnipresence of Yahweh.

The Heavens declare His glory, and the earth shows His handywork; and without controversy, Yahweh has not left Himself without witnesses to declare the glory of His power and the greatness of His name. For the nihilist man, I issue not a challenge to meaningless debate, but in the Spirit of love and service I encourage you to emulate the Bereans (Acts 17:11), and search with due diligence to see if these things I profess are so.

And if you will not hear me, then perhaps you will hear the testimony of rocks and stones crying out that Yahweh is the memorial name of the Creator of Heaven and earth:

Hear...The Lachish letters written between 589–587 BC on ostraca (potsherd/clay) using the name of Yahweh frequently.

Hear...The Moabite stone written about 830 BC commemorating the victory of Moab over Yisrael, whereby Moab's King Mesha declares "I took from them the vessels of Yahweh..." spelling the name exactly as in the Old Testament.

Hear...The ostraca of Tell Arad; hear the Elephantine Papyri of Egypt; or the Khirbet Beit Lei, and what of the ivory of Fort Shalmaneser: all with inscriptions of Yahweh.

Conclusively, each of the four-letter depictions differ in grammatical style, while maintaining the context and content of Yahweh's sacred name as it was dispensational revealed. To a large degree, I have deliberately avoided scholarly analysis, intellectual apologia, and various schools of thought on this subject matter that clarity might have precedence over clouds of confusion. In my quest to inform and acquaint within the constrictions of this work, I'll try to be brief in my explanation of each Tetragrammaton as follows:

This four-character description is widely accepted as the pictographic symbols that ancient Hebrews used to give identity and reference to the Being and object of their worship, i.e., Yahweh. It is believed to predate Noah's flood. A type of hieroglyphic name but specific to the Hebrews. In keeping with its historical discovery and placement, it is first among the four Tetragrammaton descriptions imprinted in the upper left corners on every page of this book.

This four-letter description is universally accepted as the Paleo-Hebrew name of Yahweh, which He concealed from Abraham, Isaac, and Jacob (Ex. 6:3), but revealed it to Moses during the burning bush encounter. (Ex. 3:13–15) It is by this sacred and sanctified name (Lk.12–2) that Yahweh wanted to be known and worshipped by His Hebrew people whom he would mightily deliver out of Egyptian slavery for His name's sake, during which enslavement they lost the identity of El Shaddai and became steeped in idolatry. Generationally, this four-letter description of Yahweh's name is rightly imprinted in the upper right corner on every page of this book as the second description of Yahweh's name by which he chose to be known to His people initially and to all the nations of the world throughout various dispensations.

446

YHWH

This four-letter description of Yahweh's name postdates seventy years of the Jewish peoples' captivity in Babylon. Jewish scholars unanimously agree that this rendition of Yahweh's name is the inspiration of Modern Hebrew, revived and survived out of an attempt by the Masoretic Jews to suppress the sacred name of Yahweh due to a gross misunderstanding of Scripture (Deut. 5–11) and an over-zealous application of their misunderstanding when in fact they desecrated the Scriptures by removing Yahweh's name from the Old Testament all "6,823" times it was mentioned, placing in its stead the Hebrew word Adonai, which translates to master or lord in English. This is history's third introduction of the sacred name of Yahweh, and it is deliberately imprinted in the lower left corner on every page of this book as a testament to what modern Hebrew appreciates as Yahweh's sacred name.

YHWH

Without delving into deeper doctrines of consonants and vowels and how they phonetically transliterate the communication of Yahweh's sacred name, this four-letter description is the English version of the Tetragrammaton, as previously introduced, it's the four-letter name of Yahweh. The pronunciation and phonetics of Yahweh's name has been the subject of much scholarly debate and division for more than four centuries since the erroneous arrival of the name "Jehovah," but the simple truth is that his name is pronounced the same today as it was when he first ascribed it to Himself in eternity past. In our current dispensation in which we now live, it ranks as the fourth four-letter description of Yahweh's sacred name and is uniquely imprinted in the lower right corner on every page of this book in constant commemoration of the sacred name of Yahweh.

Hear O Yisrael, Yahweh is our Sovereign, Yahweh is One!

YHWH

BOOK DESIGN AND LAYOUT

Beginning with *The Master Identity Thief* front cover, the mosaic design is the first layer of symbolism in this text. It is comprised of individuals' faces that are multi-ethnic, inter-generational, and gender-inclusive to depict the diversity found in the identity theft victimization epidemic. The pronounced photo of me as the author and master identity thief portrays the piercing, calculating gaze I held only for the numbers each face would represent. If you look a little closer into those beautiful brown eyes of the master identity thief, you'll see the faces of both my beloved parents situated as the sight of my first targets and victims of identity theft.

On the back cover, there are further layers of imagery for *America's Domestic War*. With the American flag intentionally and symbolically skewed, this cover reveals how innocent lives were turned upside down by this stealth crime, placing the US in distress from the havoc that data breaches and identity theft crimes have wreaked on the innocent lives of American citizens. Look closer at the cracks in my skin and understand that they symbolize the hairline fracture of a broken spirit that led to the countless breaches and manipulation of victims' personal data.

My face, shadowy and situated behind the red stripes, hints of prison bars and underscores the serious and legitimate need for criminal justice and prison reform in America's justice system. The binary pixelated ones and zeroes are a constant reminder of the cybersecurity threats that are matters of national security as well as for the everyday American citizen that individually contributes, complements, and completes the existence of its democracy as a collective republic.

Within the material, the opening volume of this work is comprised of thirteen chapters, which are representative of the thirteen stripes on the American flag. In the second volume that follows, there are fifty legislative proposals aimed at identity theft correlating to the fifty stars and fifty states of the United States of America—no place is exempt.

The second volume, *America's Domestic War: A Cyber Crisis of Identity Theft,* is comprised of seven chapters, symbolic of Biblical completion, covering the three major categories of identity theft as I experienced and apprehended each of them during my time as the master identity thief.

The overall letter and spirit of this work is meant to cross four genres:

1. A spiritual overtone opens the first chapter, and throughout the manuscript you will witness the constant struggle between the flesh and the spirit (Galatians 5:17, NKJV); how my life was enslaved to the sin nature for a season; and ultimately how the fruit of redemption was materialized and manifested, among other things, through the publication of this work.

2. The patriotic and political undertone is both real and relevant, advocating for Congressional, senatorial, and presidential considerations of the fifty legislative bills, meant to serve as a guide to solve, reverse, and resolve the growing epidemic of identity theft.

3. While the book itself is a memoir that captures my story from an amateur petty thief to becoming the master identity thief, its autobiographical nature reflects our national story surrounding identity theft. I hope to grab hold of the hands of my national siblings and walk them through my egregious psychology and nefarious experiences so that they might avoid similar pitfalls.

4. While this work started out as a public confession and conscience-clearing exercise, in seeking guidance and direction through prayer and meditation, I quickly discovered the need and developed the conviction to educate my constituents, my country, and our communities. Thus, the resultant manuscripts are didactic and serve dual purposes: entertainment and

education to more broadly convey its lessons and warnings. With much sacrifice and due diligence, I have labored to deliver a book that earns your time and attention.

Finally, this work has a total of twenty chapters, symbolic of America's wait in the bondage (Gen 31:38–41, Judges 4–5, NKJV) of systemic pride and proof that willful ignorance has been perfected, and that at this appointed time (Habakkuk 2:3, NKJV) "...Yahweh has chosen the foolish things of the world to put to shame the wise, and Yahweh has chosen the weak things of the world to put to shame the things which are mighty; and the base things of the world and the things which are despised Yahweh has chosen, and the things which are not, to bring to nothing the things that are, that no flesh should glory in His presence." (1 Cor. 1:27–29, NKJV)

My prayer is and will remain that this expert testimony will create a cultural shockwave that strikes at the heart of America's ongoing domestic war, and that through the rediscovery of my own identity others will come to find and protect theirs as well, now and for generations to come.

From me to America, with the best of intentions,

DAW

ACKNOWLEDGMENTS

To my sponsors, who prefer anonymity over notoriety, among whom are Trina Harris, Dr. Jay Perniciaro, and my late and beloved friend, Jimmy McGraw, whom, against their preference to my disclosure, were and remain my friends, foundation, and fortresses throughout all my entrepreneurial aspirations and endeavors. It is with the utmost gratitude and deepest humility that I literalize my gratefulness and manifest my appreciation for each of you and the monetary seeds you've sown into the literary harvest of what the world will now read. On behalf of each and every victim of identity theft and repentant perpetrator of identity theft, I thank you for helping me to publish, market, and promote this work. By the authority invested in me, may all of Heaven bless you in this life betimes and forever in the life to come. Thank you!

To my publishing guardian, Scribe Media, thank you Bailey, Mark, Erin and Cindy, Money-Matthew, and Zach, who guided me from the first letter to the last period of this work. You guarded me from myself at those critical moments when decisions had to be made to keep this work from being a book only I would be interested in reading. And Sir CEO JT McCormick, I would be remiss if I didn't personally thank you for looking past my initial ignorance and naïveté as an aspiring, overzealous author and believing in me enough to take specific and special interest in my project and personally oversee it as your own. Thank you and y'all!

To each of my children, Kaleb Kar'Micah Williams, Madisen Marie Williams, Darquise Noel Williams, and Emoni Jane-Marie Williams, for without your collective impatience, intolerance, and forced understanding of my need to go on a literary hiatus during the summer and winter months to complete this project, its reality would still be in the distant future. Each of you worked my nerves but contributed and motivated me in ways unspeakable. Y'all are my biggest accomplishments in life, and I love you for you, respectively. Thank y'all!

To Dr. Thomas J. Durant, my personal friend and author of one of two forewords for this work, your unwavering commitment to my cause, sagacious counsel, scholarly advice, and intellectual symposiums over the many lunches and shared brownies baked by your beloved wife Ms. Anne, have finally paid off as we originally discussed on the date of our intentional introduction eight years ago. I am grateful for you and to you. Thank you!

To Mr. Joe Louis Smith (a.k.a., JoeLSerious) and Ms. Frances R. Smith, my "Day-1s." If intelligence and wisdom had different names, they would belong to the both of you as a first and last name combined. Together, y'all embraced me, welcomed me into your scholar community, and cultivated the rawness of my intellect in ways that will carry me for the remainder of my days. Thank you for y'all!

To my friend and confidant, Mr. Darryl G. Thornton, author of this work's second foreword. My gratitude for your sacrifice, commitment, and contribution is without measure. From the day of our introduction at Greater King David Church in Baton Rouge, LA, you understood the confessed frailties and failures of my sinful nature and never once did you pass judgment on my past criminalities. Your integrity and insight are exceptional, and I'm grateful to have you as a Big Brother for life. Thank you!

To my filmmaking, scriptwriting, and culinary artist friend Barry Berman, who gave me pushback on every aspect of this work. It worked and has made me a better, more disciplined writer. Although I neither welcomed nor wanted to hear it then, I now appreciate your frankness and the candor you exhibited throughout the entire book-writing process. Thank you!

To my criminal defense team, namely: Mr. Lavalle B. Solomon, the late Mr. Paul Kidd, Sr., Mr. Ross Barnett, Jr., Mr. Gary Jordan, and Mr. Rodney Baum, whose effective assistance of counsel, individually and collectively, navigated me through the tricks and traps of America's criminal justice system that's designed to induce recidivism and perpetuate incorrigibility. I am grateful for the potential each of you saw in me in spite of our racial differences, and I remain thankful for the fulfillment of your promises to take care of me when

I was too naive and narcissistic to make better decisions for myself. I owe you every word of this acknowledgment, and in retrospect I now understand that each of you were providential commas and periods properly placed then for a greater purpose now. To say the least, I appreciate you and y'all!

To my brothers in technology, Shakil Ahmad, Aditya Saini, and Rahul Dass, whose sympathetic recommendations reconciled my palate back to Indian cuisine, thank you. I admire each of you for the innovative and ingenious suggestions you made to the "Disruptive Technology" we have designed and developed that will forever change the way in which the world engages as consumers and merchants in the hidden networks of transactional security. In this single regard, we've done well, my brothers.

To my astute attorneys, Patrick Mckenzie and Bryan Stewart of Morris, Manning, and Martin, LLP of the Atlanta Office. The vision and ideas of my intellectual properties would have drowned in dreams if it had not been for both your patience with me as I was starting up DuckPond Technologies, Inc. and developing its products. Your wise counsel and steadfast commitment to client services in your respective areas of expertise equates both of you to Rock Star Attorneys in my book. I am grateful that Morris, Manning, and Martin, LLP, positioned and made you available to meet me in due season. Thank you!

To my Father in the Faith, Bro. Sedrick Pierre, to whose spirit I am eternally connected as wet is to water. Only Yahweh himself knows the depth of my gratitude to Him, for you. You are my Earthly, Heavenly advisor, and I don't know exactly how nor if I could ever thank you enough for our time spent together in the days of Texarkana to present. When and wherever this acknowledgment is read, you are honored. In Yahshua's name, if Yahweh's name means anything at all... Thank you!

To Leetric "The Photographer" Walker, my childhood and lifelong friend. If a picture is worth a thousand words, then the photos of both covers, and more especially the photos of my parents displayed in my eye pupils have captured and captivated my attention, and now the attention of America, since the day we mutually selected them to be cover-worthy. Your artistry is unique, and I'm grateful to be a pictorial product of it. Thank you!

To Nellie Webster, you have inspired much of this work in some of the most unusual ways. I thank you for "motivating" me when complacency was before me and contentment was behind me. By Yahweh's grace, I used your sharp and selective words of encouragement to pierce and push me across the finish line. I did it. Thank you!

To Brannan Sirratt, my senior editor and literary visionary. If I could write in the spiritual language that I communicate when speaking in tongues, only Heaven could translate and convey my profound appreciations for you. In his book, *On Writing | A Memoir of The Craft*, on page 10 of the third foreword, Mr. Stephen King remarks that the ability "to write is human, to edit is divine" as he documents his admiration for his editor, Chuck Verrill. I echo this same sentiment for and to you, "B." You were divine. Thank you!

To Dr. Lisa Vosper, the *queen* of all things. You have been my bridge over turbulent waters and my serenity and safe during tumultuous times. Some things, especially the Queen's things, are spiritually initiated and instigated before they find physical manifestation, and if anything can be said about grace in my life, I'd be the first to testify before heaven that my indebtedness to you makes me so unworthy and undeserving of your least devotions and last heartfelt considerations. You are indeed a gift of Yahweh's grace shown to me. I am profoundly grateful for the sacrifices you have made as I've dedicated myself to "working on building your battery." Some of us believe that "less is more," and perhaps this is true in most instances. Thus, I will pause my expression of love and gratitude for you here and deliver in full measure as we continue to live our lives for His glory and work through the psychology of why *Men Take Showers and Women Take Baths*. The rest is intuitive. Selah. Thank you!

YHWH

Dartanyon Antwaun Williams was the student teachers loved to hate and one of his classmates' favorites. He graduated with a near 4.0 GPA and technical training certifications, then promptly set it all aside to pursue criminal aspirations. The unprecedented sophistication of his crimes earned him consultancies with the FBI, Secret Service, Louisiana Bureau of Investigation, Louisiana State Police, and US Attorney's Offices for the Eastern and Middle Districts of Louisiana, helping their respective agencies better understand, prevent, and mitigate identity theft. He is an advocate, consultant, content expert, evangelist, serial entrepreneur, public speaker, and founder of the software firm DuckPond Technologies, Inc. and The DAW Group, LLC.

www.duckpond.tech
www.thedawgroup.com
www.dartanyonawilliams.com
www.themasteridentitythief.com

CPSIA information can be obtained
at www.ICGtesting.com
Printed in the USA
LVHW031407120320
649845LV00001B/1